Spinning Laughter

Spinning Laughter

Profiles of 111 Proposed Comedy Spin-offs and Sequels that Never Became a Series

by **Richard Irvin**

BearManor Media
2016

Spinning Laughter: Profiles of 111 Proposed Comedy Spin-offs and Sequels that Never Became a Series

© 2016 Richard Irvin

All Rights Reserved.
Reproduction in whole or in part without the author's permission is strictly forbidden.

Publicity photographs are from the author's private collection

For information, address:

BearManor Media
P. O. Box 71426
Albany, GA 31708

bearmanormedia.com

Typesetting and layout by John Teehan

Published in the USA by BearManor Media

ISBN—1-59393-197-2
978-1-59393-197-1

Table of Contents

Acknowledgments xi
Preface xiii

Introduction
    Spin-offs and Sequels 1
    Spin-offs and Imitations 4
    Front-door Pilots and Anthology Series 6

**Part 1: Proposed Sitcom Spin-offs and Sequels
in the 1950s: The "Firsts" of Many** 9
    Chuck Goes to College 9
    The Mertzes 11
    My Wife Irma 13
    The Plumber and His Daughters 15
    Teenage Idol 16

**Part 2: Proposed Sitcom Spin-offs in the 1960s:
The Thomas-Leonard Impact** 19
    Aloha, Kimi 22
    Always April 24
    The Bill Bendix Show 25
    Emmy Lou 27
    The Jack Carter Show 28
    Moko and Tatti from Outer Space 30
    Munroe 32

Pandora 33
The Pat Buttram Show 34
The Roberta Sherwood Show 35
Shape up Sergeant 37
Thataway 38
The Two Musketeers 39
Wagon Train "Prairie Hillbillies" Spin-off 41
Which Way'd They Go? 42
Wide Open Spaces 44
Zelda 45

Part 3: Proposed Sitcom Spin-offs and Sequels in the 1970s: Cutting-Edge, Nostalgic, and In-Between 49

After the Honeymoon 54
Barney and Me 56
The Blonde 58
Bo and Sam 59
The "Castaways" on Gilligan's Island 60
The Councilman 63
Della and Son 65
Father Knows Best Reunion 66
Goober and the Truckers' Paradise 68
Horshack 70
Jersey Bounce 73
Kelly's Kids 74
Lenny & Squiggy in the Army 75
The Lucie Arnaz Show 77
Margie's Little Margie 78
Pam 80
Pinky Tuscadero 81

Potsie and Ralph and Maxine 87
The Rita Moreno Show 88
We Love Annie 89
Whatever Happened to Dobie Gillis? 91
Wojo 93
Young Love 95

Part 4: Proposed Sitcom Spin-offs and Sequels in the 1980s: Trying to Satisfy One Network's Demand 97

The Academy 99
Almost American (aka *Night School*) 101
Almost Home 102
The Art of Being Nick 103
The Big Apple Blues 105
Bring Me the Head of Dobie Gillis 106
Carlton Your Doorman 109
The Center 110
Charmed Lives 112
The Coneheads 114
The Dick Butkus Project 117
The Eddie Mekka Project 118
Family Business 119
Fenster Hall 120
Flatfoots 122
Gilligan's Island: The Second Generation 123
Jackee 124
Jo's Cousins 125
Kat Mandu 126
The Last Word 128
Late Bloomer 129

The Lisa Whelchel Project 130
Max 132
Mr. Bill's Real Life Adventures 133
Mr. Moe's 135
Mona 136
The Munster's Revenge 138
Nick Derringer, PI 140
The Parkers 141
A Piece of the Pie/Carlos and Chuck 142
Schneider 143
Taking It Home 144
That's My Mama Now! 146
The Tony Orlando Show 147
Three Apartments 148
W*A*L*T*E*R 149
We the People 151

Part 5: Proposed Sitcom Spin-offs and Sequels in the 1990s: Not Your Typical Fare 153

Almost Family 154
The Chatterbox 156
Clarissa Now 157
Daddio 159
Enemies 160
Fair Exchange 161
Goin' for Mine 162
Harlan and Merleen 163
The Jackie Chiles Show 164
Krusty the Clown 166
Laverne Todd Show 167

    The Lost Resort 169
    The Mighty Quinns 170
    Radio Free Trumaine 172
    Related by Birth 173
    Roseanne's Gay Family Project 175
    The Young Americans 178

Part 6: Proposed Sitcom Spin-offs and Sequels in the 2000s: Spin-offs for a New Generation 181

    Arwin! 182
    The Carmichaels 183
    The Farm 184
    Gibby 187
    Goin' Hollywood 188
    Mary and Rhoda 189
    Monsignor Martinez 191
    Mystik Spiral 194
    The Patakis 197
    What's Stevie Thinking? 198
    Witchright Hall 198
    The Xtacles 200

Appendix: Proposed Spin-offs and Sequels Listed by TV Series that Spawned Them

    Proposed Sequels 203
    Proposed Spin-offs 203

Endnotes 207
Index 217

Acknowledgments

I WOULD LIKE TO THANK the following writers, actors, producers, and directors for their contributions to this work: Bob Ari, James Baio, Mitchell Bank, Harry Basil, Ted Bergman, Ron Bloomberg, Pat Carroll, Marcy Carsey, Patrick Cassidy, Ann B. Davis, Barton Dean, Elinor Donahue, Rich Eustis, Noanna Dix Feldman, Bruce Ferber, Jeff Franklin, Steve Granat, Bradley Gregg, Richard Gurman, Richard Hawkins, Gary Jacobs, Irma Kalish, David Ketchum, Carl Kleinshmitt, Sheila James Kuehl, Jerry Mayer, Philip Charles MacKenzie, Arnold Margolin, Melanie Mayron, Eddie Mekka, John Mengatti, Rita Moreno, Andrew Nichols, Natalija Nogulich, Jo McDonnell Parker, Bill Persky, Deborah Pratt, Jerry Rannow, Rene Rivera, Stan Rogow, Jerry Ross, Mark Rothman, Robert Sand, Susan Silo, Jeff Silver, Paul Tigue, Adam Vernier, William Lucas Walker, Sam Weisman, and Michael Weithorn.

I would also like to thank the staff at the following libraries for their assistance: the Motion Picture Reading Room of the Library of Congress, the Howard Gotlieb Archival Research Center at Boston University for access to the Max Shulman Collection, the University of Illinois—Urbana for copies of scripts related to proposed spin-offs from *Happy Days*, and the Department of Archives and Special Collections at Loyola Marymount University for information from the Donna Reed Collection. And a special thanks to my friend Garry Settimi for his help and encouragement with this book.

Preface

FOR THOSE WHO HAVE READ Lee Goldberg's works on unsold television pilots (*Unsold Television Pilots*, Volumes 1 and 2), one can't help but notice the number of projects that were planned as spin-offs from popular television series. There is a continuing fascination among diehard television fans about spin-offs of characters and episodes from one series into another as witnessed by articles that appear in print and electronic media with titles such as "25 Totally Unnecessary Spinoffs," "The 19 Best Spinoff TV Shows of All Time," "12 Amazing TV Spinoffs that Almost Happened," "10 TV Spin-offs that Are Better than the Originals," and "15 Worst TV Spin-offs Ever." Most people remember popular comedy spin-offs like *Frasier*, which spun off from *Cheers*, and *The Andy Griffith Show*, which first appeared as an episode of *The Danny Thomas Show*. Some may even remember less successful attempts such as *Joey* from *Friends* or *The Golden Palace*—a sequel to *The Golden Girls*. This book deals with another category of spin-offs and sequels—those that were proposed but never became a series.

Unlike many books about television pilots that present short descriptions of each project, this work provides background information, a complete summary of the storyline, and comments from several writers, producers, directors, and actors involved with the attempted spin-off or sequel.

Potential spin-offs or sequels take several forms. Many actually aired as episodes of the comedy series from which they planned to be spun off. Some were filmed but never aired. For others, scripts or treatments were written but never produced, while still others were "concepts" discussed by producers and actors which never went into development. The latter is a particularly difficult category to document since one never knows if such concepts were merely floated for publicity purposes or if they were serious undertakings for a possible spin-off series. For example, there were rumors that the supporting characters of Jack McFarland (Sean Hayes) and Karen Walker (Megan Mullally) from the ground-breaking comedy *Will & Grace* would be spun-off into a series of their own or that at least the Sean Hayes character would get his own series or that the Karen Walker character would. The only documentation about such a possible spin-off seems to be an interview in which Megan Mullally said, "I was going to do a spinoff, but then they spun off a character from *Friends*, Joey, that did not go very well. They decided they wanted me to host a talk show instead, which also didn't go particularly well."[1] If a pilot, script, or treatment was not developed for a possible spin-off or sequel and there is little documentary evidence of a serious endeavor undertaken to create a spin-off or sequel, then such projects have been excluded from this book. This work makes no claims that it covers every possible comedy spin-off or sequel ever attempted over the past sixty years. However, the book does include the vast majority of such projects broken down by the decade in which they were conceived and/or produced.

While almost every hit situation comedy has had a spin-off proposed at some point during its run, there have even been spin-offs contemplated from sitcoms that were only moderately successful. In at least one case, a sequel pilot emanated from a series that aired only four episodes.

This work covers potential spin-offs and sequels beginning with those proposed in the mid-1950s and continuing through 2013. Attempted comedy spin-offs are listed in alphabetical order for each decade beginning with the 1950s and continuing through the 2000s. At the beginning of each part, background information is provided about the factors influencing comedy spin-offs during each decade.

Introduction

Spin-offs and Sequels

Generally, there are two types of television series spin-offs. Spin-offs involve a different situation from the original series and include either:

1. the same supporting or secondary characters from the original show who usually become the main characters in the spin-off; or
2. a new character who was introduced on a "special" episode of the original show.

The first type of spin-off is often referred to as a "character spin-off." The latter type of spin-off is known as a "planted spin-off" or a "backdoor pilot" and is usually created by the writers of the original series or at the direction of network management. Such episodes allow networks and production companies to spend less on the cost of the pilot while also obtaining audience reaction.

In between the two broad types of spin-offs is a hybrid type where a new character is introduced on a few episodes of a series and then a backdoor pilot starring that character airs as an episode of the original series. For example, on *All in the Family*, Bea Arthur appeared as Edith's cousin Maude on an episode of that series and later, another episode of *All in the Family* served as the pilot for Arthur's own series.

Spin-offs are not the same as sequels, which are rarer than spin-offs. A sequel is a series that has a different situation from the original show but the same main characters and same actors as the original. Sequels should not be confused with remakes. A remake is a series that involves the same situation and characters as the original but with different actors than the original. For example, the 2010 version of *Hawaii Five-O* is a remake of the 1968 to 1980 series starring Jack Lord just as the 1967 Raymond Burr drama *Ironside* came back again in a 2013 remake that quickly vanished from the air. Remakes of situation comedies are rarer than reboots of dramatic series. The attempted 2002 remake of the 1960s series *Family Affair* is a good example of a comedy revival. The original sitcom about wealthy bachelor Bill Davis, who was raising his young nephew and two nieces after their parents were killed in an automobile accident, ran on CBS for five seasons. The WB network tried a remake of the series in September 2002 with entirely different actors in all the roles, but this attempt lasted for only sixteen episodes, of which fourteen actually aired.

A radio series titled *The Great Gildersleeve*, which coincidentally had a premise similar to *Family Affair*, is probably the earliest example of a situation comedy spin-off. The long-running radio comedy *Fibber McGee and Molly* first introduced the character of Throckmorton P. Gildersleeve, who proved to be so popular that a spin-off series was developed in which Gildersleeve, a bachelor, came to raise his orphaned niece and nephew. The comedy premiered in 1941 and ran until 1957. In 1955, a syndicated television version of the series lasted for thirty-nine episodes.

Sometimes a project is labeled a "spin-off" that doesn't really fit the definition. For example, a 1989 pilot titled *Nikki and Alexander* has been termed by *Variety* to be a spin-off of *Night Court*, but the only thing that the pilot had in common with *Night Court* was that Reinhold Weege created both projects. *Night Court* focused on the antics of Judge Harry Stone (Harry Anderson) and his staff. *Nikki and Alexander* starred Tim Matheson as Alex, a writer who had just broken up with his girlfriend, and Irene Ferris as Nikki, a Russian who worked at the United Nations for a married U.S. negotiator with whom she had an affair. After the end of the affair, Nikki knocks on Alex's apartment and asks if he has a room to rent. He allows her to stay in his spare bedroom and from that a relationship develops. However, the only association between *Night Court* and *Nikki and Alexander*, other than the fact that Weege created both, is that Irene Ferris had previously been featured as Ludmila Federova, an attractive blonde Russian functionary, on an episode of *Night Court* titled "Russkie Business," which is probably best remembered for a cameo appearance by Johnny Carson at the end.

Crossovers are also not the same as spin-offs. Crossovers occur when the characters from one television series appear on another series after both series have been on the air for a period of time or, for promotional purposes, when a new series will debut in a few days after characters from that series are featured on an episode of an already-established series. An example of the first type of crossover involving two comedies is when the Danny Williams's family from *The Danny Thomas Show* guest starred on an episode of *The Lucy-Desi Comedy Hour*. In return for this appearance, Lucy and Desi as Lucy and Ricky Ricardo appeared on an episode of *The Danny Thomas Show*. A crossover between two comedies produced by James Komack, *Welcome Back, Kotter* and *Mr. T and Tina*, is an example of the promotional type of crossover. To introduce *Mr. T and Tina* to viewers, Pat Morita, who played the Mr. T character, appeared on the second season premiere episode of *Welcome Back, Kotter*. In that episode, the high school where Mr. Kotter taught had a career day, and Mr. T shows his inventions to the students. The second season premiere of *Kotter* occurred two days before the debut of *Mr. T and Tina*, and so presumably Mr. T's appearance on that show would help boost the audience for *Mr. T and Tina*. The students from *Kotter* then did a cameo appearance at the beginning of the first episode of *Mr. T and Tina* to introduce that series to viewers.

Three comedies that debuted in the sixties—*The Beverly Hillbillies*, *Petticoat Junction*, and *Green Acres*—are probably most associated with crossover appearances among their casts, leading some to believe that *Petticoat Junction* spun off from the *Hillbillies* and that *Petticoat Junction* in turn spawned *Green Acres*. While all three rural sitcoms were produced by Paul Henning and were broadcast by CBS, neither *Petticoat Junction* nor *Green Acres* was a spin-off. Actress Bea Benaderet played Cousin Pearl Bodine on *The Beverly Hillbillies*. Paul Henning, who had worked with Benaderet on *The George Burns and Gracie Allen Show* before the *Hillbillies*, decided to create a series for her titled *Petticoat Junction*. However, Benaderet's character on her own series was named Kate Bradley, not Pearl Bodine. Later in *Petticoat Junction*'s run, after Benaderet became ill with cancer and passed away, characters from the *Hillbillies* series, like Granny (Irene Ryan), guest starred on *Petticoat Junction* and supporting characters such as Fred Drucker (Frank Cady) appeared on *The Beverly Hillbillies*.

Green Acres, starring Eddie Albert and Eva Gabor, took place in the same setting as *Petticoat Junction*—Hooterville. But *Green Acres* did not originally air as a back-door pilot on *Petticoat Junction*. The Eddie Albert series premiered on September 15, 1965. About a week later, Albert and Gabor, as their characters Oliver and Lisa Douglas, were featured on a crossover episode of *Petticoat Junction* staying at the Shady Rest Hotel before moving to their newly-purchased farm. After that both series featured numerous crossovers between their supporting casts.

Probably the first true situation comedy spin-off from a television show was the 1955-56 half-hour version of *The Honeymooners* that began as a sketch on *The Jackie Gleason Show*. The Gleason variety hour that gave rise to *The Honeymooners* proves that not every sitcom spin-off emanates from another situation comedy. While sitcoms are the most common source for comedy spin-offs and sequels, as will be described later in this book, proposed sitcom spin-offs also came from Western series as well as from variety shows.

Television spin-offs and sequels date back to the mid-fifties with some of the first proposed comedy spin-offs related to shows produced by entertainer-actor George Burns. However, the "Golden Age of Spin-offs" occurred in the 1970s and can be credited to Fred Silverman, the head of network programming for CBS from 1970 to 1975, then president of the ABC Entertainment Division from 1975 to 1978, and finally president of NBC form 1978 to 1981. Silverman encouraged the spin-off of *Maude* from *All in the Family* and then *The Jeffersons* from the same series. *Maude*, in turn, spun off *Good Times*. From *The Mary Tyler Moore Show*, *Rhoda*, *Phyllis*, and *Lou Grant* were spun-off. When Silverman moved to ABC in May 1975, he suggested the spinoff of *Laverne & Shirley* from *Happy Days* followed by the spin-offs of *Mork & Mindy* and *Joanie Loves Chachi*. According to former CBS programmer Alan Wagner, "Fred kept urging us to think of spin-offs. 'Why not?' he would say, 'It's a good source of supply. Familiar characters are good soil in which to grow new programs.'" [2]

Spin-offs and Imitations

Sometimes a pilot is labeled as a "spin-off" when, instead of characters from a comedy being featured on their own show, it is the generic situation from a series that is proposed as a "spin-off." A good example of this is the effort to make a female version of *M*A*S*H*, which Twentieth Century Fox tried very hard to get on the air.

No character from *M*A*S*H*, either permanent or temporary, appeared in any of the female-centered pilots, and none of the pilots aired as an episode of *M*A*S*H*. However, the distaff versions of *M*A*S*H* have been sometimes labeled "spin-offs" based on taking place in the same time period and locale and within a medical setting like *M*A*S*H*.

The first such pilot was initially titled *Nurses*, then *Nurses in Korea*, then *TLC Corp*, and finally *Handle with Care*. Written by Woody Kling, Dawn Aldredge, Marion C. Freeman, and Jim Parker and directed by Alan Rafkin, this attempt focused on a group of nurses during the Korean War assisting doctors and engaging in various hijinks.

Brian Dennehy appeared as Colonel Marvin Richardson, the commanding officer of this M*A*S*H unit, and Mary Jo Cartlett played Major Charlotte Hinkley, the head nurse. The pilot centered on Nurse Jacqueline "Jackie" Morse (Didi Conn) and Nurse Elizabeth "Liz" Baker (Marlyn Mason). Other characters in *Handle with Care* included Shirley "Scoop" Nichols (Betsy Slade), the unit organizer; Nurse Sophia, nicknamed "Turk" (Jeannie Wilson); and Corporal Carp (Robert Lussier), a nasty little man who liked to inform Major Hinkley of any schemes her nurses might be up to.

In the pilot, Liz and Jackie are planning a ten-day leave in Tokyo. Major Hinkley is laying down the law about her nurses pulling pranks. If any other pranks occur, Hinkley threatens to cancel all leave. The nurses are treating a young soldier, Corporal Tillingham (Ted Wass,) who has shrapnel in his back and needs surgery in Tokyo. Since he will soon turn twenty-one, Jackie wants to give him a birthday party to boost his morale before he has surgery. After Corporal Carp informs Hinkley of the party plans, she orders him to spy on the nurses. When the nurses catch Carp secretly watching them, they tie him up. However, Carp frees himself and informs Hinkley that there is a party going on. Of course, Hinkley cancels all leave, but she does allow Jackie and Liz to accompany Tillingham to Tokyo for his surgery and to stay for ten days.

This pilot aired May 9, 1977, but never became a series. Twentieth Century Fox subsequently decided to put together another attempt, this one called *Fighting Nightingales*. The pilot, broadcast on January 16, 1978, involved Major Kate Seele (Adrienne Barbeau), an easy-going, but dedicated head nurse; Captain Margaret "Irish" McCall (Erica Yohn), a by-the-book career nurse; and Lieutenant Angie Finelli (Livia Genise), a street-smart native of Brooklyn welcoming a new nurse to Korea—Lieutenant Hope Phillips (Stephanie Faracy), fresh from finishing school. When Phillips learns that the enemy is not only just over the hill but also right in the post-op tent, she wants to go back home, particularly when she finds the optimistic Colonel H. Jonas Boyette (Kenneth Mars) less than helpful. But after a night of grueling work, Hope gets her feet on the ground and decides to stay. As with *Handle with Care*, *Fighting Nightingales*, directed by George Tyne and written by Alan Uger and Barry Sand, did not become a series.

A more recent example of a popular situation comedy that has been termed a "spin-off" is the pilot *How I Met Your Dad*, which many have termed a spin-off of *How I Met Your Mother* even though the pilot did not contain any of the characters from the latter show nor did it air as an episode of that show. *How I Met Your Mother* told the story of Ted Moseby (Josh Radnor) meeting the mother of his children. *How I Met Your Dad* had the same premise, but from the female point of view. The series would have focused on Sally's (Greta Gerwig) search for a new husband after divorcing her first spouse Gavin (Anders Holm).

Attempts such as these pilots are better labeled as imitations or copies rather than as spin-offs.

Front-door Pilots and Anthology Series

During the 1950s and 1960s, television networks scheduled many anthology series—something like a mini-movie of the week—containing a different dramatic story with each episode. Many of these shows would often air "front-door" pilots which the producers hoped would become their own series. For example, the western series *The Rifleman* first aired as a pilot on the anthology series *Dick Powell's Zane Grey Theater*. Differentiating between a front-door pilot that aired as a special episode of a series to see if it would be a viable candidate for a spin-off and a burned-off pilot that had already been rejected by a network is difficult. Some anthology series, like *Vacation Playhouse,* broadcast as summer replacements for a popular show, consisted solely of rejected pilots.

Examples of pilots that aired as episodes of an anthology series are two episodes from the science fiction series *The Twilight Zone*, both dealing with guardian angels coming to Earth to help someone.

The first attempt, titled "Mr. Bevis," in season one of *The Twilight Zone* centered on eccentric James B.W. Bevis (Orson Bean) who drives a 1924 Rickenbacker, wears a bowtie, and likes kids, but has difficulty conforming to the dictates of a nine-to-five office job. One day, Bevis is fired from his job, his old car locks bumpers with another vehicle and ends up on its side, and he has to walk home to his apartment where he finds that he has been evicted. Bevis goes to a bar where he sees J. Hardy Hempstead (Henry Jones), his guardian angel. Hempstead has been the guardian angel for several of Bevis's ancestors and now allows Bevis to live his day all over again with some changes. He has Bevis dress more appropriately for the office and has him pay his rent on time, drive a new sports car, and maintain a clean desk. Instead of being fired, Bevis's boss gives him a raise. But Bevis doesn't like his new life and wants to go back to the way things were. Hempstead makes this happen, and Bevis goes out to find another job and a new apartment. To show that he still has a guardian angel, Hempstead also gives Bevis his old car back.

CBS rejected this pilot because Rod Serling, its writer and the creator of *The Twilight Zone,* would not be around to supervise the writing of the episodes for the series since he was working on a screenplay for his drama *Requiem of a Heavyweight.* However, "Bevis" did air as an episode of *The Twilight Zone.*

Later Serling reworked the idea more from the guardian angel's point of view in a May 25, 1962, episode of *The Twilight Zone* titled "Cavender Is Coming." Jesse White played an apprentice angel named Herman Cavender who hasn't received his wings yet. He is given the mission to go to Earth to help Agnes Grep (Carol Burnett) in order to earn his wings. Like Bevis, Agnes is fired from her job as a theater usher when she messes up. Cavender appears to her on the bus that is taking her home and reappears in her apartment. He wants to make Agnes independently wealthy since she has difficulty holding on to a job. Cavender deposits money into her bank account, gets her new clothes, and holds a society party for her. However, Agnes, like Bevis, doesn't like her new lifestyle. She tells Cavender that she was happier back in her original apartment with her old friends. He allows her to resume her previous way of life and discovers that cash and contentment are not the same. Back in Heaven, Cavender's boss sees that Agnes is happy and informs Cavender that he will be assigning him similar missions.

Like "Mr. Bevis," "Cavender is Coming" never went beyond the pilot stage.

More recent examples of pilots that aired as part of an anthology series come from ABC's *Love, American Style,* a series that usually included three separate segments involving "love" in its various manifestations. Unlike many anthology series from the 1950s that aired pilots so networks could access their viability as a potential series, *Love, American Style* often burned off already rejected pilots as segments of the series. For example, "Love and the Young Unmarrieds," that aired as part of the second season of *Love, American Style,* started out originally as a pilot titled *God Bless Mr. Ferguson,* starring John McMartin as Reverend Peter Ferguson who attempts to convince a young couple that they should marry and not simply live together.[3] Rejected by the network, the pilot was then edited to be a segment of *Love, American Style.* A more famous example is the segment of *Love, American Style* titled "Love and the Happy Days," shown in 1971. First pitched to ABC in 1970 by its creator Garry Marshall, the network rejected it. Paramount, which produced the pilot as well as *Love, American Style,* decided to air the pilot as part of that anthology series which Marshall termed "... the graveyard for dead pilots."[4] Re-pitched to ABC after the success of the movie *American Graffiti,* the pilot became the hit show *Happy Days.* Such cases are rare. However, comedy pilots from anthology series, either those rejected before airing or rejected afterwards, are not considered potential spin-offs for the purposes of this book.

Networks like spin-offs because of their predictability. Network heads know which characters on a series are popular with viewers and so might lead to a successful series of their own. In the case of back-door pilots, while the characters might be new to viewers, at least airing such a pilot as an episode of a successful series allows a sampling by the television audience that a regular pilot might never receive.

The proposed spin-offs and sequels described in this book are all ones that seemed like a good idea at the time, but never became a series.

PART 1

Proposed Sitcom Spin-offs and Sequels in the 1950s: The "Firsts" of Many

IN ADDITION TO THE THIRTY-MINUTE *Honeymooners* comedy with Jackie Gleason, Art Carney, Audrey Meadows, and Joyce Randolph—the first sitcom spin-off—premiering in October 1955, the fifties also brought the first examples of the different types of comedy spin-offs and sequels defined in the Introduction: *My Wife Irma*, the first attempted comedy sequel; *Chuck Goes to College*, the first potential spin-off of a regular supporting character from a series; *The Plumber and His Daughters*, the first proposed spin-off of an occasional character appearing on a comedy; and the first back-door pilot, *Teenage Idol* from *Mr. Adams and Eve*. These projects as well as an attempt to spin-off the Mertzes, the neighbors from the iconic comedy *I Love Lucy*, are described in this part.

Chuck Goes to College

This first proposed spin-off of a character from one series to another featured Dwayne Hickman as Chuck McDonald, the character he portrayed on *The Bob Cummings Show*. The Cummings show concerned a playboy bachelor photographer, Bob Collins (Cummings), who lived with his sister Margaret McDonald and her son, Chuck. If it had been picked up as a series, *Chuck Goes to College* would have centered on pre-med student Chuck, his steady girlfriend, Carol Henning (Olive Sturgess), who attended a nearby college for girls, and his roommate Jimmy (Jeff Silver) and their various escapades. Note that the character of Carol Henning was named after the daughter of the writer-creator of the Cummings show—Paul Henning.

Before he starred as Dobie Gillis, Dwayne Hickman appeared as Chuck McDonald on *The Bob Cummings Show*.

Background

Henning, who later created *The Beverly Hillbillies* and *Petticoat Junction*, wrote the spin-off pilot which Bob Cummings himself directed. Producers of *The Bob Cummings Show* and the spin-off included Henning, Cummings, and entertainer George Burns. The spin-off, based on an episode of the Cummings show titled "Chuck at College," aired on February 28, 1957.

The Pilot

Chuck McDonald begins attending Gridley College for Men with his friend Jimmy. Mr. Bassett, the men's counselor at Gridley, informs Chuck that he will be under particular surveillance because of his uncle's well-known reputation with women. Two upperclassmen visit Chuck's dorm room and ask him to arrange a date for one of them—a student named Madison (portrayed by Jody McCrea, the son of movie actor Joel McCrea). The upperclassmen want the prospective date to meet Madison in Chuck's room. Knowing it is impossible for him to sneak a girl into the dormitory, Chuck decides to have his roommate Jimmy dress in drag as a female named Gertrude. When the upperclassmen stop by again to meet the girl Chuck got for Madison, Madison finds Gertrude very attractive. But then Mr. Bassett comes by, dismisses the upperclassmen, and looks for the girl that he thinks is hiding in Chuck's room. He finds Jimmy, but not his alter ego Gertrude. Later at the malt shop, Madison asks Chuck to fix him up with Gertrude for an upcoming dance.

Postscript

Marketed to all three networks at the time, *Chuck Goes to College* never sold. Dwayne Hickman remained with *The Bob Cummings Show* for the most part until it ended in 1959. He then went on to play the lead in *The Many Loves of Dobie Gillis*.

Jeff Silver, who played Chuck's friend Jimmy on the pilot, went into the Army in January 1957 right after completing filming of this episode unaware that *Chuck Goes to College* was being marketed as a spin-off series.[5]

The Mertzes

William Frawley and Vivian Vance would star as their characters, Fred and Ethel Mertz from the *I Love Lucy* show, in this attempted spin-off which would have no doubt portrayed their life managing an apartment building in New York City, including Ethel's ongoing attempts to pry money out of her skinflint husband.

Background

Desi Arnaz, the head of Desilu, the production company he owned with his wife Lucille Ball, came up with the idea in 1958 for a spin-off staring Vivian Vance and William Frawley as Ethel and Fred Mertz, who

Fred and Ethel Mertz (William Frawley and Vivian Vance) from *I Love Lucy*

were the Ricardo's neighbors on *I Love Lucy*. However, Vivian Vance, who refused to appear with irascible William Frawley on any series without Lucy and Desi, strongly opposed Desi's plan for a spin-off.[6]

The two co-stars of *I Love Lucy* never really had a good working relationship. As described in the book, *Meet the Mertzes*, Vance rejected the idea of a spin-off with Frawley ". . . because she could not stomach the notion of costarring on an even more full-time basis with a man as crude and insulting as she found Frawley to be. She would not even film a pilot episode, even after Desi Arnaz agreed to pay her a $50,000 bonus. When Frawley learned of Vance's refusal, he was irate, if only because the eternally money-conscious actor—who had a well-earned reputation as a cheapskate—would have been paid a much-higher salary than he currently was earning."[7]

The Concept

One might speculate about the premise of a Mertzes spin-off. During the run of the *Lucille Ball-Desi Arnaz Show*, the one-hour version of *I Love Lucy*, the characters of Fred and Ethel had moved to Connecticut to live in the guest house on Lucy and Ricky's property. Fred, in charge of raising chickens on the Ricardo's estate, still owned an apartment building in New York City which was being managed by Mrs. Trumbull (Elizabeth Patterson). If the idea of a spin-off had been developed, it no doubt would have involved Fred and Ethel moving back to the city to resume managing their apartment building and dealing with the problems of their tenants.

Postscript

While Vivian Vance would never reprise her role of Ethel Mertz after the *Lucille Ball-Desi Arnaz Show* ended, she did later appear as Lucille Ball's sidekick Vivian Bagley on *The Lucy Show* for several seasons. William Frawley subsequently starred as "Bub" on *My Three Sons* until health issues forced him to retire from that series.

My Wife Irma

My Wife Irma, a potential sequel to the comedy *My Friend Irma*, would have focused on quirky Irma Peterson Briston and her understanding husband, Harvey—a New York millionaire.

Background

Broadcast by CBS from January 1952 to June 1954, *My Friend Irma* starred Marie Wilson as stereotypical dumb-blonde Irma Peterson, the secretary for an attorney, who roomed with a level-headed female friend. During the final season of *My Friend Irma*, Irma acquired a new boyfriend, Joe Vance (Hal March), an employee of Spic and Span Cleaners. Her previous love interest, Al (Sid Tomack), something of a con-artist, always seemed to take advantage of Irma. Near the end of the series, both Al and Joe would propose marriage to Irma with her leaning toward marrying Joe.

The Concept

Cy Howard, the creator of *My Friend Irma*, proposed a sequel to CBS dealing with Irma's marriage not to Joe Vance but to a Park Avenue millionaire. As Howard put it in a news article, "This is going to be the story of what happens when Irma goes Park Avenue. It will be the Cinderella story. Irma is going to marry one of the richest men in the world."[8] Irma would become Mrs. Harvey Briston. Although never cast, actor Steve Dunne, who subsequently starred in the short-lived comedy *Professional Father,* was reportedly under consideration for the part of Irma's husband.

The sequel, planned for the fall 1954 season on CBS, never materialized. If the concept had become a series, apparently Irma's new husband would have replaced her roommate in *My Friend Irma* as the level-headed part of the team.

Postscript

After *My Friend Irma*, Wilson made several other situation comedy pilots during the 1950s, always playing the "dumb blonde" type of character, but none of the pilots ever became a series. Writer-producer Cy Howard subsequently worked as a writer on two pilots starring show business legends. Ethel Merman appeared as Maggie Brown in a 1963 pilot of the same name playing a widow raising a daughter and running a nightclub next to a Marine base. Actress Bette Davis portrayed *The Decorator,* another unsold pilot from 1965, in which she appeared as an interior designer who liked to move in with the families who contracted for her services in order to determine what they liked.

The Plumber and His Daughters

In this proposed spin-off of a character from *The George Burns and Gracie Allen Show*, Howard McNear would appear as Cusperd Jantzen, a widowed plumber raising four beautiful unmarried daughters—Jean (Jody Warner), Joy (Yvonne Lime), June (Darlene Albert), and Joan (Mary Ellen Kaye). The comedy would have explored Jantzen's efforts to marry and his daughters' modeling and dating activities.

Background

The character of Cusperd Jantzen first appeared on an episode of *The Burns and Allen Show* in spring 1957. In the episode titled "The Ring," Gracie gives her engagement ring to her son Ronnie so he can present it to a girl with whom he wants to go steady. Gracie has her best friend and next-door neighbor, Blanche Morton (Bea Benaderet) make up a story that Gracie lost the ring down her kitchen sink drain. George calls plumber Jantzen to retrieve the ring. In the following week's episode, Jantzen asks Gracie to watch his four daughters while he goes to San Diego to meet a possible marriage prospect.

The Cusperd Jantzen character appeared in a number of other episodes of *The George Burns and Gracie Allen Show* with Gracie normally trying to find a wife for him but with no luck. For instance, in another episode, Gracie places an ad in the newspaper to attempt to get a suitable wife for Jantzen. The ad claims he is thirty-five years old. When she receives a reply from a woman who is thirty, the lady, upon seeing that Jantzen is really in his fifties, declines to pursue a relationship.

The Concept

In May 1957, Burns said that he planned to spinoff the Howard McNear character into his own series.[9] As Yvonne Lime Fedderson (Joy Jantzen) recalls "…I do remember playing one of the daughters of the widowed plumber. We had a lot of fun working together and I know George Burns truly thought *The Plumber and His Daughters* could be an interesting series. Unfortunately it didn't work out."[10]

Postscript

Howard McNear would become more famous for his role as Floyd Lawson, the barber, on *The Andy Griffith Show*. Yvonne Lime subsequently starred with George Burns's son Ronnie on the short-lived comedy *Happy* about a baby who expresses his thoughts directly to the TV audience. She later married producer Don Fedderson, responsible for shows such as *My Three Sons* and *Family Affair*. The actresses who played the other Jantzen daughters, for the most part, ended their television acting careers after *The Burns and Allen Show* ceased production.

Teenage Idol

This proposed spin-off from *Mr. Adams and Eve* which starred then-husband and wife, Howard Duff and Ida Lupino, featured a young Patrick Wayne as a shy teenager who wants to become a rock 'n roll star, like his idol, Swivelhips Jackson. Presumably, if the pilot had become a series, its focus would have been on the life of a 1950s teenage rock star.

Background

Written by Louella MacFarlene, who subsequently scripted episodes of *Dennis the Menace* and *Hazel*, and produced by Bridget Productions owned by Ida Lupino and Howard Duff and named after their daughter, the *Teenage Idol* pilot aired on July 8, 1958, as the final episode of *Mr. Adams and Eve*.

As part of publicity for the pilot, Duff and Lupino announced a nationwide search in March 1958 for a young man who could sing, act, and play the guitar—a combination of Elvis Presley and Tommy Sands. Auditions were to be submitted in the form of tape recordings and a full-length photograph.[11] Over 1,500 auditions were submitted. Darrell Howe, a former tractor-trailer truck driver, won the search and was cast along with Patrick Wayne, the son of John Wayne. Supposedly, three songs from the pilot were to be recorded and released before this episode of *Mr. Adams and Eve* aired.

The Pilot

The Adamses approve their housekeeper Elsie's (Olive Carey) hiring of a young man to help with her duties. The teenager turns out to be her nephew from Kansas, Walter Hannigan (Patrick Wayne), who is very shy but is a great fan of rock 'n roll star Swivelhips Jackson (Howe) and wants to be just like him. Walter constantly plays Swivelhips's records. The Adamses conspire to mold Walter into a teenage copy of his idol with mixed results.

Postscript

After *Teenage Idol*, Darrell Howe made a few appearances on television series such as *The Virginian* and *Felony Squad* in which Howard Duff starred. Howe appeared in one movie, 1961's *Anatomy of a Psycho* with Ronnie Burns (son of George Burns). Patrick Wayne had a lengthier career as an actor, appearing on several television series such as *The Rounders*, *The FBI*, and *Fantasy Island*. Later he became Chairman of the John Wayne Cancer Institute.

Except for the planned sequel to *My Friend Irma* which would have been produced by CBS, all the spin-off attempts during the 1950s were conceived or produced by production companies owned by the stars of their own series—George Burns's McCadden Productions, Lucy and Desi's Desilu, and Lupino and Duff's Bridget Productions. This trend would continue in the 1960s with actor-owned companies seeking successful spin-offs from their own series.

PART 2

Proposed Sitcom Spin-offs and Squels in the 1960s: The Thomas-Leonard Impact

THE FIRST COMEDY SPIN-OFF from a situation comedy premiered in 1960. Many may think that this spin-off was *The Andy Griffith Show* which originated as a back-door pilot on *The Danny Thomas Show*. The Griffith series debuted on October 3, 1960. But *Pete and Gladys*, featuring a secondary character, Pete Porter (Harry Morgan) from the 1950s sitcom *December Bride*, debuted weeks before *The Andy Griffith Show* on September 19, 1960.

Produced by Desilu and created by Parke Levy, *December Bride* starred actress Spring Byington as widow Lily Ruskin, who lives with her daughter and son-in-law and who often becomes involved in "Lucy-like" predicaments with her best friend Hilda Crocker (Verna Felton). Pete Porter, the next door neighbor on *December Bride*, had a never-seen wife named Gladys about whom Pete would always make wisecracks. A year after *December Bride* ended its run on CBS in 1959, *Pete and Gladys*, with Gladys played by Cara Williams, debuted. The comedy focused on the zany adventures of redheaded Gladys and her sarcastic husband Pete. Parke Levy created this spin-off which ran for two seasons.

The Andy Griffith Show did become the most popular comedy spin-off from the 1960s. In a February 1960 installment of *The Danny Thomas Show*, Andy Griffith first appeared as Sheriff Andy Taylor with Ron Howard as his son Opie. Frances Bavier, who would later play Aunt Bee on the Griffith show, played the role of the town widow. Don Knotts as Deputy Barney Fife did not appear in the pilot but joined the series when

Danny Thomas (standing) and his producing partner Sheldon Leonard (seated)

it debuted. The *Thomas* episode had Danny Williams (Thomas) traveling through Mayberry and being arrested by Sheriff Taylor for running a stop sign.

The Andy Griffith Show, created by Thomas's producing partner Sheldon Leonard, ran for eight seasons and became the first of three spin-offs from *The Danny Thomas Show* picked up as a series. The other two were *The Joey Bishop Show* and *The Bill Dana Show*. The Griffith show itself led to two other spin-offs in the 1960s: *Gomer Pyle USMC*, starring Jim Nabors, and *Mayberry RFD*, which featured Ken Berry as Sam Jones, head of Mayberry's town council, who became the main character on that show when Andy Griffith decided to end his own series.

All of the Thomas-Leonard comedies revolved around a strong central character. As Sheldon Leonard wrote in his autobiography: "Nonprofessionals have the mistaken idea that 'ideas' are the foundation for television success. Not true. Ideas grow on every tree. Personalities are what count. Name a personality and any writer can pitch a dozen 'ideas' that would work for him or her."[12] Most of the sitcoms Thomas and Leonard developed followed a formula similar to *The Danny Thomas Show*—a male lead character who had both a domestic life and a work life. Generally, the series title included either the name of the actor who portrayed the central character or the central character's name.

An episode of *The Danny Thomas Show*, "Everything Happens to Me" broadcast on March 27, 1961, served as the back-door pilot for the first iteration of *The Joey Bishop Show*. In the pilot, comedian Joey Bishop plays an inept booking agent who forgets to reserve a hotel room for a very tired Danny Williams and so invites him to spend the night at his home, which he shares with his parents and siblings. Because the first season of the Bishop show did not score high in the ratings, the format changed in the second year to have Bishop's character star on his own talk show.

Concerning *The Bill Dana Show*, Dana played Jose Jimenez, a comical Hispanic character which he originated on *The Steve Allen Show* before being featured on several episodes of Danny Thomas's comedy and then getting his own series as a bellhop in a hotel. *The Bill Dana Show* was a character spin-off from *The Danny Thomas Show* and not a back-door pilot like the Griffith and Bishop series. Neither comedy enjoyed the success of *The Andy Griffith Show*. Dana's sitcom lasted for only two seasons, while Bishop's show ran for four seasons.

The tremendous popularity of *The Andy Griffith Show* brought a deluge of attempts to imitate this success with many episodes of established series airing as back-door pilots, most of which involved a central male or female character as had the spin-offs from Danny Thomas and Sheldon Leonard. Three potential spin-offs aired on *The Donna Reed Show*, three on *Mister Ed*, and three other little-known pilots from *The Danny Thomas Show* along with several others as detailed in this part. As with spin-off attempts in the 1950s, most of the proposed comedy spin-offs in the 1960s had production companies owned by actors behind them. Such companies were seeking to expand their complement of series while at the same time reducing expenses by making certain episodes of their existing series back-door pilots.

Not only did back-door comedy spin-offs air as installments of situation comedies, but also as episodes of some Western series such as *Wagon Train*, *The Rifleman*, and *Laredo*, with the leads in such attempts not being the typical Western hero, but more of an anti-hero for comedic purposes.

Aloha, Kimi

Myoshi Umeki starred as a head nurse nicknamed "Mac" who works at the Pacific View Clinic in Honolulu with Dr. Kendall (Crahan Denton), Dr. Paul Phillips (James Douglas), and orderly/taxi driver Rudy Meyer (Harvey Lembeck, who had previously played Corporal Rocco Barbella on *The Phil Silvers Show*). Umeki's character, as the "power behind the throne," essentially managed the doctors at the clinic.

Background

During the first six months of 1962, *The Donna Reed Show* aired three pilots for possible spin-off series, all produced by ToDon, Reed's production company with her then husband Tony Owen. Owen and Reed's company, however, never succeeded in getting another series besides *The Donna Reed Show* on television.

Written by Paul West, who had also scripted several episodes of *Father Knows Best*, and directed by Norman Tokar, *Aloha, Kimi* aired January 25, 1962. An Oscar winner for Best Supporting Actress for the film *Sayonara*, Myoshi Umeki had appeared on a 1961 episode of *The Donna Reed Show* titled "The Geisha Girl" in which she played the wife of a new doctor who treats her husband in the traditional manner all Japanese women care for their spouses—by waiting on them hand and foot. Donna decides to teach her the American way of life by taking her shopping. She buys new clothes and has her hair styled differently and decides to adapt to American customs.

Actress Myoshi Umeki from her first appearance on *The Donna Reed Show* in "Geisha Girl"

The Pilot

Donna Stone (Reed) and her doctor husband Alex (Carl Betz) fly to Honolulu when a patient of Dr. Stone's from the fictional town of Hilldale where the Stones lived, Penny Palmer (Susan Gordon), falls off her surfboard and can't walk. Kimi takes Dr. Stone to see Penny. He and Dr.

Kendall diagnose hysterical paralysis, and they try to recreate everything that happened on the day of the accident by giving Penny sodium pentothal. Kimi speaks with Penny after she is given the medication. Through Kimi, the doctors discover that Penny saw Dr. Phillips in a Navy uniform as she was coming out of the anesthesia after her accident and envisioned him as her late father, a Navy pilot, which caused the paralysis.

Postscript

The title of the back-door pilot was changed from *Aloha, Miki* to *Aloha, Kimi* presumably because the name "Miki" may have been confused for a man and the name "Kimi" would not be. As a sidebar, in the Donna Reed Show Collection at Loyola Marymount University is a letter from Tony Owen to Al Schneider of ABC about this pilot stating that, although a good part of the action is supposedly taking place in Hawaii, practically the entire production was shot in Hollywood. However, to create the impression that the Stone family is flying to Hawaii, ToDon acquired stock footage from United Air Lines of a plane in flight and landing in Hawaii. The letter informed ABC that the arrangement to use the footage involved no consideration of any kind to ToDon and that, when Tony Owen and Donna Reed planned to fly to Honolulu for Thanksgiving week in 1961, they would be flying on Pan-Am.[13]

Always April

This back-door pilot from *The Ann Sothern Show*, in which Ms. Sothern played the assistant manager of a New York City hotel, centered on a young woman named April Fleming (Susan Silo), who aspired to be an actress. A retired show business couple, Guinevere Lang (Constance Bennett) and David Fleming (John Emery), were April's parents.

Background

Like other major television stars at the time, Ann Sothern had her own production company, Anso, that produced her series and its potential spin-offs in association with Desilu. Desilu and Anso each owned half of the projects. *Always April* was one of two spin-off pilots (see *Pandora*) which aired during the final season of the Sothern show. Probably best remembered for writing and producing *Murder, She Wrote* with Angela Lansbury, Robert Van Scoyk penned *Always April*, which Richard Whorf directed. The back-door pilot aired February 23, 1961.

The Pilot

Ann Sothern's character Katy O'Connor discovers a girl living in room 1022 at the Bartley Hotel whom she thinks is destitute because she has been eating only peanut butter. April tells Katy that she has run away from school to be an actress. Katy calls April's parents in Vermont. Initially, her mother, Guinevere, doesn't believe that her daughter is in New York, but then realizes that Katy may be right. She and her husband go to the city to bring their daughter back home. April wants to stay in New York to pursue acting, but her dad doesn't support her interest in becoming an actress. Katy suggests that April's father, who now raises sugar maple trees in Vermont, should sit in on April's acting class to see if she has any talent. Katy and the parents go to the class where, at the direction of the teacher played by Leonid Kinskey, April and Erskine Wild (Marty Ingels) act out a scene from *The Taming of the Shrew* done with a Brooklyn accent. April's mother reveals that she has been coaching her daughter, and the parents perform on stage to show how the scene should really be done. When April replaces her mother in the scene, her dad agrees that she has the talent to be an actress. April returns to Vermont with them since her mother has allowed the acting class to use their barn as a summer theater.

Postscript

Reminiscing about making the pilot, Susan Silo said, "It was a most enjoyable experience for me as a teenage actor to be with these very GROWN UP and talented movie actors." She went on to say that she was treated like a daughter by everyone, especially her mentor, Ann Sothern.[14]

Susan Silo later became an in-demand voice actress working on animated series such as *Curious George*. Constance Bennett, the sister of actress Joan Bennett, had starred in several movies during the thirties and forties. She passed away at age sixty in 1965. John Emery, once married to stage and film star Tallulah Bankhead and romantically involved with Joan Bennett, died in 1964 at age fifty-nine.

The Bill Bendix Show

William Bendix appeared as Bill Parker, the good-hearted owner of a lodge in this pilot from the fantasy sitcom about a talking horse called *Mister Ed* that starred Alan Young as Wilbur Post and Connie Hines as his wife Carol. If it had become a series, *The Bill Bendix Show* would have focused on Bendix's well-intentioned but not always well-thought out plans for his family, lodge, and community.

Background

Al Simon, head of television production for Filmways which produced *Mister Ed*, had previously worked for George Burns's production company, McCadden Corporation, and, as such, gained experience in doing back-door pilots for the McCadden anthology series *Panic! The Bill Bendix Show* was the first of three *Mister Ed* back-door pilots. The others, *Emmy Lou* and *Moko and Taiti from Outer Space,* are profiled later in this part.

Initially written by Lou Derman and Bill Davenport, Norman Paul and Willy Burns re-did the script for the June 1961 Bendix pilot which veteran director John Rich helmed. Entertainer George Burns (Willy Burns's brother) had an ownership interest in *Mister Ed* from when his company produced the first *Mister Ed* pilot.

The Pilot

Titled "Pine Lake Lodge," the Posts are spending a weekend at the lodge owned by Bill Parker (Bendix). Parker's niece Ann (Coleen Gray), who has a young daughter, Cindy, helps Bill run the place along with Martha (Nancy Kulp), the housekeeper and waitress. Bill attends a fundraising meeting for the Pine Lake Summer Camp for children and volunteers to make picnic tables and benches for the camp. When Bill cannot persuade a local lumber yard to donate the wood, he decides to cut down a tree on J.F. Thompson's (Will Wright) property without asking permission since Thompson is a notorious skinflint. Bill enlists Wilbur Post's help in downing the tree, but they both flee the scene after a forest ranger stops nearby. However, unbeknownst to them, a birdwatcher takes a photo of Bill and Wilbur running away. When J.F. Thompson informs Bill of a witness to the tree-cutting incident, Bill admits that he and Wilbur felled the tree. After Wilbur explains the reason for what they did, Thompson agrees to donate the wood for the outdoor furniture.

Postscript

William Bendix continued to do guest appearances on various television series after this pilot failed to sell. In 1964, he teamed up with Martha Raye to star on a comedy titled *Bill and Martha* about a butler and maid who inherit a mansion and maintain it on a rental basis. CBS initially bought the series and planned to air it on Sundays at 9:30 p.m., but, due to Bendix's fragile health at the time, the network canceled the series before it ever aired and substituted *The Joey Bishop Show* in its place. Bendix sued CBS for over $2.6 million for supposedly spreading false rumors about his health. However, a few months after filing the suit, he passed away at age fifty-eight from stomach cancer which brought on malnutrition and pneumonia.

Emmy Lou

Featuring teen actor Noanna Dix as Emmy Lou, this proposed series, also known as *The Trials and Tribulations of Emmy Lou Harper*, dealt with the escapades of a young girl as she seeks love and attention from the opposite sex.

Background

The second back-door pilot from *Mister Ed*, titled "Ed the Matchmaker," aired on April 29, 1962, as the final episode of *Mister Ed*'s second season. *Emmy Lou*, the United Features syndicated cartoon by Marty Links (Martha Arguello), served as the basis for this pilot. Apparently, Herb Browar, an executive at Filmways, saw the cartoon in the newspaper and brought it to producer Al Simon's attention, who thought that it would make a great series. The comic strip first appeared in newspapers in 1944 under the name of "Bobby Sox" and had a previous treatment on television as an episode of *Shirley Temple Theatre* in November 1960 with Bernadette Withers in the title role. Ben Starr and Robert O'Brien wrote the *Mister Ed* episode which Art Lubin, who directed most of the series episodes, helmed.

The Pilot

"Ed the Matchmaker" features love-crazed teenager Emmy Lou Harper (Noanna Dix) whose family has moved next door to Wilbur and Carol Post. Emmy Lou asks Wilbur for a hair from Mister Ed's tail to make a love potion. She wants to win the affections of Arthur (Peter Brooks), a grocery delivery boy who mumbles his lines because he is always eating apples. Arthur eventually asks Emmy Lou to the movies but has to cancel the date because of a flat tire. Emmy Lou auctions off some of her stuff to raise money for a new tire, but then Arthur's car battery goes dead. Finally, Mister Ed, pretending to be Wilbur, phones Emmy

Lou and offers to pull Arthur's car to the drive-in movie. Actor George O'Hanlon and actress Jeff Donnell appeared as Emmy Lou's parents.

Postscript

Reminiscing about making the pilot, Noanna Dix recalls doing the screen test for the role of Emmy Lou several times with different actors trying out for the roles of her mother and father. "One thing that I vividly remember is that because my hair is naturally dark blond, they dyed my hair black to match the cartoon character. Since I was so young (about thirteen years old at the time), the studio didn't want to permanently dye my hair, so we used a product called 'Tiz' rinse which washed out."[15] Dix says that the horse, Mister Ed, was amazing to work with, and she remembers a sort of invisible string attached to the horse's mouth and, when his trainer would tug on it slightly, the horse would start to "talk." She recalls George Burns, wearing a beret to cover his bald head and smoking a very large cigar, stopping by one day to watch the filming of the episode. According to Ms. Dix, ABC picked up the pilot as a series to take over the time slot of *The Donna Reed Show* when Reed decided to retire from her series. However, Donna Reed changed her mind about leaving her comedy, and by then it was too late in the season to find another time slot for *Emmy Lou*.

The Jack Carter Show

Variety reported on September 9, 1962, that an episode of *The Danny Thomas Show* would serve as a back-door pilot for a sitcom centering on comedian Jack Carter. In the pilot, Carter appears as himself—a nightclub entertainer.

Background

On *Make Room for Daddy*, subsequently called *The Danny Thomas Show*, Thomas played nightclub performer Danny Williams, who was trying to balance his life on the road as an entertainer with his family responsibilities.

The Jack Carter episode, titled "Danny's Replacement," aired on October 8, 1962, as the second episode of the tenth season of the *Thomas* show. Written by Jack Elinson and Charles Stewart, Thomas's producing partner, Sheldon Leonard, directed this installment. Long-time writers for *The Danny Thomas Show*, Elinson and Stewart also crafted episodes

Part 2: Proposed Sitcom Spin-offs and Sequels in the 1960s • 29

From left to right, Sid Melton, Danny Thomas, and Jack Carter in "Danny's Replacement," an episode of *The Danny Thomas Show*

of *The Bill Dana Show*, *The Andy Griffith Show*, *The Joey Bishop Show* and *Gomer Pyle USMC*.

The Pilot

Danny Williams is booked for a European tour, but can't leave until he finds a replacement at the Copa Club where he regularly performs. Danny thinks that comedian Jack Carter might be the perfect replacement. Danny tries to sell Charlie Helper (Sid Melton), the manager of the club, on Jack. Jack arrives and says he has a lot of ideas for increasing the club's profits. He also mentions that he will work for less money than Danny and indicates that he can start as soon as Danny leaves for Europe.

To Danny, he says, "The audience will be so sick of laughing, they'll be glad to see you again."

While performing that night, Danny has Jack come up on stage to say "hello," but then Jack proceeds to take over and do his own act.

The next day, Danny informs his agent of how embarrassed he was by Carter's performance, and he is worried that he might not have a job to come back to. Danny says that Jack isn't right for his replacement and that he has changed his mind about touring Europe. When Jack arrives, Charlie Helper lets him know that Danny isn't going to Europe. Jack looks crestfallen but takes it in stride since he has been lined up as a replacement for Danny should Danny not go on the tour. Danny changes his mind again and decides to go to Europe. He says goodbye to Jack who promises to "step in his shoes, not step on his toes."

Postscript

The Jack Carter Show never became a series. Later in his career, Carter was up for the role of Oscar Madison in TV's *Odd Couple* but lost the part to Jack Klugman. He also lost the part of the father-in-law on *The King of Queens* to Jerry Stiller. Even though Jack Carter never got his own situation comedy, he continued to work steadily in Las Vegas as well as in television guest appearances starring in series ranging from the original *Hawaii Five-O* to *Shameless*.

Moko and Tatti from Outer Space

This third back-door pilot from *Mister Ed* featured two characters from Mars, one of whom would periodically come to Earth and enter the minds of unsuspecting people, radically changing their personalities.

Background

Written by Norman Paul and Willy Burns and directed by Art Lubin, *Moko and Tatti from Outer Space* combined live action and rudimentary animation. Simply titled "Moko," this back-door pilot aired May 17, 1964.

Moko and Tatti were animated characters living on Mars. Richard Deacon voiced Tatti, the older, more sensible of the two; Dave Willock did the voice of the prankish Moko. Moko traveled back and forth between Earth and Mars, while Tatti remained on Mars and scolded Moko about his behavior.

Paul and Burns described Moko and Tatti in their script as: "…two irregular globs. The glob that is Moko conveys an impish quality. The glob that is Tatti has an intellectual appearance. Both voices should have a slight echo chamber effect, and each voice should be different. Tatti's is serious; Moko's lighter, with a mischievous quality to match his appearance."[16]

The two Martians discussed their differences thusly,

> Tatti: "Moko, I'll never understand you. You are the only distracting element in the perfect society we have here on Mars."
> Moko: "But I haven't been to a party for more than 2000 years."
> Tatti: "Parties! Moko, we have achieved serenity here. With our great intellect we discovered the formula for discarding our physical bodies and have become pure essence of mind."
> Moko: "I'm bored, Tatti… I'd like to taste a piece of steak, smell a rose… dance with a woman…."
> Tatti: "A woman? Oh, yes, I do remember… Back on Earth they still have two sexes. Thank goodness we have evolved past that stage."
> Moko: "I think we took a wrong turn some place."

The Pilot

At this point in the *Mister Ed* series, Carol and Wilbur Post's neighbors were Gordon and Winnie Kirkwood (Leon Ames and Florence MacMichael). Moko travels to Earth to fly into people's ears and make them lose their inhibitions. The Posts are invited to a party the Kirkwoods are having for a very uptight general to whom Gordon once reported. Moko first takes over Gordon Kirkwood's mind to have him invite Gloria Laverne (Joan Tabor), an attractive blonde client of Wilbur's, and her young friends to the affair. Moko enters Kirkwood's body again at the party to have him dance the twist with Miss Laverne, and then he takes over Wilbur's mind and body and that of General Lucius Bromley's (Robert Barrett). Both dance with the actress, and the next day, all have hangovers from drinking the punch that Moko had spiked. During the episode, Moko travels back and forth between the two planets and is lectured by Tatti about his mischief making.

Postscript

If the pilot had become a series, apparently each week Moko would have visited another human and drastically change his or her personality. For example, Al Simon recalled that Jack Benny might have appeared on an episode with Moko turning the miserly Benny into a spendthrift.

Munroe

This pilot came out of an episode of the *Dennis the Menace*-like sitcom titled *McKeever and the Colonel* and takes place at Camp Boone where Augie Gitchy (Guy Marks) and Corporal Ira Bobbit (Jan Stine) are in charge of a trouble-making dog, Munroe, for the K-9 Corps.

Background

Originally called *The Munroe Story*, this 1963 pilot was based on the final episode of *McKeever and the Colonel* titled "McKeever Meets Munroe" about a dog in the K-9 Corps. Both the pilot and *McKeever and the Colonel* were produced by Four Star Productions, another Hollywood production company owned by actors. Dick Powell, Charles Boyer, and David Niven were the principal stockholders in the company. Actress Ida Lupino was the fourth star but owned no stock. Scripted by James Poe and produced and created by Harry Tatelman, *Dobie Gillis* director Stanley Z. Cherry helmed the pilot.

McKeever and the Colonel centered on Cadet Gary McKeever (Scott Edmund Lane) who attended a military school run by Colonel Harvey Blackwell (Allyn Joslyn) and his aide, Sergeant Barnes (Jackie Coogan). McKeever and his buddies at the school, Tubby (Keith Taylor) and Monk (Johnny Eimen), always seemed to be getting into some sort of trouble.

The Pilot

Munroe has a habit of chasing cats, including the colonel's mother-in-law's cat. James Flavin plays the colonel and Verna Felton his mother-in-law. Augie Gitchy decides to teach Munroe a lesson by procuring a lion for him to chase thinking that will break the dog of his cat-chasing habit. However, the lion tamer they go to mistakenly gives them the wrong lion. He provides them with a man-eating lion instead of the tame one. Gitchy puts Munroe into the building with the lion, and the lion ends up chasing Munroe. While this cures Munroe of his habit of chasing cats, Gitchy still has to return the lion to its owner. He tries to trap the lion in a net, but inevitably Munroe, the colonel, Bobbit, the colonel's secretary Selma (Joan Freeman), and he all get caught in the net. Finally, the lion's owner comes to the base and gives Munroe the scent to track the lion. However, the dog finds the colonel's mother-in-law's cat instead. Eventually the mother-in-law locates the actual lion and gets it back into its cage.

Postscript

As with *Shape up Sergeant* (see below), two versions of *Munroe* were made—one version with scenes including McKeever and his cohorts and one without—the latter to be presented to potential advertisers who might sponsor a series based on the pilot.

Pandora

The second proposed spin-off from *The Ann Sothern Show*, titled *Pandora*, starred Pat Carroll as a secretary for a movie star. An honest, small-town girl, Pandora is not used to working in Hollywood for a popular actor in feature films.

Background

According to Ms. Carroll, this spin-off came about because she had done an episode of *Private Secretary* titled "Susie for President" where the character played by Ann Sothern runs for president of the Midtown Secretaries League. In *Private Secretary*, Sothern's first television series, she portrayed the assistant to Peter Sands (Don Porter), a New York talent agent. The two actresses worked well together on the episode, and Sothern proposed a spin-off series for Carroll which in some respects seemed like a remake of *Private Secretary*.

The episode, written by John Fenton Murray and Benedict Freedom and directed by Richard Whorf, aired March 16, 1961.

The Pilot

Pandora Peterson (Carroll) has just left her small town and moved to Hollywood. Katy O'Connor, who happens to be visiting friends in Hollywood, calls an employment agency to hire a secretary for movie star Tony Bardot (Luke Anthony). Katy gets klutzy Pandora, who turns out to be an excellent typist, but swoons when she is introduced to her boss, Tony. Tony's chauffeur, Gabby (singer Guy Mitchell) instructs Pandora to make sure she keeps the door to the house locked so that when he and his boss are out no fans break in. When a sightseeing bus comes by and one of the passengers gets out to take some photos, the passenger, who is a big fan of Tony Bardot, lays down on the doormat. Thinking that the woman has fallen, Pandora invites her in, followed by the rest of the bus passengers who loot the house for souvenirs. Bardot comes home and is mobbed. He fires Pandora, but, before she leaves, she tells him that he is not neighborly and is not handsome. Liking Pandora's honesty, he rehires her.

Postscript

In describing Ms. Sothern, Pat Carroll remarked, "From her years on stage and in film, she had garnered much knowledge and used it intelligently and well." Concerning *Pandora*, Carroll felt that the script was very weak and the character undefined. She stated further that, ". . . if Miss Ann was willing to use her money and time in its behalf, who was I to carp? I said to myself: 'Do the best you can and devil take the hindmost.' The devil probably heard me and took care of that spinoff."[17]

Pat Carroll subsequently played Bunny, Charlie Helper's wife on *The Danny Thomas Show*, and also became a regular on *Too Close for Comfort* and *She's the Sheriff*.

The Pat Buttram Show

Another back-door pilot from *The Danny Thomas Show*, this potential spin-off featured the homespun humor of Pat Buttram as Harvey Bullock, an ex-nightclub entertainer, who spends his free time traveling the country striking up acquaintances with strangers. If Jack Carter in his back-door pilot bore a resemblance to the Danny Thomas character on the Thomas show in that they were both nightclub entertainers, then Pat Buttram was somewhat like Andy Griffith—both having a down-home sense of humor.

Background

As with the proposed Jack Carter vehicle, country comedian and actor Pat Buttram was also reported by *Variety* on July 1, 1963, as appearing on an episode of *The Danny Thomas Show* that might lead to his own self-titled sitcom. Danny Thomas himself directed this October 14, 1963, episode titled "Here's the $50 Back" from a script by Jack Elinson and Charles Stewart.

The Pilot

Bullock comes to Danny's apartment, hugs Danny, but Danny can't quite remember him. Harvey announces that he doesn't have his seal act anymore because of health reasons related to the seal. Danny asks him what brought him to New York, and he responds that it is an issue of money. Harvey wants to return the $50 he says he borrowed from Danny a while back. Harvey is now in the pest control business in Arkansas and says he will be staying at the Waldorf Astoria during his vacation. Danny and his wife Kathy invite Harvey to stay with them. Kathy and the kids all take to Harvey, but Danny admits to still not having recognized him.

While receiving a shave at the barbershop, Danny tells his barber about Harvey and says he cannot honestly remember the guy. The barber describes a similar situation a friend of his experienced, saying that the man had to be legit because he had come back to pay his friend $50. Williams recognizes an uncanny similarity to his situation, the seal story, and everything.

Danny returns to his apartment and lets Harvey know that he has been found out. Harvey relates a story to Danny about a man who lives in Arkansas, has an act, but loses his partner. He goes into a new business, but misses show business, and talks about needing to be out with friends from his show biz days. Harvey apologizes and tries to leave, but Danny gives Harvey the $50 back so that he can visit his family again. Harvey says he plans to visit Jack Benny next. After Harvey leaves, Kathy gives Danny a big kiss for being so kind to Harvey.

Postscript

Buttram subsequently starred as Mr. Haney on *Green Acres* for several seasons later in the 1960s and early 1970s. The character Buttram played on this episode of *The Danny Thomas Show*—Harvey Bullock—was the name of one of the writers for the series. The real Harvey Bullock also wrote for several other comedies including *The Andy Griffith Show*, *Gomer Pyle, USMC*, and *Hogan's Heroes*.

The Roberta Sherwood Show

The story of a piano teacher raising three sons and living with her brother is the premise of this attempted spin-off from *The Donna Reed Show*. Similar to Reed's character on her series, *The Roberta Sherwood Show* was another "mother knows best" type of comedy.

Background

The Roberta Sherwood vehicle, the third pilot produced by Donna Reed and Tony Owen's company, aired on May 3, 1962. Actress Eva Marie

Saint's husband, Jeffrey Hayden, directed the episode titled "Donna Meets Roberta" from a script penned by Sumner Long.

The Pilot

Donna Stone sees Roberta Summers (Sherwood) at a charity bazaar in Westfield where Donna and Alex learn from a friend of his that Roberta is selling her house. Roberta doesn't know that in the near future a new shopping center will be built on the land where her home is located, increasing its value. At the bazaar, Roberta belts out "Up a Lazy River" for the attendees. She used to be in show business but now gives piano lessons from her home and is raising three boys—Don, Jerry, and Bobby (played by the Lanning brothers, Roberta Sherwood's real life sons, who were respectively twenty-one, eighteen, and thirteen at the time of the pilot)—all of whom sing and play instruments. Roberta lives with her brother Dudley Brockton (Gale Gordon), owner of a drugstore. Alex is interested in buying Roberta's house, but Donna feels guilty about him not divulging the shopping center project to her. He buys the house for $500 more than the asking price. Donna is disappointed in him, and Roberta is disappointed with Dudley for selling what she considers a white elephant for more than the asking price. When Bobby gets sick, Roberta calls Dr. Stone to come and treat him for the measles. Both Alex and Roberta confess the truth about the home purchase, and Alex backs out of the deal. In the end, the Stone family is invited to Dudley's birthday party where Roberta and her sons sing "We're Singing" (the song "We're Traveling" with special lyrics for the occasion).

Postscript

For the purposes of selling this pilot to potential advertisers, Roberta Sherwood informs viewers at the end that the episode gave them a peek at her family, and she shows vignettes from possible future episodes—one where Dudley finds a two-year-old girl left at his pharmacy with a note from the mother asking him to take good care of her baby; a scene where Don and Jerry argue about a girl their mother has invited to stay with them who turns out to be very pretty; one where Bobby is beaten up by a girl who just moved in next door; and a scene where the boys are rehearsing with their mother and do a rock 'n roll version of one of her songs. However, no other actual episodes were filmed beyond these vignettes.

Roberta Sherwood resumed her musical career after this back-door pilot failed to sell, and Gale Gordon continued his long career in television. After appearing as a regular on *Our Miss Brooks*, *Make Room for Daddy*, and *Pete and Gladys*, he replaced Joseph Kerns as Mr. Wilson's brother on *Dennis the Menace* and had his most famous roles as Mr. Mooney and Harry Carter starring with Lucille Ball on *The Lucy Show* and *Here's Lucy*. Speaking of *The Lucy Show*, Roberta Sherwood and her son Bobby appeared on a 1964 episode of that series playing a singer and her son who move in with Lucy when Lucy's roommate, Viv (Vivian Vance) temporarily moves out.

Shape up Sergeant

Shape up Sergeant, about a female military sergeant, Ann Gruber, played by Ann B. Davis, was another back-door pilot from the one-season comedy *McKeever and the Colonel* that aired on NBC from September 1962 to June 1963 on early Sunday evenings.

Background

Initially titled *Get with It,* Ms. Davis recalls making the pilot for *Shape up Sergeant* but doesn't remember its specific storyline. She did note that Beverly Wills, the daughter of comic actress Joan Davis (*I Married Joan*), co-starred with her in the pilot.[18] Apparently, the October 1962 episode of *McKeever and the Colonel* in which she starred was used as the pilot for *Shape up Sergeant* with additional material written by Johnny Bradford and Barry Blitzer and presumably the scenes with the McKeever cast deleted.

The Pilot

Between the end of *The Bob Cummings Show* and before her role in *The Brady Bunch,* Ann B. Davis played a WAC sergeant on an episode of *McKeever and the Colonel* titled "Too Many Sergeants." In that episode, the head of McKeever's military school doesn't think that his assistant, Sergeant Barnes, is being strict enough with the cadets, and so he calls in Sergeant Ann Gruber. Gruber inspects the honor guard and finds infractions such as McKeever having a frog under his helmet and McKeever's friend Tubby with bubblegum in his rifle. She puts the boys on KP for a week. McKeever thinks that Gruber needs a man to make her more easygoing. He and his friends believe that Sergeant Barnes would be ideal for Sergeant Gruber. They plant candy and flowers in Gruber's room and leave Sergeant Barnes under the impression that Sergeant Gruber stole a photo of him. What they don't know is that Sergeant Gruber already has a boyfriend—weight-lifting Sergeant Swatlaski (Mike Muzurki), who is insanely jealous. When Sergeant Barnes asks Gruber on a date, her boyfriend visits and, thinking that Barnes is trying to take away his girlfriend, he proposes, and they elope to Las Vegas.

Postscript

Beverly Wills, who was to be featured in *Shape up Sergeant* if it had become a series, died in a house fire on October 24, 1963, along with her grandmother and two sons. Her mother, actress/comedienne Joan Davis, had passed away from a heart attack two years earlier.

Thataway

Dudley Lester (Chad Stuart) and Newton Weeks (Jeremy Clyde) are two actors, part of Famous Players International, touring the West and getting into all sorts of trouble in this proposed comedy spin-off from the NBC Western *Laredo*.

Background

Thataway, produced by Howard Christie, who had done the proposed *Wagon Train* hillbilly spin-off (see below), featured the 1960s British musical duo of Chad and Jeremy. The back-door pilot titled "That's Noway, Thataway" aired as a January 20, 1966, installment of *Laredo*, the Western about the exploits of three members of the Texas Rangers—Reese Bennett (Neville Brand), Chad Cooper (Peter Brown), and Joe Riley (William Smith), and their senior officer Captain Edward Parmalee (Philip Carey).

The proposed comedy series was originally conceived as a half-hour sitcom based on the Bob Hope movie *The Paleface*. Later, it evolved into a one-hour pilot dealing with a troupe of traveling actors with *The Paleface* title being dropped for legal reasons. *What a Way to Go* became the new title for the attempted series, but it too was changed, becoming *Thataway*.

Actor Howard Morris (Earnest T. Bass from *The Andy Griffith Show*) directed and Vincent Bogert and Gene L. Coon wrote this back-door pilot. Bogert had been a comedy writer for *Duffy's Tavern*, *The Phil Silvers Show*, and *The Garry Moore Show*, while Gene L. Coon had done scripts for *Wagon Train* and *Star Trek*.

The Pilot

Dudley and Newton's former manager has vanished with the money the townspeople of Three Forks, Texas, had paid to see a show, and Dudley and Newton are being threatened with arrest. Texas Rangers Joe and Chad intervene, and Dudley and Newton leave town in a horse and buggy with a trunk of costumes singing "These Are Hard Times." They go to Whiskey Flats where they find the town without a preacher. Newton asks Dudley to masquerade as the town's new minister, Preacher Jones, hoping to make money from Sunday collections. Newton pretends to be one of Preacher Jones's converts. In town, they meet gunfighter Ben Conrad (Peter Graves) who wants to marry Belleflower Ferne (Marlyn Mason). Conrad wants Preacher Jones to perform the marriage ceremony, but Dudley as Jones doesn't want to go through with it. Both Dudley and Newton, however, are afraid that Conrad will kill them if he doesn't get married. Newton becomes Conrad's best man, and Dudley works up the courage to perform the ceremony. The two try to delay Conrad and his new wife from going on their honeymoon but are not successful. Meanwhile, Chad and Joe find that the Pecos Kid, the outlaw they are searching for, is really Ben Conrad. Newton and Dudley disguise themselves as robbers to hold up the stage carrying Conrad and his new wife The duo wants to get Belleflower away from Conrad, but Conrad gets the drop on them. Dudley and Newton's buggy then knocks Conrad unconscious just as Chad and Joe come to arrest him.

Postscript

NBC did not pick up the series reportedly because it already had scheduled *The Monkees*, a comedy about a rock quartet, and thought that having two competing recording groups in two series was one too many.[19]

The Two Musketeers

The third proposed spin-off from *The Danny Thomas Show*, titled *The Two Musketeers*, starred Ross Martin as Bertie and Bernard Fox as Britisher Alfie—mismatched roommates sharing an apartment.

Background

The character of Alfie Wingate had been introduced in earlier episodes of the Thomas show. Danny had met Alfie while in London visiting the pub where Alfie worked as a waiter. When Alfie mentioned that he planned to visit New York, Danny suggested he contact Charlie Helper at the Copa. Alfie thinks that Danny is offering him a job, and he does eventually become a waiter at the club.

Danny Thomas directed the pilot starring Martin and Fox. Airing December 16, 1963, veteran comedy writers R.S. Allen and Harvey Bullock scripted the episode. Allen and Bullock worked on various situation comedies including the Griffith show, *Hogan's Heroes*, and *Love, American Style*. Bullock also helped to write *The Andy Griffith Show* reunion movie *Return to Mayberry*.

The Pilot

In the opening scene of "The Two Musketeers," Bertie approaches Danny Williams at the Copa wanting to borrow money to pay off a debt he owes to Big Joe. Apparently, Danny has bailed Bertie out several times before, but doesn't want to do it again. Alfie enters the club talking about trying to find a place to live. When Bertie overhears this, he suggests Alfie room with him. Bertie offers to rent a room to Alfie in his apartment for $50 a week, but Alfie gets him to lower the rent to $25 a week.

Bertie then argues with his landlady over the fact that he has promised Alfie three meals a day, meals that the landlady will have to prepare. To get out of feeding Alfie, Bertie takes various steps to make him believe he has already eaten. For example, Bertie fast-forwards the clocks to persuade Alfie that it is bedtime, and, the next day, Bertie has the landlady bring in a tray of dirty dishes to convince Alfie that he has already had breakfast. Bertie tells Alfie that he has amnesia and that is why he doesn't remember eating. He also says that Alfie should eat only carrots to cure his amnesia.

Since Bertie still hasn't paid his debt, Big Joe comes by the apartment to collect. Bertie asks Big Joe to give him another half hour to pay, and Joe leaves. When Alfie emerges from his room, carrot in hand, looking quite dizzy, he says he is leaving and going back to England. Bertie sits Alfie down and confesses the whole set up and the lies he told to take advantage of Alfie. He says that Alfie is not really sick and explains why he needed the money. Alfie offers his heirloom watch to Bertie to pay off Big Joe. Joe returns, and Bertie shows him the watch but has guilty feelings about turning it over to him. Bertie decides to return the watch to Alfie. He informs Big Joe that he should get on with beating him up since he won't be giving him the watch. Big Joe then opens the apartment door, letting in Danny Williams, who had made a bet with Joe. Danny had paid off Bertie's debt thinking that Bertie would be giving Alfie's watch to Joe. Danny thanks

Bertie for not giving away the watch. In the final scene, Bertie promises Danny that he will be better and will pay Danny back, turning to Alfie to ask about hawking the watch for money.

Postscript

After appearing on several installments of *The Danny Thomas Show*, Bernard Fox became better known as Malcolm Merriweather on episodes of *The Andy Griffith Show* and as Dr. Bombay on *Bewitched*. Ross Martin later played Artemus Gordon on *The Wild, Wild West*.

Wagon Train "Prairie Hillbillies" Spin-off

In this proposed spin-off from the Western *Wagon Train*, Jeanette Nolan (the wife of the star of *Wagon Train* at the time, John McIntire) appears as Bella McKavitch, L.Q. Jones as her son Esdras, and Morgan Woodward as her other son Ciel in a comedy pilot about a somewhat lovable but conniving family in the Old West.

Background

Produced by Universal, *Wagon Train*, which began on NBC in September 1957 and moved to ABC in September 1962, chronicled the migration of settlers from Missouri to California for eight seasons. *Wagon Train* aired a back-door pilot for a comedy titled "Charlie Wooster—Outlaw" on February 20, 1963. *Wagon Train's* producer, Howard Christie, who had been involved with the *Ma and Pa Kettle* film series, told *Variety* that this episode was "…our answer to *The Beverly Hillbillies*."[20] Virgil W. Vogel directed and Leonard Praskins penned this installment of *Wagon Train*.

The Pilot

Charlie Wooster, the cook for wagon master Chris Hale, is knocked unconscious and kidnapped along with his supply wagon holding a $5,000 Army payroll of which he is unaware. The kidnappers, Esdras and Ciel McKavitch and Scotty (Mickey Sholder), a teen boy the family "adopted," think Charlie is the wagon master, but their mother Bella knows he is not. Charlie fibs to the guys that he knows where the Army payroll is and claims he is an experienced robber. Bella becomes attracted to Charlie and tells him that she feigns illness to get her sons to do things for her. She says that she will have her sons kidnap a minister so she can marry Wooster, and the two tie the knot.

Charlie finds some gold coins near his wagon and finally discovers it holds the Army payroll. He learns that Scotty also found where the payroll is hidden. At night, with Scotty's help, Charlie escapes to the nearby town, but is recaptured by Esdras and Ciel.

After Charlie asks Scotty to warn the wagon train that Esdras and Ciel want to kidnap Chris Hale to get to the Army payroll, Scotty is captured by the sheriff. Charlie, Esdras, and Ciel go to the wagon train with the intention of kidnapping Hale, but the brothers are caught before they can take the wagon master hostage. They all go back to the McKavitch house where the sheriff has found Bella with the gold from Charlie's supply wagon. Scotty divulges that Charlie's marriage in not valid since Bella's previous husband is still alive in prison.

Postscript

According to Morgan Woodward, who played Ciel, the producers of *Wagon Train* were so pleased with how this episode turned out that they started to develop the project into a series, but it never came to fruition.[21] Woodward appeared in a total of eleven episodes of *Wagon Train* playing various characters.

Which Way'd They Go?

This comedy pilot focused on the Jackman family. Neb Jackman (Peter Whitney) lives on a rundown farm with his three sons—Moss (Mickey Manners), the bright one of the group (which isn't saying much), Haslim (Conlan Carter), the dumbest one, and Bo (John Craig), the strong one.

Background

Which Way'd They Go? aired on April 1, 1963, as the next-to-the last episode of *The Rifleman*. *The Rifleman*, which, as mentioned in the Introduction, had been a spin-off from *Zane Grey Theater*, premiered on ABC September 30, 1958, and ran for five seasons. The Western starred Chuck Connors as Lucas McCain and Johnny Crawford as his son Mark. Arthur Browne Jr. wrote, and Arnold Laven, one of the producers of *The Rifleman*, directed the Jackman back-door pilot. The Jackman family had appeared on a prior episode of *The Rifleman* titled "Lou Mallory" dealing with Neb Jackman selling what he perceived as a worthless piece of land to a businesswoman only to discover that, with the railroad coming to town, the land was more valuable than he had originally believed. The same actors who played Neb and Haslim Jackman in the comedy pilot appeared in the "Lou Mallory" episode. Actors Thom Carney and Mel Carter portrayed Moss and Bo Jackman on the "Lou Mallory" episode.

The Pilot

The Jackmans are being evicted from their farm for failure to pay taxes. It seems that someone in the family had forgotten to plant the corn crop. Neb had tasked Haslam to do the plantin', Bo the pickin', and Moss, the shuckin'. However, Haslam had fed the corn seed to their chickens, and, as it turns out, Neb was the one who forgot to plant it.

The Jackmans abandon their farm and head to Pair-O-Dice, a town currently without a sheriff because no one in the town wanted the job. When the Jackmans enter the saloon and hear the word "job," Neb becomes the sheriff and his boys the deputies. Beatrice King played Miss Goldie Drain, a dance hall girl; Dallas McKennon appeared as Judge Maze; and Vitto Scotti portrayed Marcello Carbini, the banker—all residents of Pair-O-Dice.

Meanwhile, Lucas McCain receives a note from Micah, the sheriff of North Fork where McCain lives, that a gang of bank robbers headed by Wade Stack (Leo Gordon) has broken out of prison and may be headed to Pair-O-Dice to rob the bank because the town has no sheriff. Lucas is asked to ride to the town to warn them. On his way, he is knocked unconscious by Stack's gang who take his note. When the gang arrives in the town, the head of the bank recognizes them and gets Neb and his sons to arrest them. However, the gang says they were sent by Micah to warn the town of the bank robbers and show the Jackmans the note. Wade Stack tells Neb that he and his boys can watch the bank at night and his gang will relieve them in the morning. The next morning, after the Jackmans return to the sheriff's office, Haslam sees a wanted poster for Wade Stack. Bo and Moss are able to knock out most of the gang except for Wade whom Haslam collides with and the money from the bank lands in Neb's arms. The townsfolk throw a party for their heroes—Neb and his sons.

Postscript

This proposed spin-off has been termed "the worst *Rifleman* episode ever" and represented *The Rifleman*'s producers Levy, Gardner, and Laven's first (and apparently last) venture into comedy. Two versions of the pilot were filmed—one that included the appearances of Chuck Connors and Johnny Crawford, and one without.

Wide Open Spaces

This second attempt by Donna Reed and Tony Owen for a comedy series other than Reed's own show starred William Windom and Patricia Breslin as a city couple with two young sons who move to a small farm.

Background

Jeffrey Hayden directed this episode, which aired March 8, 1962, from a script by Sumner Long who later wrote the play and movie *It's Never Too Late*. The original title, *Country Cousins*, had been rejected for *Wide Open Spaces* when it was found that "Country Cousin" had been the title of a *Father Knows Best* episode. A subsequent title, *The Good Life*, was abandoned as well in favor of *Wide Open Spaces*.

William Windom and Pat Breslin had appeared as a married couple earlier in the season on an episode of *The Donna Reed Show*. In "All Is Forgiven," they had played Ed and Millie Corwin, bickering friends of the Stones who decide to separate. Donna thinks she can get them back together if they adopt a child. Alex knows of a baby boy up for adoption at the hospital because the young mother can't afford to raise him. Donna invites the Corwins to dinner and has the baby there for them to see. However, the young mother comes by and explains her situation, and Ed promises her husband a job. Millie thinks Ed is wonderful for offering a job to the young husband, and they make up.

The Pilot

David Adams (William Windom) and his wife Millie (Pat Breslin), friends of the Stones, recently relocated to a small farm with their two young sons—Steve and Les (played by Stephen and Leslie Barringer). Jimmy Hawkins appeared as the Adams's farm hand "Jimmy." Donna and Alex visit the Adamses and experience the pleasures of farm life. However, Millie is not so pleased to be living on the farm. She thinks their lifestyle is aging her and her husband, while she believes that Alex and Donna look younger. However, when Millie and David comfort an aging draft horse on the brink of death and are able to revive it, Millie changes her mind about going back to the city.

Postscript

Jimmy Hawkins, who portrayed the farm hand in the pilot, had played Donna's daughter's boyfriend Scotty on several episodes of *The Donna Reed Show*

The actors who played Millie and David's sons—Leslie and Stephen Barringer—appeared in other television series from the 1960s such as *The Andy Griffith Show* and *Lassie*. However, as with many child actors, both left show business after they grew up and returned to their native Canada. Leslie Barringer passed away at age sixty from emphysema. Known as the "Bard of Queen Street," he spent his final years composing "poems for a penny" for tourists in Toronto.

Zelda

This pilot, a spin-off from *The Many Loves of Dobie Gillis*, featured the character of teenage Zelda Gilroy played by Sheila James Keuhl. Dobie Gillis, the target of Zelda's affections on the Gillis comedy, was never mentioned in this spin-off attempt. Zelda, who had the highest IQ in Central High, played the cello, guitar, piano, and contrabassoon and knew various dances like the tap, ballroom, and classical. She had the same kind of monologues to open the show that Dobie had with *The Thinker* statue. Zelda lived in a small apartment above the garage where her dad, Harry (Joe Flynn), ran a small auto body repair shop. Her mother Ruth (Jean Bryon) was a tall blonde in her mid-thirties. Zelda seems to have inherited her dad's looks. She is short, has dark hair, and a button nose.

Background

Created by Max Shulman, *The Many Loves of Dobie Gillis*, which ran on CBS from 1959 to 1963, starred Dwayne Hickman as a teenager pursuing cars, money, and especially girls. Bob Denver appeared as beatnik Maynard G. Krebs, Dobie's best buddy, while intelligent, but not beautiful in the traditional sense, teenage Zelda had a crush on Dobie and wanted to marry him.

Written by Max Shulman, the 1961 pilot for the Zelda character was produced and directed by Rod Amateau, who had formerly directed *The Burns and Allen Show* and *The Bob Cummings Show* and, for a short time, had been married to George Burns's daughter Sandra. Zelda's parents had appeared on two episodes of *Dobie Gillis*— "Dobie Spreads a

Rumor" and "Here Comes the Groom." However, in those episodes, her family was not the same as the one portrayed in the *Zelda* pilot. In the *Dobie* episodes, Zelda's dad Walter (Dabbs Greer), a white collar worker, lived with his family in a modern house. In "Dobie Spreads a Rumor," Zelda's mother (Jane Walker) and her dad had five daughters in addition to Zelda. Anna Capri, Jeri Lou Jones, Sherryl Alberoni, Larraine Gillespie, and Glenda Padgett played Zelda's unnamed sisters. In "Here Comes the Groom," actress Joan Banks appeared as Zelda's mother Edna.

The Pilot

The storyline of the actual *Zelda* pilot, titled "The Treehouse of the August Moon," had Zelda trying to get Benbow Teed, a photography nut, to fall in love with her since it seemed that most students in her high school were going steady. She goes to see Benbow in the school's photographic dark room, but he pays more attention to entering the shutter bug magazine contest than to Zelda. She decides to take up photography to get him interested in her. When Benbow sees her in the park taking pictures, he lets her carry his flash equipment. Zelda then accompanies Benbow to shoot photos of deer in the woods. However, he has difficulty taking good pictures of the deer since he can't get close enough without scaring them away. Zelda recommends that they build a tree house so they can get better photos. Benbow kisses Zelda for coming up with the idea.

When Benbow goes to the hardware store to buy nails to build the tree house, he meets Priscilla Dockstader and is instantly attracted to her. Despite this, Zelda invites Benbow to accompany her to the woods to take more photos of deer where she reveals the already-built tree house she constructed. Both climb up to the platform which then collapses since Zelda did not use enough nails in building it. As the structure breaks, Zelda exclaims to Benbow that she loves him. He responds by saying he still loves Priscilla. Zelda tries keeping him from tumbling by grabbing on to his collar, but she can't prevent him from falling and breaking his leg. Later, Zelda helps him when he is on crutches. She says that Benbow now loves, respects, and admires her, and they go steady.

The Alternative Pilot Script

Max Shulman wrote an alternative pilot script for *Zelda* which apparently was never filmed. This script titled, "It's a Long, Long Way from

May to September," described a different way Zelda sought to impress Benbow. The script begins with Zelda still trying to find a boyfriend. She attempts to initiate a relationship with Calvin Epperson, a French major, by speaking French to him. When he shows no interest, Zelda approaches Max Amateau, a lepidopterist who wears glasses. The last name of "Amateau" was a reference to producer/director Rod Amateau. Zelda goes to the woods with a butterfly net to meet Max, but when things don't work out with him, she goes after Benbow Teed.

Benbow would like Zelda to buy him a $134 Kolb Metternich lens for his camera, but later tells her to forget about the lens. He just doesn't want a girlfriend. Zelda's friend Elizabeth Barret, a female jock, says that boys are no good for Zelda. However, Elizabeth admits that she does like men such as Marlon Brando, Roger Moore, and President Kennedy. Zelda tells her parents about Benbow and the lens he wants, but her mother says that buying such a gift is no way to get a boyfriend.

Zelda goes back to see Elizabeth, who is alone at home and afraid of burglars. Zelda says she will stay with her if Elizabeth pays for her to babysit. However, Zelda decides not to take any money from her friend. She ends up getting enough money from a gentleman by the name of Fred Distelfink, a portly man in his sixties, who pays Zelda for information about teenagers. Distelfink, a newspaper sportswriter, has just been assigned the "Susie Spear" advice column for teenagers at his paper.

When Zelda next sees Benbow, he shows her the new Kolb Metternich lens that he received for his birthday. Zelda had just bought him the same type of lens. Benbow thinks she is great and asks her out on a date.

Postscript

As Ms. Kuehl recalls, everyone thought that the pilot had a good chance to become a series, but no network picked it up. Rod Amateau took Sheila for a walk around the studio lot and told her that Jim Aubrey, then-President of CBS, put the kibosh to the series because he thought she seemed "just a little too butch." At the time, Sheila was deeply in the closet about her sexuality. She had a relationship with another woman and had been kicked out of her sorority at UCLA when they found some letters from the woman among her things. But, being the early sixties, no one made this public.[22]

The 1970s would usher in a new era of comedy spin-offs. Instead of backdoor pilots airing as episodes of popular series, the seventies saw a majority of spin-offs featuring characters from hit series. Two writer/producers in particular were responsible for many of the spin-offs that became series during the 1970s—Norman Lear and Garry Marshall. In addition, Grant Tinker, who, with his spouse Mary Tyler Moore founded MTM Enterprises, established an environment conducive to talented writers who created both original and spin-off series.

PART 3

Proposed Sitcom Spin-offs and Sequels in the 1970s: Cutting-Edge, Nostalgic, and In-Between

As noted in the Introduction, the 1970s were marked by the number of successful comedy spin-offs mainly from producer Grant Tinker and his wife, Mary Tyler Moore, writer/producer Norman Lear, and writer/producer Garry Marshal. Each, however, had their own unique approach to comedy. MTM and Norman Lear broke several sitcom traditions in creating their series, while Marshall had the talent for producing new comedies that seemed like old ones.

The influence of the Danny Thomas/Sheldon Leonard comedies of the 1960s could be seen in the sitcoms produced by Grant Tinker's company, MTM Enterprises, with strong central characters as their focal point. After all, Mary Tyler Moore had starred as Rob Petrie's wife Laura on *The Dick Van Dyke Show*, one of Thomas and Leonard's rare comedies that did not start as a spin-off from *The Danny Thomas Show*. Like the Thomas and Leonard series, *The Mary Tyler Moore Show* had a central character, Mary Richards (Moore), who not only led a personal life with friends such as Rhoda Morgenstern (Valerie Harper) and Phyllis Lindstrom (Cloris Leachman), but also had a career working at a Minneapolis TV station for her boss Lou Grant (Ed Asner). Unlike the Thomas-Leonard series which always had male central figures, the Moore comedy revolved around a single working female character who did not seek, as her primary goal, a husband and marriage.

Although not a writer himself, Tinker headed a production company that quickly became known as one that permitted its writers "…almost limitless independence and authority."[23] He hired the writing team of James L. Brooks and Allan Burns to create *The Mary Tyler Moore Show*. They had previously developed the comedy-drama *Room 222* for ABC, one of the first series on network television to feature a black lead character. As with Mary Tyler Moore, Brooks also had a connection to Danny Thomas and Sheldon Leonard. He had written episodes for the Sheldon Leonard-produced *Accidental Family* starring Jerry Van Dyke as well as for *The Andy Griffith Show* and *Mayberry RFD*. Furthermore, Leonard had hired Brooks as story editor on *My Friend Tony*, a 1969 detective drama that Leonard produced.

As *The Danny Thomas Show* had done, *The Mary Tyler Moore Show* also had several spin-offs picked up by CBS as their own series. Beginning in September 1974, the character of Rhoda Morgenstern spun-off from the Moore show. The 1975 TV season saw Mary Richard's landlord Phyllis Lindstrom featured on her own spin-off developed by Ed. Weinberger and Stan Daniels. Finally, after *The Mary Tyler Moore Show* ended, Ed Asner's character Lou Grant appeared on a one-hour dramatic series—the first such spin-off from a comedy. Later, in 1979, *Trapper John MD* premiered becoming the second dramatic series spin-off from a comedy, in this case, *M*A*S*H*. After the *Rhoda* and *Phyllis* spin-offs, *The Mary Tyler Moore Show* became more like an ensemble comedy revolving around the television station where Mary worked with most of her friends being her work colleagues.

After the moderately successful *Rhoda*, which ran for four and a half seasons, and the less-than-successful *Phyllis*, which lasted for only two seasons, the producers at MTM decided against doing another spin-off starring Sue Ann Nivens (Betty White), one of Mary's colleagues at work. "To soften her up enough to be a leading lady would destroy her character à la *Phyllis*, to marry her off was a chance they weren't about to take after *Rhoda*."[24] The producers decided to develop a whole new comedy for White, *The Betty White Show*, which expired after thirteen weeks.

The second major influence on comedy spin-offs during the 1970s came from writer/producer Norman Lear with his ground-breaking comedy *All in the Family* based on the British series *Till Death Do Us Part*, which premiered in 1971. While not impacting the type of comedies Lear produced, as was the case with MTM Enterprises, Danny Thomas did influence the career of Norman Lear. Thomas first hired Norman Lear and his then writing partner Ed Simmons to work in show business as writers for his stand-up comedy act.

Prior to *All in the Family*, which featured conservative bigot Archie Bunker (Carroll O'Conner), his patient wife Edith (Jean Stapleton), their daughter Gloria (Sally Struthers), and Gloria's husband, liberal Mike Stivic (Rob Reiner), sitcoms dealt mostly with non-controversial family and friends issues like growing up, dating, getting married, raising kids, and finding a job. The white, mostly middle-class world in which comedies existed prior to *All in the Family* tended to be hermetically sealed from larger societal issues. *All in the Family* brought a new diversity and relevance to comedies not only in handling topics like racism, feminism, homosexuality, and the Vietnam War, but also in featuring characters from diverse racial, ethnic, religious, and socio-economic backgrounds.

All in the Family resulted in more successful spin-offs than any other comedy series. At the urging of Fred Silverman, then head of CBS programming, Lear spun off Edith's cousin Maude (Bea Arthur) into her own series in 1972. Maude, a liberal and opinionated matriarch of her family, was the polar opposite of Archie Bunker, the conservative and narrow-minded patriarch of his. Maude's family included fourth husband Walter (Bill Macy), daughter Carol (Adrienne Barbeau) and grandson Phillip (Brian Morrison and then Kraig Metzinger). In *Maude*'s second season, her maid Florida Evans (Esther Rolle) got her own comedy titled *Good Times* about a lower-class black family struggling to make ends meet. In the *Maude* episode, "Florida's Good-bye," Florida informs Maude that she is quitting because her husband Henry, a fireman, received a promotion and she wants to spend her time at home raising her kids. However, when *Good Times* premiered, Florida's husband's name changed to "James." No longer a fireman, he held down several part-time jobs to support his family, and the family lived in Chicago, not New York City as in *Maude*. Apparently, the changes were made because the producers thought more substance could be found with the focus on a poor black family than a semi-prosperous one.

It didn't take Lear long, however, to develop a spin-off based on an upper-middle class African-American family. The Bunker's next-door neighbors, the Jeffersons, got their own spin-off in 1975 when George Jefferson's (Sherman Hemsley) dry cleaning business became a success, and he, his wife Louise (Isabel Sanford) and their son Lionel (Mike Evans) moved to a high-rise deluxe apartment on Manhattan's East Side. Later in the decade, the Archie Bunker character became the central focus of a sequel to *All in the Family* called *Archie Bunker's Place* after Archie purchased the neighborhood bar and the Jean Stapleton, Sally Struthers, and

Rob Reiner characters had left the series.

Lear's production company, Tandem, which he owned with Bud Yorkin also developed the hit comedy *Sanford and Son* on NBC that starred Redd Foxx as irascible junk-dealer Fred Sanford and Demond Wilson as his loyal son Lamont. This series resulted in *Grady*, a short-lived 1975 spin-off featuring Fred's friend, Grady Wilson (Whitman Mayo), who moved into a middle class neighborhood in Los Angeles to be with his daughter and her family. After Foxx decided to leave *Sanford and Son* in 1977 and his co-star Demond Wilson refused to appear on the series because of a salary dispute, *The Sanford Arms* spin-off took the place of *Sanford and Son*. This comedy, which lasted for only four low-rated episodes, featured Teddy Wilson as Phil Wheeler, who bought the Sanford house from Fred and was turning the rooming house next door into a resident hotel.

Finally, in 1978, Lear's company created the comedy *Diff'rent Strokes* about Philip Drummond (Conrad Bain), a Park Avenue millionaire, adopting two black children. This series gave birth to the 1979 comedy *The Facts of Life*, featuring the Edna Garrett character (Charlotte Ross), the Drummond's housekeeper, becoming the house mother at a private school and dealing with the problems of teenage girls.

Perhaps not remembered as much as the MTM and Lear comedies, writer/producer Danny Arnold created *Barney Miller*, the iconic 1970s comedy about a group of detectives working out of a precinct in Greenwich Village. As with the Lear sitcoms, it dealt with topical issues and, at least initially, the comedy centered mainly on the life and times of Detective Barney Miller—both his work and domestic life. Danny Arnold's focus on the personal life of Barney Miller in the first season of the show was no doubt influenced by his work with Sheldon Leonard on the 1969 to 1970 comedy, *My World and Welcome to It*, about the life and work of cartoonist John Munroe. Arnold won an Emmy for producing this series based on the works of James Thurber. Arnold would spin-off the Abe Vigoda character *Fish* from *Barney Miller* into his own series which had a relatively brief run lasting for a season and a half and would attempt a spin-off of the Max Gail character as described later in this part.

Perhaps in reaction to the topical comedies of Lear and Arnold and the female-centric shows of MTM which appealed to adults, writer/producer Garry Marshall created "retro" comedies like *Happy Days* and its spin-off *Laverne & Shirley* set in the 1950s that seemed like the old-fashioned sitcoms of that era and that appealed mainly to young people.

Part 3: Proposed Sitcom Spin-offs and Sequels in the 1970s

One of Marshall's first writing jobs for situation comedies was for the Danny Thomas-produced comedy *The Joey Bishop Show*. Marshall, with then-writing partner Jerry Belson, also scripted episodes of *The Danny Thomas Show* and *The Dick Van Dyke Show*. If the MTM, Lear, and Arnold comedies were considered revolutionary at the time, then Garry Marshall's shows were counter-revolutionary.

However, like the series produced by Thomas and Leonard on which Marshall had worked, *Happy Days*, starring Ron Howard from *The Andy Griffith Show* as Richie Cunningham, was a central character comedy. Set in 1950s Milwaukee, Wisconsin, the sitcom initially revolved around the teenage life of Richie with his family and friends. The comedy aired for ten seasons, and, as it evolved, Richie's friend, the "super cool" Arthur "Fonzie" Fonzarelli (Henry Winkler) became the most popular one on the show and eventually replaced Richie as the main character.

When Fred Silverman left CBS to assume the presidency of ABC Entertainment in May 1975, he asked Garry Marshall about spinning off the Fonzie character into his own series. Marshall responded that "Without Fonzie, you'll go back to *Father Knows Best*" and offered instead the concept for what would become *Laverne & Shirley*.[25] The characters of Laverne DeFazio and Shirley Feeney first appeared on an episode of *Happy Days* broadcast on November 11, 1975, titled "A Date with Fonzie" as dates for Richie Cunningham and the Fonz. Outspoken, somewhat pessimistic Laverne and naïve, optimistic Shirley got their own spin-off series beginning in January 1976 which ran for seven and a half seasons.

Marshall's other big hit spin-off during the 1970s, *Mork & Mindy*, starred Robin Williams as Mork from the planet Ork. Mork first appeared on the *Happy Days* episode titled "My Favorite Orkin," a play on the title of the 1960s comedy about a man from Mars called *My Favorite Martian*. In the episode, Richie Cunningham is alone at home watching television when Mork knocks on the door and introduces himself. Mork says he has come to Earth to collect a human specimen to bring back to his planet. After deciding to take Fonzie instead of Richie back to Ork, Richie wakes up and realizes it was all a dream. However, when *Mork & Mindy* became a series in September 1978, for rerun purposes, the *Happy Days* episode had a new ending added where Mork explains that he decided to let Fonzie go and traveled back to 1978 to continue his mission on Earth.

Another 1970s situation comedy, *Out of the Blue*, is often mentioned as still another spin-off from *Happy Days*. The series starred James Brogan as an angel named Random who has to perform good deeds on Earth to earn his wings. Random appeared on an episode of *Happy Days* on September 18, 1979, airing nine days after the debut of *Out of the Blue* on September 9. While *Out of the Blue* had been intended as a *Happy Days* spin-off, the appearance by Brogan on that show after the premiere of his series turned out to be more of a promotional crossover event than a spin-off. *Out of the Blue* lasted for only twelve episodes.

Somewhat in between the cutting-edge comedies of the seventies and the retro sitcoms of that decade were series created by actor-producer-director-writer James Komack. His most successful comedies were *Welcome Back, Kotter* and *Chico and the Man*, each starring a stand-up comic—Gabe Kaplan and Freddie Prinze. Both had ethnically diverse casts as in a Lear comedy, but the storylines were more like comedy sketches in the set-up/joke style which appealed mainly to younger viewers. Komack attempted several spin-offs during the seventies but none ever became a series.

Echoing the one trend during the seventies for nostalgia, several fondly remembered shows from the 1950s and 1960s were revived. Danny Thomas returned in a sequel to his fifties and sixties series in *Make Room for Granddaddy*, and Ozzie and Harriet Nelson came back in *Ozzie's Girls* where two young women—one black, one white—move into the Nelson house after David and Ricky had moved out on their own. Each series ended after a single season. The 1970s also saw attempted sequels to *Gilligan's Island*, *Father Knows Best*, and *The Many Loves of Dobie Gillis*.

While most of the comedy spin-offs, as mentioned above, that were picked up as a series were produced by MTM, Lear, or Arnold, the majority of spin-off attempts profiled below were in the mold of nostalgic characters like Richie Cunningham and not more modern representations like Mary Richards, Barney Miller, or Maude Finley.

After the Honeymoon

This episode of *My Three Sons*, a spin-off featuring Don Grady as Robbie Douglas, Tina Cole as his wife Katie, and their triplet sons, would have followed the struggles of a young, white middle-class husband and wife raising a family where the husband earned a living with the wife as the homemaker.

Background

Directed by Fred de Cordova and written by George Tibbles, who had scripted the pilot for *My Three Sons* back in 1960, *After the Hon-*

Part 3: Proposed Sitcom Spin-offs and Sequels in the 1970s • 55

From *My Three Sons*, Fred MacMurray, Don Grady, Tina Cole and their three sons

eymoon aired March 20, 1971, in the sitcom's eleventh and next to last season. In the ninth season of *My Three Sons*, Katie Douglas had given birth to identical triplet boys on an episode titled "My Three Grandsons."

The Pilot
 Robbie is laid off from his position at his dad's aircraft engineering firm, but lands a job in San Francisco. He, his wife, and their sons move

to an apartment managed by Cleo Mortensen (Pat Carroll) and her husband Willis (Richard X. Slattery). Their neighbor is Clark Sullivan (Mike Minor, the son of *My Three Sons* producer, Don Fedderson), a bachelor who wants to be a singer. Katie meets other young married women living in the apartment building and feels she may be saddling Robbie with too many responsibilities so early in life, particularly after speaking with one neighbor who says she and her husband have postponed having any kids. At his new job, Robbie finds that he has to share an office with three other guys and is earning less than he did at his previous position. After a day's work, he falls asleep in a chair at home. During the day, Robbie's dad, Steve stops by to visit his grandchildren, and Katie talks with him about Robbie being tied down. As might be expected given the tone of *My Three Sons*, Steve says that just about everyone wants what Robbie has. Katie tells Robbie about what Steve said, and he agrees with his father.

Postscript

After the Honeymoon did not become a series because Don Grady decided to leave his role as Robbie Douglas. According to Fred MacMurray,

> He (Grady) wanted to go out on his own and do something else—to get away from the image he had on the show.... He spent half his life on the series. When he decided to leave, at one point, we were going to have him killed (in the script), but wanted Tina and the triplets to stay on. We didn't want to send him to Vietnam and be killed or there to be a divorce. But the network said no to the idea of him being "killed,".... So now in the script, he is going to a remote part of South America so that family can't join him.[26]

Grady went on to pursue his musical career. Tina Cole did return to *My Three Sons* for its twelfth and final season with her husband's absence explained by having Robbie transferred to Peru to supervise a construction job.

Barney and Me

A kids-show host played by Soupy Sales recruits a live talking bear to appear on his show in order to boost its ratings in this proposed spin-off of the cookie-stealing Bear from *The New Andy Williams Show*.

Background

Barney and Me grew out of a character on singer Andy Williams's second variety show for NBC which debuted in September 1969. That version of the Williams's show emphasized comedy as much as singing. It ran for two seasons and featured several strange characters such as the Little General, Walking Suitcase, Big Bird, and the Bear—a cookie-thieving animal with Janos Prohaska dressed in a bear costume. The popularity of the Bear character led the creators of the sketches, Chris Bearde and Allan Blye, to propose a spin-off series in late 1971 originally titled *The Bear and I*. Soupy Sales appeared as Pete Richards, the star of a local kids' television show called *Uncle Pete*. While Janos Prohaska, a European animal impersonator, wore the bear suit, Shepard Menkin provided Barney the Bear's voice. The spin-off aired in March 1973 on NBC as part of *Triple Play '73*, a two-hour movie presentation of failed pilots. Bruce Bilson directed the pilot from a script written by Bearde, Blye, and A.J. Crothers.

The Pilot

Kelsoe (Joe Flynn), a television executive, informs Pete Richards that due to the terrible quality of his show and low ratings, *Uncle Pete* will be canceled at the end of the week. Depressed, Pete wanders through a zoo talking to himself. To his surprise, a bear at the zoo begins talking back to Pete. The bear introduces himself as Barney but refuses to speak to other people since they are always upset when he does. Pete convinces Barney to be on his show. The zoo's owner, Jungle Johnny (Joey Foreman), is happy to get rid of the bear for $250. Pete takes Barney to his apartment, and then Joanne (Bonnie Boland), the roommate of Pete's girlfriend Sylvia (Odona Powers), arrives and thinks Pete is hiding a woman in his apartment. Pete's girlfriend comes by and eventually both she and Joanne discover Barney. After Barney begins talking to them, they believe that Barney is a man in an elaborate bear costume.

Pete has Barney on his show. The show's ratings go up, and it becomes the network's most successful program. Mr. Kelsoe plans a large press conference where he thinks Barney will have to come out of the bear suit. Meanwhile, in his office, Jungle Johnny sees that Barney is making money and says to himself that he will capture the bear again. At the press conference, Barney attempts to explain that he is really a bear, only to receive laughs and then frustration from the reporters who demand that he remove his suit. Barney runs out of the press conference. Outside, Jungle Johnny is waiting with a cage for Barney, but, in the confusion, he captures Pete instead and drives away. Later, a freed Pete is at home hearing the missing Barney discussed on the radio with everyone now realizing that Barney is a talking bear. After Barney climbs through Pete's apartment window, Pete convinces him that people now want to help and understand him. In the lobby of his apartment, Pete introduces Barney to excited reporters and young children. The kids hug Barney and say that they love him no matter whether he is human or bear.

Postscript

As many may remember, Soupy Sales himself hosted his own children's show on local television stations and in syndication in the 1960s. After *Barney and Me* failed to turn into a series, Sales returned in a new version of his iconic kids' show, *The New Soupy Sales Show*, in 1978.

The Blonde

The misadventures of Oliver Douglas's (Eddie Albert) stereotypical blonde, ex-secretary Carol Rush (Elaine Joyce) is the focus of this backdoor pilot from *Green Acres*.

Background

The episode titled "The Ex-Secretary" aired on April 27, 1971, as the final installment of *Green Acres*. Like *Pam* (see below), the other backdoor pilot from *Green Acres*, Jay Sommers, the creator of the Eddie Albert series, penned the script for this episode which Bruce Bilson, the grandfather of actress Rachel Bilson, directed.

The Pilot

Carol Rush works in the real estate office of William Oglethorpe (Richard Deacon) and lives with her sister Lillian Grant (Emmaline Henry) and Lillian's husband Harry (Cliff Norton). Carol had previously worked as Oliver Douglas's legal secretary in New York before he moved to Hooterville. Oliver calls her to see if she can recall the jeweler she took his grandfather's watch to for repairs. At the office, Mr. Oglethorpe is expecting an important client, Mr. David, who wants to buy land for a big complex he is building. Before he shows up, Mark Allan (George Furth), an attorney, comes to the Oglethorpe's to rent the office next door. When Mr. David arrives, Carol says he reminds her of someone. Mr. David is looking to sell shares in his new complex. Oglethorpe writes him a check for $10,000 worth of shares. Carol then remembers that Mr. David is also known as Horace Billingsley, whom Oliver Douglas had tried to indict in New York for swindling. Carol, along with her brother-in-law Harry, goes to David's hotel room to retrieve the check. While Carol is trying to find the check in Mr. David's room with him there, Harry becomes involved in a card game across the hall. When she calls Mr. David "Mr. Billingsley," he realizes that she recognizes him and says he will do away with her. She screams for help, but the other players in the card game won't allow Harry to leave. Two police officers then arrive to break up the game. Hearing Carol's screams, one of the officers comes to her assistance. In the end, Mr. Oglethorpe is grateful to her for the return of his check.

Postscript
This spin-off attempt certainly did not follow the trend of the cutting edge shows of the 1970s like *The Mary Tyler Moore Show* in advancing the depiction of single working women. At the time she made the pilot, actress Elaine Joyce, who portrayed Carol Rush, was married to actor/dancer Bobby Van. Van passed away from brain cancer in 1980. In 1999, Elaine Joyce married playwright Neil Simon.

Bo and Sam

This potential spin-off from *The Love Boat* centered on Bo and Sam (Michael Tucci and Philip Charles MacKenzie)—two wacky carpenters whose motto is "We Go Anywhere; We Do Anything." The slapstick antics of Bo and Sam reminded one of the early 1960s comedy, *I'm Dickens, He's Fenster* which starred Marty Ingels as Arch Fenster and John Astin as Harry Dickens—two carpenters/construction workers.

Background
Similar to an anthology series, *The Love Boat* aired different stories each week focusing on love and sentimentality. However, unlike a traditional anthology series, *The Love Boat* had regular characters—the crew of the Pacific Princess, a luxury cruise ship. The crew often became involved in the different stories on each episode. Captain Stubing (Gavin MacLeod), Dr. Bricker (Bernie Kopell), Yeoman-Purser "Gopher" Smith (Fred Grandy), bartender Isaac Washington (Ted Lange), and Cruise Director Julie McCoy (Lauren Tewes) were the original crew members.

Each show generally had three different storylines—a "heart story" about love, a "tears story" dealing with sentimentality, and a "laugh story" just for the fun of it.[27] The proposed *Bo and Sam* spin-off was the latter. The pilot, directed by Richard Kinon and written by Ben Joelson and Art Baer, who executive produced *The Love Boat*, aired as part of episode twenty-four of the second season of *The Love Boat* on March 10, 1979.

The Pilot

In honor of Stubing's fifth anniversary as captain, the crew pays two men, Bo and Sam, to craft a model of the Pacific Princess. The builders bring the model made out of matchsticks onboard, but break it and are not able to repair the model before the Pacific Princess sails. They try to rebuild the replica before the Captain's anniversary party. When Bo runs out of hairpins in putting the model back together, he and Sam find some ill-fitting suits in order to mix with the crowd on board. Bo dances with a woman whose hair is full of pins and, while dancing, takes the pins from her hair. The two men finally rebuild the model, but, in trying to hide it from the Captain, the model becomes stuck in some elevator doors and is broken in half. Bo and Sam attempt to put it back together a second time but have only thirty minutes to make the repairs. During the course of fixing it, Bo's wristwatch inadvertently comes off in the hull of the model ship.

At the party, the Captain receives ship replicas from almost everyone. When he is presented with the model Bo and Sam built, he hears the watch's alarm go off inside and breaks the model to retrieve the watch which is what he really wanted for his anniversary.

Postscript

According to Philip Charles MacKenzie, who played Sam, spin-off possibilities were mentioned during the filming of this segment of *The Love Boat*. He further remarked that he is not aware why the *Bo and Sam* did not become a series. "As far as I can recall, it just went away and I also don't know at all if there were any future script or situational ideas."[28]

The "Castaways" on Gilligan's Island

This proposed sequel to the 1960s sitcom *Gilligan's Island* starred most of the original cast running a resort hotel on the island that each week would attract new guests with their own stories similar to the ABC series, *The Love Boat*.

Background

Gilligan's Island, the tale of seven castaways marooned on an uncharted island in the Pacific, starred Bob Denver as skipper's mate Gilligan. Five passengers set sail on the Minnow, a small charter boat, captained by the Skipper Jonas Grumby (Alan Hale Jr.), when a storm knocked the boat off course and the passengers and crew ended up on an island for three years. Millionare Thurston Howell III (Jim Backus) and his wife Lovey (Natalie Schafer), movie star Ginger Grant (Tina Louise), country girl Mary Ann (Dawn Wells), and Professor Roy Hinkley (Russell Johnson) comprised the passengers.

In October 1978, a movie titled *Rescue from Gilligan's Island* reunited most of the cast except for Tina Louise and aired to tremendous ratings on NBC. The film showed the castaways finally being rescued after a hurricane strikes their island. Using their huts as rafts, they are swept out to sea and taken to Honolulu by the Coast Guard. The castaways return to their former lives, but find things are not the same. The Skipper and Gilligan visit each of the castaways to have them sign an insurance form so the Skipper can purchase a new boat which he names the Minnow II. He invites everyone for a Christmas cruise back to their deserted island, but as luck would have it, a storm comes up and they become shipwrecked again.

The ratings for the reunion movie prompted NBC to ask Sherwood Schwartz, the creator of *Gilligan's Island*, to consider producing an hour-long version of the series that would be a sequel to the original. Schwartz settled on an idea that he had originally thought about for the possible fourth season of *Gilligan*. If the ratings for the supposed fourth season of the sitcom had started to fall, Schwartz would have had the castaways rescued and Thurston Howell would have subsequently constructed a hotel on the island. The Skipper, Gilligan, and the other castaways would help run the hotel.

As Schwartz described the idea for the sequel, "The new series would be done as an hour show, with a cast of guests, bringing two or three plots to the hotel in each episode. In form it would be something like *Love Boat*."[29]

The original deal with NBC called for seven one-hour episodes of the new *Gilligan's Island* sequel to be made. However, first Sherwood Schwartz wanted to produce a pilot for the proposed series, hence the movie—*The "Castaways" on Gilligan's Island*. The one-hour pilot became a ninety-minute movie that NBC premiered on Thursday, May 3, 1979.

Sherwood Schwartz, along with his brothers Al and Elroy, penned the script for this *Gilligan's Island* movie which Earl Bellamy directed.

The Pilot

Gilligan finds two old World War II planes on the island. The Professor figures out a way to get one of them running again and everyone, except the Howells, pitch in to fix the plane. The plane is dubbed Minnow III and flies off the island only to encounter engine trouble. The Professor has everyone jettison their belongings. In the process, Gilligan falls out of the plane, but luckily has a parachute on because of the engine trouble. The rest of the castaways decide to return to the island to rescue Gilligan. After they land, the remaining good engine falls off and so returning to the island saved their lives. They find Gilligan, and the Navy rescues all of them since the Navy saw the plane disappear from radar. Mr. Howell then declares that he will build a tribute to the castaways on the island.

A year later, the Castaways Resort is completed with no phones, television, radio, or electricity so guests can enjoy the peaceful island life. All of the castaways are partners in the venture. The Howells are the hosts, the Professor does research on the island, Mary Ann conducts exercise classes, Ginger entertains, and the Skipper and Gilligan shuttle guests from cruise liners off shore to the hotel. Among the first guests are Mr. and Mrs. Elliot. Myra Elliot (Marcia Wallace) booked the resort so her husband Henry (Tom Bosley) can relax and not spend all his time running his real estate business. Dr. Tom Larson (Rod Browning) and his wife Laura (Joan Roberts) are also guests at the resort and are accompanied by a boy thought to be their son. However, the boy who came from the cruise ship turns out not to be the son of either the Elliots or the Larsons.

Myra tries to get Henry to relax to no avail. She enlists the help of the castaways in this endeavor with Mary Ann and Ginger giving Henry a massage, the Professor taking him snorkeling, and Gilligan and the Skipper going fishing with him. Subsequently, Henry overhears his wife tell the Larsons that she and her husband will not leave the island until Henry relaxes. He decides to pretend he is taking it easy by not shaving and abandoning his business suits for less formal attire. Later, Myra overhears Henry remark to the Larsons that it is all an act. Myra and Henry begin to argue, but eventually reconcile at the first luau given by the castaways. The couple decides to return in six months because Henry wants to work a deal with Thurston on building condos on part of the island.

In the second story, when no one knows who the young boy belongs to, everyone starts looking for him. Gilligan finds the boy and learns that his name is Robbie and that his parents are training him for the Olympics. Robbie Sloan is tired of training all day and left the cruise ship to get away from his parents. The boy's parents show up on the island, and Gilligan informs them that their son ran away because they made him train too hard. The boy overhears his parents say that maybe they were too demanding, and he reconciles with them.

Postscript

This sequel pilot attracted about half of the audience as the first *Gilligan* movie, and so plans to produce the additional one-hour episodes were abandoned. In 1980, *The Harlem Globetrotters on Gilligan's Island* became the final TV movie about the adventures of Gilligan and the castaways. Originally, the Dallas Cowboys Cheerleaders were to be the guests at the Castaways Hotel, but when they were not available, the Harlem Globetrotters took their place. The movie aired on May 15, 1981, and involved a power-hungry billionaire played by Martin Landau and his associate portrayed by his then wife, Barbara Bain, discovering a new element called "Supremium" and trying to get all the castaways to sign the deed for the island over to him. He obtains everyone's signature except that of Howell's son Thurston Howell IV. To obtain his signature, he bets with Howell IV on a basketball game between his team made up of robots and Howell's team, the Harlem Globetrotters. Of course, the Globetrotters win. Jim Backus who had played Thurston Howell III was too ill to appear in much of the movie. David Ruprecht played his son, Thurston Howell IV. This movie scored about the same ratings as *The "Castaways" on Gilligan's Island*.

The Councilman

Councilman Pete Peterson (Bill Daily) needs a lot of help from his two administrative assistants Jennifer (Carol Androsky) and Kris (Janet MacLachlan)—one white and one black—in carrying out the responsibilities of his office in this "power behind the throne" comedy.

Background

The Councilman, the only back-door pilot and the only potential spin-off from *The Mary Tyler Moore Show* that never became a series, aired March 4, 1972. Even though in the episode Janet MacLachlan's character was referred to as "Kris," the credits at the end listed her character's name as "Sherry Wilson."

The Mary Tyler Moore Show's director, Jay Sandrich, helmed the episode based on a script written by Jim Parker and Arnold Margolin. Parker and Margolin had worked with Allan Burns, co-creator of *The Mary Tyler Moore Show*, on the comedy *He & She* starring Richard Benjamin and Paula Prentiss. Parker and Margolin were employed by MTM Enterprises for about a year after being forced out of the Paramount series they produced, *Love, American Style*, by studio head Douglas Cramer.

The Pilot

In the last episode of the second season of *The Mary Tyler Moore Show* titled "His Two Right Arms," Lou Grant wants Mary to get newly-elected councilman Pete Peterson for WJM's Sunday afternoon interview show *Face the People*. Mary goes to Peterson's headquarters and meets his staff—Walter Ellis (Wally Taylor), his press secretary, and his two administrative assistants, Jennifer Riley and Kris Wilson. She also meets Peterson himself—an absent-minded bumbler who really needs Jennifer and Kris to set him straight on many issues. Mary advises Lou that Peterson wouldn't be right for their show, but the station's manager insists that Peterson be booked on *Face the People*. After Mary informs Jennifer and Kris that Peterson will be on the show, they think they will be able to prep him for the appearance. Jennifer, Kris, and Kris's mother, played by Isabel Sanford who went on to star as Louise Jefferson in *The Jeffersons*, along with Peterson all meet at Mary's apartment to rehearse him, but Pete does not want to be briefed. On the live interview show, his answers to questions are less than adequate, but it seems that everyone had been watching a baseball game on another channel and so little damage to his career resulted from his appearance.

If it had become a series, episodes would presumably have focused on Jennifer and Kris's continuing efforts to help their boss extricate himself from embarrassing situations.

Postscript

Commenting on this proposed spin-off, writer Arnold Margolin describes the challenges of doing a good back-door pilot:

> We were introducing three new characters with their own potential series format (two young women who work for a bum-

bling politician and are constantly trying to keep him out of trouble) into a format of an established series... Thus, with the twenty-four minutes of time we were allotted we had to service the established characters of *The Mary Tyler Moore Show* and their storylines and also introduce three new characters and give them a story that established the premise of their projected series. It was simply too many characters and too much story and we ended up not being able to either do a very good episode of the series or delineate and serve the characters and premise of the new show. I would sum it up thusly: Not a case of too many cooks, but a case of too many ingredients.[30]

Although CBS did not pick up *The Councilman* as a series, its star, Bill Daily, did become a regular on the MTM-produced *The Bob Newhart Show* which began in 1972.

Della and Son

In *Della and Son*, a proposed spin-off from *Chico and the Man*, Della Reese stars along with Franklyn Ajaye as mother and son running a catering business together in what would have been one of the first comedies about an African-American middle-class mother as an entrepreneur.

Background

Comic Freddie Prinze as Chico Rodriguez originally appeared on *Chico and the Man* partnered with cranky Ed Brown (Jack Albertson) to help Ed run his garage. James Komack, the creator of *Chico and the Man* and originally a stand-up comedian himself, hired another stand-up comic, Franklyn Ajaye, as Della Reese's son in this spin-off.

Della Reese had become part of the cast at the beginning of *Chico and the Man*'s third season in fall 1976. In a two-part episode of the comedy, Reese was introduced as "Della Rogers," the owner of a catering business, "Della-Car-Tessen," located across the street from Ed's garage. She not only managed two food trucks, but also owned the building housing Ed's garage.

Directed by Jack Donohue, who had directed episodes of many classic comedies such as *Here's Lucy* and *The Odd Couple*, and written by Jerry Ross and Gary Belkin, *Della and Son* aired June 30, 1978.

The Pilot

Della's son Tony arrives from Hawaii for a visit along with his baby son Michael. He explains that his wife Pearl is still on the islands. Tony is always coming up with pie-in-the-sky ideas to make money. His latest business venture is to make black celebrity dashikis. He is not receptive to Della's offer of being a partner in her catering business. Instead, he asks Ed for $2,000 to start his own business, but Ed turns him down. Tony finally reveals to his mother that his wife has left him and asks his mother to take care of Michael while he attempts to start his dashiki venture. Della says that she is not going to take care of the baby by herself. Later, Tony is ready to leave with Michael when Della changes her mind and offers to give him the $2,000 and to take care of her grandson. She further explains that Tony's father walked out on both of them when her son was younger and that Tony will probably do the same. Tony then reconsiders and decides to join his mother in her catering business.

Postscript

Jerry Ross, who co-scripted the pilot, recalls that "Della Reese was a well liked regular on *Chico and the Man* with a high TVQ... The pilot was shot but it didn't go anywhere because the stand-up comic who was to play her son turned out to be very uncooperative and hard to work with...Whatever charm he may have had doing stand up was lost when playing a role. Della as usual was great, a consummate professional and talented performer."[31]

While *Della and Son* never became a series, after *Chico and the Man*, Della Reese starred on *Charlie and Company* with Flip Wilson and on *The Royal Family* with Redd Foxx before appearing on her most memorable series, *Touched by an Angel*.

Father Knows Best Reunion

This project, a sequel to the 1954 to 1960 series, starred Robert Young as Jim Anderson, the head of a middle-class, middle-American family that included his wife Margaret (Jane Wyatt) and three children, Betty (Elinor Donahue), Bud (Billy Gray), and Kathy (Lauren Chapin).

Background

Written by Paul West and directed by Marc Daniels, *Father Knows Best Reunion* aired May 15, 1977. In talking about the reunion special, Robert Young said that he wouldn't rule out another series. But his co-star, Jane Wyatt responded, "I said no when this one ended (the original *Father Knows Best*) and I still say no."³² John Mitchell, president of Columbia Pictures Television, which produced the reunion movie, indicated that he wanted to do more such shows, possibly a Thanksgiving special, about now grandparents Jim and Margaret Anderson and the challenges they face growing older and dealing with the problems of their grown adult offspring.

The Pilot

Margaret is suffering from "empty nest" syndrome, and so Jim invites Bud, Kathy, and Betty to come home to celebrate his and Margaret's thirty-fifth wedding anniversary. Betty is a widow living in Chicago with two young daughters, Jenny (Cari Ann Warder), age nine, and Ellen (Kyle Richards), age seven. Her husband had been killed in an automobile accident. Bud is married to Jeanne (Susan Adams), has a ten-year-old son, Robbie (Christopher Gardner), and lives in Minneapolis where he races motorcycles and runs a motorcycle shop. Kathy, who lives in Kansas City, is single but dating Dr. Jason Harper (Hal England), ten years her senior. On her flight to Springfield, Betty meets Frank Carlson (Jim McMullan), the pilot of the airplane, whom she used to date in college. Bud is having marital problems because he is away a lot on the motorcycle racing circuit. He visits his dad and mother with his son, but without his wife. Jim subsequently calls Bud's wife and asks her to fly in to see Bud and celebrate the Anderson's anniversary. Dr. Harper also arrives for the celebration. He wants to marry Kathy, but she doesn't accept his proposal at least for now. Frank also desires a serious relationship with Betty, and Bud admits to Jeanne that she might be right about him being away from his family too much.

Postscript

Although the *Father Knows Best Reunion* received good ratings (it ranked fourth for the week), interest from NBC as well as from potential sponsors was not forthcoming for another series. However, although no Thanksgiving special resulted after the reunion movie aired as had been suggested by the head of Columbia Pictures Television, a Christmas special featuring the cast did air. Broadcast December 18, 1977, Paul West again wrote the script and, for this movie, Norman Abbott directed.

"Home for Christmas" began with Jim and Margaret expecting all their children and grandchildren to arrive for the holidays. However, one-by-one each informs their parents that they have made other plans. Jim and Margaret think that they should sell their house if they are going to spend Christmas alone. However, then Betty changes her plans and visits her parents with her two daughters. Bud phones and says he and his family will be home for Christmas as well. Kathy and her doctor boyfriend also arrive. Bud confides to his father that Jeanne is still unhappy. Jeanne relates to Margaret that she would like to live in a home of her own as well and eventually tells Bud the same thing. Betty's beau Frank has to fly by himself to Springfield when his flight from Rome comes in late to Chicago and all scheduled flights to the Anderson's home town have already left. Everyone is worried when Frank doesn't show up on time given that there is a major snowstorm hitting Springfield. Eventually, Frank arrives much to Betty's relief. On Christmas Day, Jim announces that their house has been sold. Bud reveals that he bought the house for his family. Margaret and Jim subsequently purchase a motor home to tour the country.

In reflecting on the two *Father Knows Best* movies, Elinor Donahue, who played Betty Anderson, remarked that she thought that, at most, the cast would appear in perhaps one special every year, but she doesn't recall any serious discussion of the movies leading to another weekly series. However, "doing those two specials in the one year (1977) put even that idea (of doing yearly specials) to rest."[33]

Goober and the Truckers' Paradise

This attempted spin-off starred George Lindsey as Goober Pyle—a role he had originated on *The Andy Griffith Show*. Goober Pyle sells his gas station in Mayberry, North Carolina, and moves to a small town outside of Atlanta where he and his sister Pearl (Leigh French) run a truck stop restaurant.

Background

Produced by Lindsey, Rich Eustis, and Sam Lovello, this spin-off, originally titled *Goober's Girls*, aired May 17, 1978, ten years after *The Andy Griffith Show* had ended. It was written by Eustis, Lindsey, and April Kelly. Rich Eustis and Bill Wyse directed the pilot.

George Lindsey had joined the Griffith show in 1965 portraying Goober, Gomer Pyle's (Jim Nabors) cousin. The character of Goober Pyle first appeared on an episode of *The Andy Griffith Show* titled "Fun Girls." Sheriff Andy Taylor and his deputy Barney Fife are working late doing inventory when Gomer and Goober stop by to ask Andy to go to the movies with them. They want to see a Cary Grant film, and Gomer has Goober do a Cary

Grant impression—"Judy, Judy, Judy, Judy, Judy." Gomer really likes Goober's impression; Andy not so much. After the Jim Nabors character got his own sitcom—*Gomer Pyle USMC* (the first spin-off of a spin-off)—the role of George Lindsey as Goober grew to fill the void. Lindsey not only played Goober on the Griffith show, but also on its other spin-off, *Mayberry RFD*, which featured many of the supporting characters from *The Andy Griffith Show* along with Ken Berry starring as farmer Sam Jones. Subsequently, Lindsey also appeared as Goober on the corn-fed variety series *Hee Haw*.

The Pilot

Goober and the Truckers' Paradise focuses on the misadventures of Goober and his sister trying to keep their business running. Other characters in the pilot included Charlene (Sandi Newton), the waitress at the truck stop who came with the place; Becky Pyle (Audrey Landers), Goober's niece who is fond and supportive of him; Toni (Lindsay Bloom), Goober's other sister; Eagle Keyes (John Chappell), the town's deputy who comes to the café every day for a free lunch. Bible Bill (Bill Medley), T-Bone (Brion James), Catfish (Bruce Fisher), Elwood Gunnite (Robert Towers), Troll (Mickey Jones), and Bud (Ken Johnson) are other frequent diners at the cafe. Goober has invested his life savings in the restaurant. Even though the business flourishes, he finds the cash register filled with a lot of IOUs.

As Rich Eustis remarked when describing the pilot's storyline, Goober is "…in over his head, of course, and the truckers enjoy poking fun at him, pulling practical jokes, etc., etc., but he weathers it all, and comes out on top, one way or another… by the end of the episode."[34]

Postscript

By the time the pilot aired, George Lindsey had already been informed that CBS wouldn't turn it into a series. According to Lindsey, the effort didn't sell because it wasn't very good. He indicated, "That show's failure was totally my mistake. I thought I knew how to produce a show and I didn't know and ruined it. We shot a half-hour television show and it took 14 hours to film it. I should have just stuck with the acting part of it."[35]

Rich Eustis agrees with Lindsey about the difficulty of making the pilot, but he indicates that it did come together after editing and re-shoots. Eustis received a call from a CBS executive saying that he loved it. A few days later, he ran into a friend at a restaurant who knew one of the top network executives who said "too bad about your pilot."[36] Eustis learned that some of the top executives with CBS in New York had winced at the idea of the network continuing to be known as the place to go for low-brow, country-bumpkin type comedies. At the time, CBS wanted more sophisticated entertainment in line with comedies like Mary Tyler Moore's series and not rural, nostalgic sitcoms such as *Goober and The Truckers' Paradise*.

Horshack

This proposed spin-off from *Welcome Back, Kotter* featured the character of Arnold Horshack (Ron Palillo) living with his mother and siblings. Arnold's mom has just lost her fifth husband, and Arnold attempts to become the man of the family.

Background

Welcome Back, Kotter starred Gabe Kaplan as a Brooklyn-born teacher who returns to his high school to teach a remedial academics group known as the "Sweathogs." Robert Hegyes appeared as Juan Epstein, a Jewish Puerto Rican; John Travolta played Vinnie Barbarino, the handsome leader of the group; Lawrence Hilton-Jacobs was featured as Boom Boom Washington, the hip black dude; and Ron Palillo portrayed Arnold Horshack, the not-so-bright member of the group. *Welcome Back, Kotter* had been created by "multi-hyphenate" James Komack. See also *Della and Son*, *We Love Annie*, and *Whatever Happened to Dobie Gillis?* in this part.

According to Jerry Rannow, who wrote the pilot along with his then wife Jewel Jaffe, a slightly exaggerated form of his own life story served as the back story for the Arnold Horshack character.[37] Rannow, the son of a much-married mother, had siblings with different last names and personalities. He and his spouse cast Andrea McArdle as Arnold's sister. She would later originate the role of Annie in the Broadway musical. However, they passed on Doris Roberts as Horshack's mother. Roberts later played the mother on the hit comedy, *Everybody Loves Raymond*. Ellen Travolta, John Travolta's sister, won the role of the mother.

The character of Arnold Horshack appeared in a potential spin-off broadcast on February 3, 1977, as the second part of a two-part one-hour episode of *Kotter*. James Komack directed the pilot along with Bob LaHendro and starred in it as Horshack's uncle.

Part 3: Proposed Sitcom Spin-offs and Sequels in the 1970s • 71

Ron Palillo who starred as Arnold Horshack in his own spin-off pilot from *Welcome Back, Kotter*

The Pilot

In the first part of the two-parter, titled "Has Anyone Seen Arnold?," Mr. Kotter announces a school drama festival and wants his class to put on a scene from a play. He asks for students to volunteer, and Arnold offers to do a scene from *Cyrano de Bergerac*. He is paired with Judy, a student from the over-achievers class. During rehearsals, when the other Sweathogs make fun of him, Arnold becomes upset and leaves. Later, no one can find him, and Kotter asks for someone to substitute for Arnold in the play. Vinnie Barbarino takes over and overacts in front of a student audience.

In the second part, titled "There Goes Number 5," the actual pilot for the spin-off, Horshack has been gone for two days, and everyone is worried. He reappears and asks Kotter how to become a father since he wants to be head of his family. Arnold Horshack's stepfather, Mr. O'Hara, a taxi driver and Arnold's mother's (Ellen Travolta) fifth husband, has died. She hopes to find another husband soon to support her family which includes, in addition to Arnold, daughter Judy (Elyssa Davalos), a younger daughter Doris (Andrea McArdle), and younger son Manny (Dean M. Salomon). At dinner, Arnold announces that he will take care of the family to the laughter of his siblings. On the roof of his apartment building, Arnold talks with Goldie (Susan Lawrence) about his Uncle Harry who used to own a costume shop and dress as a chicken.

The next day, Arnold goes to see his uncle to ask for a job. Harry (James Komack) now owns a clothing store called "Orshacks of Fifth Avenue" having dropped the "H" from his last name. Harry says he will give Arnold a job if he forgets that Harry once owned a costume shop. Meanwhile, Arnold's mother has found a potential new husband at the bowling alley. But Arnold's siblings agree to let him try to be head of the house. His mother advises him that she has a talent for making things work out.

In the last scene, Arnold returns to Kotter's class saying that he has gotten a part-time job but will still attend school.

Postscript

Rannow feels that what really sunk the Horshack pilot was the "red" dress. He and his writing partner wanted the mother character to wear a red dress when she goes to the bowling alley to meet a new, potential mate. ABC insisted that they could not have Arnold's mom in a red dress since it is the color of passion. Even though in the scene Ellen Travolta wore a red dress, the network re-shot the scene with her in a frilly blue and white dress. As Rannow remarked, "By opposing the network so boldly we lost the game to another spin-off (from *Barney Miller*) called *Fish* with Abe Vigoda. As far as I know Abe never wore a red dress."[38]

Ron Palillo thought that the pilot to be a really good show with a great supporting cast. "However, in hindsight, if it had been successful, I would probably have been playing Arnold Horshack for the rest of my life. At the time, it would have been a feather in my cap and would have been very lucrative but it would have sealed my fate as an actor.... So it was probably for the best—but it was certainly a heartbreaker when it happened." [39]

Jersey Bounce

Eugene Conigliaro (Greg Antonacci) and Mickey Long (Gene Davis) are a couple of wannabe young mobsters in Newark, New Jersey, who will do almost anything to get jobs with the mob in this comedy-drama spin-off from *The Rockford Files*. Eugene, who always wears a cap, and Mickey, the handsome stud, work out of a pizza shop owned by Eugene's dad Beppy (Simon Oakland). A comedy about aspiring members of the New Jersey mob was a unique concept at the time.

Background

Written by David Chase and directed by former *Hogan Heroes* actor Ivan Dixon, *The Rockford Files* episode titled "Just a Coupla Guys" aired on December 14, 1979, as the next to last installment of the series. The characters of Eugene and Mickey had appeared on a prior episode of *The Rockford Files* titled "The Jersey Bounce."

The Pilot

Jim Rockford (James Garner) flies to Newark, New Jersey, at the behest of the daughter of former mob boss Joseph Lombard. Rockford is robbed at the airport and becomes stranded at a police station. Meanwhile, Mickey and Eugene think that if they solve the case of who is throwing dead animals on the lawn of the retired mobster's estate, it will ingratiate them in the eyes of Lombard, who may help them with other pursuits. They find the boy who is tossing dead chickens on the estate, not knowing that he is the son of Tony Martine, part of the crime family to which Lombard once belonged. Tony wants Lombard, who is now a born-again Christian, to intervene with a Cardinal to have his dead cousin Vincent buried in consecrated ground. Martine first tries to shoot up Lombard's estate. Upon learning of this, Mickey and Eugene think they can identify who did it. But Lombard is not interested in their help. However, after Lombard's daughter is kidnapped by the Martine family, Rockford becomes involved. Martine wants to hold Lombard's daughter until the former mob boss convinces the Cardinal to permit the cousin to be interred in a sacred place. Mickey and Eugene locate Vincent's body in a restaurant and want to exchange it for the daughter. The police arrive at the restaurant where they find not only Vincent's casket being stored for final burial, but also Lombard's daughter.

Postscript

In reviewing the episode, *Variety* said ". . . the show suffered a split personality, taking on the familiar 'Rockford' charm when Garner was on screen, lapsing into amateurish tedium when spinoff possibilities were being mined."[40] Networks were apparently not interested in a series that mixed the mob with comedy. David Chase, who wrote the pilot, would later create a series for HBO focused on the New Jersey mob—*The Sopranos*.

Kelly's Kids

Kelly's Kids was an attempt to portray a more ethnically diverse family for television viewers. This proposed spin-off from *The Brady Bunch* starred Ken Berry and Brooke Bundy as adoptive parents of a Caucasian boy, an African-American boy, and an Asian-American boy.

Background

Directed by Richard Michaels and written by the creator of *The Brady Bunch*, Sherwood Schwartz, who had previously devised *Gilligan's Island*, the *Kelly's Kids* episode aired on January 4, 1974.

The Pilot

Ken Kelly (Berry), who does a nightclub act, and his wife, Kathy (Bundy), friends of the Bradys, adopt eight-year-old Matt (Todd Lookinland—the brother of Mike Lookinland who played Bobby Brady on *The Brady Bunch*). Because Matt is sad about the friends he left at the orphanage, Kathy suggests to Ken that they should adopt more kids. They see Mrs. Phillips (Jackie Joseph, then Mrs. Ken Berry) at the orphanage and decide to adopt Matt's friends—Steve (Carey Wong), an Asian-American, and Dewayne (Billy Attmore), an African-American. When their bigoted neighbor, Mrs. Payne (Molly Dodd) discovers the couple has adopted three kids, two of whom are minorities, she thinks that the kids, particularly Steve and Dewayne, will be destructive. The two boys overhear their parents discuss the problem with Mrs. Payne and decide to run away along with Matt. They end up at the Brady's house where Carol Brady serves them hot chocolate until Ken and Kathy arrive to take them home.

Postscript

Sherwood Schwartz's attempt to bring a relevant sitcom to television in the 1970s dealing with racism and other social issues was no doubt influenced by popular comedies at the time like *All in the Family* and *Maude*. Although ABC did not turn *Kelly's Kids* into a series, twelve years later, CBS bought the concept and put on *Together We Stand*, a comedy about the Randalls—David, a basketball coach played by Elliot Gould, his wife Lori (Dee Wallace Stone), and their kids. The Randalls decided to adopt a girl after being told they couldn't conceive. Subsequently, Mrs. Randall did become pregnant and gave birth to a son. Later, at the encouragement of a social worker, they adopted a six-year-old African-American girl and a fourteen-year-old Vietnamese boy. The series lasted for only a few weeks at the beginning of the 1986-87 television season. Later that season, the comedy came back as *Nothing Is Easy* after Gould left the show. CBS added the retooled comedy to its Sunday night line-up in January 1987 with Gould's character having died in an auto accident. Lori Randall returned to work and also went to school to become a stenographer. After two low-rated episodes on Sunday, the series went on hiatus again only to return on Fridays in late March for five more episodes, after which it disappeared for good.

Lenny & Squiggy in the Army

Created by Garry Marshall, *Lenny & Squiggy in the Army*, a potential spin-off from *Laverne & Shirley*, featured the misadventures of Leonard "Lenny" Kosnowski (Michael McKean) and Andrew "Squiggy" Squiggman (David L. Lander) in the military.

Background

Starring Penny Marshall and Cindy Williams, *Laverne & Shirley*, like *Happy Days*, was set in the 1950s. Roommates Laverne and Shirley worked at the Shotz Brewery in Milwaukee. Squiggy and Lenny, their neighbors in the apartment building where they lived, were truck drivers at the brewery

Only a few weeks after their first appearance on *Laverne & Shirley*, Fred Silverman, head of ABC Entertainment, proposed that Lenny and Squiggy should star in their own series.[41] Garry Marshall developed a spin-off for Michael McKean and David Lander where the two go into the Army. The pilot, filmed in 1976, featured actor Vern Rowe in the cast along with George Memmoli who played Lenny and Squiggy's sergeant. McKean and Lander used some of the comedy bits they had developed while with the improv group, The Creditability Gap, in this spin-off.

The Pilot

Not much is known about the specific storyline of the pilot other than the obvious that it dealt with Lenny and Squiggy's initiation into the U.S Army. Both Mark Rothman, a writer and co-creator of *Laverne & Shirley*, and Eddie Mekka, who played Carmine on the comedy, witnessed the taping of *Lenny & Squiggy in the Army*. Rothman indicated that the pilot had a very thin storyline, while Mr. Mekka said that Lenny and Squiggy were the icing on the cake for *Laverne & Shirley*, and that, if you remove the cake (i.e., Laverne and Shirley), you only have the icing left. And so, *Lenny & Squiggy in the Army* never made it past the pilot stage.[42] If it had become a regular series, apparently the "Colonel Boogie March" would have been its theme song.

Postscript

Paramount supported the pilot, but ABC ultimately became concerned that taking Lenny and Squiggy out of *Laverne & Shirley* might damage the popularity of that series.

Lander and McKean stayed with *Laverne & Shirley* almost to the end of the comedy. They made their final appearance together on a February 22, 1983, episode titled "Please Don't Feed the Buzzards" that had the duo discovering a treasure map in an old suitcase they got at a swap meet and going into the California desert, along with Laverne's dad Frank and Carmine Ragusa looking for the treasure. All they find is a bottle of

Napoleon brandy which they all drink after getting lost and with buzzards circling above. Eventually, soldiers rescue them when clearing the area for a military bomb test.

The Lucie Arnaz Show

Lucie Arnaz starred with her mother Lucille Ball in Ball's third sitcom for CBS titled *Here's Lucy*. In a pilot for her own series, Lucie's character, Kim Carter, moves out of her mother's place and into an apartment to try life on her own.

Background

Foreshadowing the pilot for *The Lucie Arnaz Show* (aka *Kim*), in the twentieth episode of season four of *Here's Lucy* titled "Kim Moves Out," Kim dates Peter Sullivan (Tim Matheson). Lucy worries when Kim is late in coming home from her date. After all, Peter is a writer with a beard which apparently, at the time, meant that he couldn't be trusted. When Kim comes home, Lucy is asleep on the couch. She covers her mother with a blanket and goes out early the next day to have breakfast with Peter. When Lucy awakes, she thinks that Kim stayed out all night, but Kim points out that Lucy had a blanket over her when she woke up proving that Kim had not been gone all night. Kim tells her mother that she treats her like a little girl and decides to move out. Lucy suggests that Kim take an apartment over the neighbor's garage. Kim moves, but her mother still comes by every day to help.

Called "Kim Finally Cuts You-Know-Who's Apron Strings," a February 21, 1972, episode of *Here's Lucy* was the real pilot for Lucie Arnaz's own series. Produced by Lucille Ball's production company, long-time Lucy writers Madelyn Davis and Bob Carroll Jr. wrote the pilot, which Coby Ruskin directed.

The Pilot

Kim has moved to an apartment at Marina Del Ray managed by Lucy's brother Herb Hinkley (Alan Oppenheimer), an amateur songwriter. She is working for a public relations firm and has met a British race car driver at an auto show named Ronnie Cumberland (Lloyd Batista). Lucy has given Kim a book on self-defense, and she practices some tactics with her friend and neighbor Sue Ann Ditbenner (Susan Tolsky), a tour guide at the Museum of History.

Kim goes out on a date with Ronnie who takes her to a movie about the Indianapolis 500. They come back to her apartment, but are then interrupted by Herb and Sue. When Ronnie leaves early, Kim gets mad at Sue and her uncle for barging in. The next night, Kim and Ronnie have a candlelight dinner, and he comes on to her very strongly. She has to use her self-defense tactics to get rid of him.

Postscript

This episode of *Here's Lucy* ranked twenty-sixth for the week. Supposedly, if the pilot had sold, Lucille Ball would have made occasional visits to Kim's apartment. In speaking of the proposed spin-off, Lucie Arnaz pointed out that the premise was not exactly ground-breaking. She remarked, "We tried it, but it didn't work. Actually, I'm just as glad. If I ever do my own series, I want it to have a more interesting character than Kim Carter and a more interesting premise than just the usual one of the single girl trying to make it."[43]

Arnaz did subsequently star on her own self-titled comedy in April 1985. She played a young single psychologist named Jane Lucas, who writes a newspaper advice column and co-hosts a radio call-in show in addition to having her own private practice. Adapted from a British sitcom called *Agony*, the series lasted for only six episodes.

Margie's Little Margie

Margie Albright (Gale Storm) from *My Little Margie* grows up and encounters the same problems with her daughter that Margie's dad Vern (Charles Farrell) had faced with her in this proposed sequel to the 1950s comedy *My Little Margie*.

Background

In the original *My Little Margie*, Margie Albright, who lived with her father Vern, an investment counselor, in New York City, always tried to get around Vern's parental dictates in typical 1950s sitcom fashion. For instance, when Margie decides she wants to move to a ground floor apartment instead of living on the tenth floor, she attempts to convince her dad that he walks in his sleep. Or when her father refuses to take Margie to London with him, she hires a man to pretend he is going to elope with her as soon as her dad leaves for England.

Lee Karson, who had worked on Gale Storm's second comedy *Oh! Susanna*, developed a treatment in 1974 for a sequel to *My Little Margie*.

He, along with Gale Storm and her husband Lee Bonhell, formed Showtime Productions in 1974 to develop the series. However, it appears that no pilot ever resulted from this treatment.

The Proposal

In *Margie's Little Margie*, Margie Albright Mayfield now has a teenage daughter of her own and has become more conservative as she has matured. Like her dad before her, Margie is plagued by her daughter's

Gale Storm and Charles Farrell from *My Little Margie*

escapades. After she grew up, Margie went to college, became an English professor, and landed a job teaching at Westbrook University in Southern California. Her father, now "Grandpa Vern," took the wealth he made as an investment counselor and purchased an exclusive racquet club in Palm Springs. Mirroring real life, actor Charlie Farrell did own a racquet club in Palm Springs. Vern is now less conservative than previously when raising his own daughter Margie. Margie had married Fred Mayfield, and they had Margaret Mayfield Jr.—Margie's "Little Margie." After Fred died, Margie is raising her daughter on her own.

Postscript

If the treatment would have resulted in a series, it would have explored topics like Margie protecting her obstinate, self-willed daughter from trouble, trying to understand the new morality, worrying about her dad's latest fling, maintaining her position on the faculty at the university, coping with student problems, and attempting to live a private life of her own with some of her own male admirers.

Gale Storm never really made a comeback on television after her second comedy *Oh! Susanna* ended. Battling alcoholism and eventually overcoming the disease, Storm appeared infrequently on TV in the late 1970s and 1980s as a guest star on shows like *The Love Boat* and *Murder, She Wrote*.

Pam

This spin-off from *Green Acres* deals with conflicts between a traditional father, Bob Carter (Don Porter), and his more liberated daughter Pam (Pamela Franklin) attempting to run a hotel in Hawaii together.

Background

Pam was one of two back-door pilots (the other titled *The Blonde*, described earlier in this part) that aired as the final two episodes of *Green Acres*, the surreal sitcom about rural life in Hooterville with Eddie Albert and Eva Gabor as Oliver and Lisa Douglas. Both pilots were rushed into production by Jay Sommers, the creator of *Green Acres*, when it appeared that his series was not going to be renewed. Vince Sherman directed and Jay Sommers penned this episode, titled "Hawaiian Honeymoon," which aired March 16, 1971.

The Pilot

Bob Carter, a widower, manages the Moano Rexford, a hotel in Hawaii with his daughter Pam, who had been raised in England by an aunt, hence her British accent. Molly (Mary Mayumi) is the hotel's desk clerk, and Charlie Lee (Pat Morita, later Arnold on *Happy Days*) is a waiter at the hotel. Pam attends the University of Hawaii. Two of her classmates, Lily (Donna Benz) and Richard (Dick Kay Hong), are getting married, and Pam offers them the honeymoon suite in the hotel for their wedding night. Meanwhile, Lisa Douglas decides she wants to have a fifth honeymoon with Oliver in Hawaii. The Douglases fly to Hawaii and, at the last minute, Lisa decides they should stay in the honeymoon suite at Carter's hotel. The suite has two bedrooms. Unknown to Mr. Carter, Lily and Richard stay in one bedroom, while Pam puts the Douglases in the other bedroom. She tries unsuccessfully to get Richard and Lily to leave. Oliver orders champagne and caviar for Lisa and him, but, when it is delivered, the honeymooners think it is for them. Finally, Oliver and Lisa meet Richard and Lily, and Pam explains why they are in the suite. The Douglases let Richard and Lily stay.

Postscript

Don Porter is probably best remembered for playing Ann Sothern's boss on her two comedies, *Private Secretary* as well as *The Ann Sothern Show*, and also for his role as Russell Lawrence, Gidget's dad, on the mid-sixties comedy starring Sally Field. *Pam* seemed almost like a sequel to *Gidget*.

Pinky Tuscadero

This proposed *Happy Days* spin-off featured Pinky Tuscadero (Roz Kelly), a character introduced in a three-part story as the fourth season premiere of *Happy Days*. In the spin-off, Pinky becomes a Las Vegas showgirl living with her father and giving dance lessons on the side.

Background

Supposedly, Roz Kelly was to have her own series on ABC in January 1977. On the *Happy Days* episodes in which her character of Pinky Tuscadero first appeared, Fonzie's love, Pinky, has returned to Milwaukee to do stunts in an upcoming demolition derby sponsored by Howard Cunningham's Leopard Lodge. Despite Fonzie's reluctance, Pinky participates in the

Roz Kelly and Henry Winkler as their characters, Pinky and Fonzie from *Happy Days*

derby with him. After the derby in which Pinky is injured, Fonzie asks her to marry him. She says "yes." He wants to go on the road with her and manage her career. However, he has second thoughts about the marriage when he thinks he may become "Mr. Pinky Tuscadero." He returns the check Pinky had given him for working with her, and they depart as friends.

While the marriage never happened and the Pinky character never reappeared on *Happy Days* presumably because Roz Kelly alienated the show's cast by doing unkind impressions of Fonzie, Pinky did get her own pilot written by Bob Brunner and Art Silver and produced by Garry Marshall.[44]

The Pilot

Angelina "Pinky" Tuscadero goes to Las Vegas and lands a job as a showgirl at the Oasis Hotel. In auditioning for the job, Pinky describes her background as "Former motorcycle queen, stunt pilot, all around daredevil… Also former waitress at the House of Pies, cashier at Murray's supermarket, hat check at Chicago's Plush Pigeon club… receptionist for an eye doctor…" She gets the job and becomes the unofficial leader of the other showgirls including Gladys "Cochise" Littlefeather (Shirley Kirkes), Hillary Prentiss (Taffee O'Connell), Jeannie "Sunshine" Ungar (Lynda Goodfriend), Candy Lee Lane (Jeannie Wilson), Bridget Bolton (Elaine Bolton), Ginger Malinski (Sayra Hummel), Stephanie Henderson (Robyn Hilton), Kitty Johnson (Gerri Reddick), Jill Shapiro (Jill Owens), and Karen Karamazov (Antonette Yuskis). Their wardrobe mistress is former retired chorus girl Mrs. MacIntosh (Marcia Lewis) and the stage manager is Harvey (Richard Kline).

Pinky lives with her pet dog Blackjack and her dad Emilio (Larry Haines) in an apartment where he cuts hair for some clients and she gives dance lessons to twelve year-olds including a tween named Rod (Scott Baio) who has a crush on Pinky.

In the pilot, Ginger, the soloist in one of the numbers, is dismissed by the mysterious and sinister Mr. Smith, the henchman for Major Putnam who owns the hotel. She is replaced by Hillary who is very close to Putnam, while Pinky is placed on probation for the various pranks she has pulled. At the following night's show, Pinky wants to get even with Hillary for having Ginger dismissed. When Hillary is doing her "Dance of the Seven Veils," Pinky, riding a camel, goes on stage and pours a big jug of water on her. Pinky is fired, but her dad, who just happened to have cut Major Putnam's accountant's hair, has a heart-to-heart talk with the Major about daughters and gets Pinky's job back.

Postscript

Apparently, not wanting to waste the idea of a comedy built around Las Vegas showgirls, when the *Pinky* pilot didn't sell, a rewritten script gave rise to *Blansky's Beauties* with Nancy Walker starring as Nancy Blansky, den mother to a group of Las Vegas showgirls that included the Lynda

Goodfriend character "Sunshine" from the *Pinky* pilot as well as Blackjack the dog. Scott Baio went from playing Rod to appearing as Anthony DeLuca, the younger brother of choreographer Joey DeLuca (Eddie Mekka). Joey DeLuca just happened to be the cousin of Carmine Ragusa, the role Mekka simultaneously played on *Laverne & Shirley*. During the filming of *Blansky's Beauties*, Mekka indicated that he introduced Scott Baio to the classic *Honeymooners* television series and that, between doing scenes for *Blansky's Beauties*, the two would perform Ralph Kramden and Ed Norton bits from *The Honeymooners*.[45] Nancy Blansky along with Joey, his brother Anthony, Sunshine, and another showgirl named Bambi Benton (Caren Kaye), who had not appeared in the pilot of *Pinky Tuscadero*, all lived in the same apartment. Major Putnam, represented by Mr. Big (*Happy Days* creator Garry Marshall), remained as Nancy's employer. Like the Mr. Smith character from the *Pinky* pilot, he wore dark glasses and never spoke. The Emilio character from *Pinky*, this time played by Johnny Desmond, became the maitre d' at the hotel and Nancy's boyfriend. Shirley Kirkes as Cochise, Taffee O'Connell as Hillary Prentiss, and Elaine Bolton as Bridget reprised their roles from the *Pinky* pilot. In *Blansky's Beauties*, Gerra Reddick became Jackie Outlaw, Antonette Yurkis got the role of Sylvia Silver, and Jill Owens appeared as Misty Karamazov. The Marcia Lewis character of Mrs. Macintosh from *Pinky* disappeared since that character was similar to the role Nancy Walker had.

Even though *Blansky's Beauties* was set in the present day, some have considered the series to be a spin-off from *Happy Days* since Nancy Blansky appeared on an episode of that sitcom as Howard Cunningham's cousin from Las Vegas. However, the *Happy Days* episode, titled "The Third Anniversary Show," really focused on Howard Cunningham throwing his wife a surprise anniversary party with Richie, Joanie, and their friends making the preparations while showing scenes from previous *Happy Days* episodes. Near the end of the episode, Nancy Blansky appears as Howard's cousin who had introduced him to his wife Marion. Nancy and Howard then do a soft shoe routine. The episode aired a week before the debut of *Blansky's Beauties*. Walker's appearance on the show was really more a crossover promotion for her upcoming series than a spin-off from *Happy Days*.

Blansky's Beauties premiered on February 12, 1977, on ABC and lasted for thirteen episodes. In the debut episode titled "Blansky's Biking Beauty," Roz Kelly as Pinky Tuscadero is featured as her original stunt motorcyclist character dressed in pink, of course, and not as a Las Vegas showgirl. In the episode, Major Putnam is unhappy because business is off and he wants a new finale for Nancy's show to woo back customers. Pinky Tuscadero, a friend of Joey DeLuca's cousin Carmine from Milwaukee, visits Las Vegas and is hired by Nancy to guest star in the Las Vegas stage show's finale jumping her motorcycle over twenty showgirls. When Pinky performs her stunt, she misses landing on her target and instead crashes through a wall. Major Putnam then demands a different finale since everyone wanted to watch Pinky perform and not gamble. This episode marked Roz Kelly's final appearance as Pinky in a Garry Marshall-produced show.

With the unsold *Pinky* pilot and the quick cancelation of its revamped successor in the form of *Blansky's Beauties*, one might think that would be the end to Garry Marshall's quest to create a sitcom about Las Vegas showgirls. However, Marshall tried once more to rework the concept. Titled *Legs*, the one-hour pilot, a combination variety and comedy show, aired on NBC on May 19, 1978. Lynda Goodfriend again played a Las Vegas showgirl, this time named Angie Vitola. Caren Kaye also appeared as a showgirl named Stacy Turner, the leader of the other showgirls who took care of her nine-year-old sister Melissa (Tammy Lauren), and Marcia Lewis, who had played Mrs. MacIntosh in *Pinky Tuscadero,* came back as Norma Kay Bates, a widow trying to make a living in show business as a singer and comedienne while raising her fifteen-year-old son Franklin, played by, who else but Scott Baio. Originally called "Big Mama Bates," Norma Bates's material consisted of humor like, "I'll tell you, it's not easy raising kids in Las Vegas. I have a fifteen-year-old son and I told him to go out and play. He asked me for a cup of nickels." For the uninitiated, slot machines used to take coins instead of only paper money as they do now.

Stacy, Angie, and Norma all lived together in the same apartment. Cochise (Shirley Kirkes) and Bridget (Elaine Bolton), characters from *Pinky Tuscadero* and *Blanksy's Beauties*, also reprised their roles as showgirls in *Legs*. Major Putnam continued to be the owner of the Oasis Hotel with the mysterious character of Mr. Smith acting now as a consultant for all the hotels in Vegas.

The initial draft pilot script, titled "Give Me a Home Where the Chorus Girls Roam," was changed to "The Odd Family." In the script by Walter Kempley and Marty Nadler, the showgirls at the Oasis Hotel are complaining that only one shower works in their dressing room. Stacy demands that the Major have more than one working shower and ultimately goes to Mr. Smith to intervene with the Major on behalf of the showgirls. Meanwhile, Norma's son Frankie arrives in Las Vegas to stay with his mother. However, after attending school, he decides that he hates the city and wants to leave. His teacher sends a note to his mother saying that Frankie is a disruptive force in the classroom. The teacher wants to visit with Norma to discuss her son's situation. After the teacher's visit, Frankie announces his intention to go back home. Norma thinks that she should quit her job and go back to New Jersey with Frankie and get a job as a waitress. Stacy talks with Frankie and says that things cannot be the same as they were before his dad died and that he should help his mother. Later, while Norma is appearing on stage and about to say farewell and Frankie is watching her, he asks her to sing another song and says that he wants to remain in Vegas.

Although *Legs* scored poorly in the ratings coming in 56th out of 57 shows, NBC thought that, with some further changes, it might be successful. With the title changed to *Who's Watching the Kids?*, the comedy became part of NBC's fall 1978 schedule. In *Who's Watching the Kids?*, Scott Baio now appeared as Lynda Goodfriend's brother, Frankie "the Fox" Vitola; and the Norma Bates character vanished. However, Marcia Lewis, who had played Norma, assumed the role of Mitzi Logan, the emcee at the club where the girls performed as well as the girls' landlady. Elaine Bolton as Bridget and Shirley Kirkes, this time playing a showgirl named Venus, were also in *Who's Watching the Kids?*.

Stacy and her sister along with Angie and her brother all lived together in the same apartment. Actor Larry Breeding appeared as their next-door neighbor Larry Parnell, a TV reporter, who helped to watch the young kids while the two showgirls were performing. Jim Belushi, brother of comic actor John Belushi, played Bert Gunkel, Larry's friend and cameraman, who lived in the same building as the others and also helped to watch the kids. The comedy premiered on NBC in September 1978 and lasted until mid-December of that year.

Who's Watching the Kids? was Garry Marshall's final attempt at building a situation comedy around Las Vegas showgirls. After it ended, Scott Baio and Lynda Goodfriend returned to their roles on *Happy Days*. Lynda Goodfriend played Richie Cunningham's girlfriend Lori Beth. Tammy Lauren went on to the Marshall-produced comedy *Angie*, and then appeared on his short-lived sitcom *Out of the Blue*, while Marcia Lewis co-starred on Garry Marshall's *Goodtime Girls* about three young women working in Washington DC during World War II.

Potsie and Ralph and Maxine

In *Potsie and Ralph and Maxine*, Richie Cunningham's friends from *Happy Days* are like a young "odd couple" living as roommates at college with a female friend named Maxine.

Background

Certain episodes of *Happy Days* foreshadowed the proposed 1979 *Potsie and Ralph and Maxine* spin-off, whose concept seemed something like another version of *The Odd Couple* with Jack Klugman and Tony Randall which Garry Marshall had produced before *Happy Days*. In "The Apartment," which aired November 1, 1977, Richie, Potsie, and Ralph look for a place of their own and finally rent one from Chachi's mother. Richie dislikes the constant arguing between Potsie and Ralph over such things as Ralph's cooking and Potsie doing the laundry. Potsie ends up dyeing everyone's clothes green because he mixed the whites with the dark colored clothes. Fonzie says that he will help Richie move out. Richie does eventually leave after telling Ralph and Potsie that he has to move because he is homesick.

Another episode that hinted at a Potsie and Ralph spin-off aired in 1979 as part of *Happy Days*'s season six. Titled "Ralph v Potsie," the two are still arguing about being roommates. Fonzie suggests that they write to "Ask Aunt Fannie," an advice columnist in the local paper. Unbeknownst to Ralph and Potsie, Richie has temporarily gotten the job as "Aunt Fannie." Aunt Fannie advises the two to divide their apartment in half with a line down the middle. Potsie has the half with the bathroom and the refrigerator, while Ralph gets the half of the apartment with the front door and the stove. This leads to the pair talking about going their own ways. After Fonzie informs them that Richie is Aunt Fannie, Richie admits that he gave them bad advice. The Fonz suggests that the pair needs to communicate better with each other.

The Concept

Apparently, no script was ever written for the Ralph and Potsie spin-off. Melanie Mayron, the first choice for the role of Maxine in the proposed project, recalls the spin-off idea being presented to her as a concept with her playing Ralph and Potsie's friend. At the time, she was interested in feature film roles and so turned down the part.[46] Mayron later starred on the drama series *Thirtysomething* as Melissa Steadman.

88 • *Spinning Laughter*

One wonders if the characters of Potsie and Ralph would have been outrageous enough to support their own series in the Garry Marshall tradition of the Fonz, Mork, and Laverne and Shirley.

Postscript

According to Donny Most, "The talk of a spinoff was a year before I left the show and it was a very close call. The network almost went for it, but at the last minute Fred Silverman decided not to do it. And I was not unhappy about that decision. I was kind of relieved. I was not mourning the fact that it did not happen."[47] Reluctant to pull the Potsie and Ralph characters out of *Happy Days*, thinking it could affect the success of that series, ABC decided against pursuing the project.

The Rita Moreno Show

Rita Moreno played Rosa Delores, an aspiring show business star, in this attempted spin-off from the one season sitcom *On the Rocks*, about four inmates of Alamesa Minimum Security Prison. Rosa's attempts to find work in the entertainment business would have been the focus of the series.

Background

Dick Clement and Ian LaFrenais penned the March 29, 1976, episode titled "I'll Never Forget What's Her Name." John Rich, who had helmed several episodes of *All in the Family* as well as *The Brady Bunch* and the sequel to *The Danny Thomas Show* called *Make Room for Granddaddy*, produced and directed the back-door pilot.

According to Rita Moreno, the pilot resulted from ABC seeing her performance in the 1975 Broadway play *The Ritz*, set in a gay bathhouse.[48] Moreno appeared as Googie Gomez, a third-rate entertainer at the Ritz who had big show biz aspirations. She based her character in the *On the Rocks* back-door pilot on Gomez.

The Pilot

Hector Fuentes (Jose Perez), one of the prison inmates, has a visitor—his second cousin Rosa Dolores (Rita Moreno), who is on her way to Hollywood to become a star. She wants to borrow $50 from him to fix her car. Coincidentally, Howard Weston (Hamilton Camp), who has just been released from the Alamesa Prison, sees Rosa in the local diner

Part 3: Proposed Sitcom Spin-offs and Sequels in the 1970s • 89

where she is arguing with the mechanic who now wants $75 to repair her vehicle. Howard says he will fix her car for free if she takes him to California. Rosa arrives in West Hollywood to stay at her friend Lillian's (Yvonne Wilder) place. Howard stops by and then moves in. Trying to find someone to represent her, Rosa and Howard go to see agent Paul Horn. She performs a medley of songs for two guys in the office, one of whom she thinks is Horn, but they turn out to be there to repossess Horn's piano. Howard answers the phone before Horn returns to his office and volunteers Rosa for her first job.

Postscript

Rita Moreno never had much luck starring in her own situation comedy. In 1978, she attempted another pilot featuring her as a former showgirl who takes a job as a social director at a Pocono Mountains resort which she unexpectedly inherits when the owner dies. This pilot, like the one from *On the Rocks*, did not become a series. Moreno tried again in 1986 for a comedy series playing a toy designer with a husband and three kids in a pilot titled *Rita* that didn't sell.

Moreno also starred in the original pilot for *Empty Nest*, a spin-off from *The Golden Girls*, where she appeared as neighbor Renee Corliss with Paul Dooley as her physician husband George. Renee has empty nest syndrome after her daughter goes to college. This pilot did not test well with a sample of viewers who said that the leads had no chemistry together, that the pilot had a depressing premise, and that it relied too much on appearances by the cast from *The Golden Girls*.[49] Redone with Richard Mulligan in the lead role, *Empty Nest* ran for seven years on NBC.

We Love Annie

In this potential spin-off from *The Courtship of Eddie's Father*, Anne Meara played Annie Dempsey, who works for an agency that offers a wide variety of services to its clients. The series would have followed the antics of Annie as she tried to serve the clients who availed themselves of Landon's Listen-In.

Background

Bill Bixby played Tom Corbett, a widowed dad with a young son, in *The Courtship of Eddie's Father*, based on the movie of the same title. The comedy was developed by James Komack, who played Norman Tinker on

Anne Meara and Brandon Cruz from *The Courtship of Eddie's Father* back-door pilot, *We Love Annie*

the series, a photographer at the magazine where Tom Corbett worked. Komack wrote and directed *We Love Annie,* his first attempt at a back-door pilot. This episode of *Courtship* aired on March 1, 1972. The comedy duo of Anne Meara and her husband Jerry Stiller had starred in an earlier season three episode of *Courtship* where they played Tom's new neighbors who drove him crazy with their kindness.

The Pilot

Tom has contracted with Landon's Listen-In message service to answer his home phone when no one is available. The service is owned by Mr. Landon (Jerry Stiller) and staffed by Annie Dempsey (Meara), Jeff (Jon Breakfield), who writes children's stories, and Kathy (Yvonne Wilder). In addition to being a message service, Landon's Listen-In provides other services such as walking dogs and planning parties.

Tom and his son Eddie (Brandon Cruz) come down with colds as does their housekeeper Mrs. Livingston (Myoshi Umeki), who stays at her home. Annie volunteers to babysit Eddie while Tom goes into the office for an hour. She has all the calls from the message service directed to the Corbett's phone which keeps her very busy. She also brings Bruce, a St. Bernard, to dogsit. At dinner, after Tom returns from work, Annie drinks too much wine and falls asleep on the Corbett's couch. The next day she cooks breakfast for Tom and Eddie, but then catches what she thinks is a cold. Her boss, Mr. Landon, comes by furious that she is not catering a party she was scheduled to work. Annie discovers that she really doesn't have a cold; she is just allergic to the dog, and, to save her job, Tom agrees to write an article about Landon's Listen-In services.

Postscript

We Love Annie never made it past the pilot stage. In addition to creating *Welcome Back, Kotter* and *Chico and the Man*, as noted above, Komack developed several other situation comedies in the 1970s such as *Mr. T and Tina*, *Roller Girls*, *Sugar Time!*, and *Snip* all of which met with a quick demise. NBC canceled *Snip*, starring comedian David Brenner, before it even premiered.

Whatever Happened to Dobie Gillis?

In this sequel to the original *Dobie Gillis* series, Dobie is married to Zelda, who is now a law student; has a sixteen-year-old son Georgie (Steven Paul); and runs his father's grocery store. Dobie's dad, Herbert Gillis (Frank Faylen), still works at the grocery store and lives with Dobie and his wife.

Background

James Komack, the producer of the sequel, had hired Max Shulman to write the script but was unhappy with the result. Komack reportedly told

Shulman that he didn't understand the character even though Shulman had created Dobie. Komack fired Shulman from the project and brought in Peter Meyerson and Nick Arnold, who had written episodes of *Welcome Back, Kotter,* to come up with a new script. As Dwayne Hickman remarks in his autobiography, "In the two weeks we rehearsed Komack's Dobie, every day we got page after page of rewrites, so by the time we filmed the show we were under-rehearsed and the script was flat and devoid of any humor."[50] The pilot aired on CBS on May 10, 1977. Lorenzo Lamas, in his first television role, appeared as Lucky, a friend of Dobie's son.

The Pilot

On his fortieth birthday, Dobie is having a mid-life crisis. Maynard arrives wearing long robes and has become something of a traveling guru who makes bad puns. Dobie says he doesn't want any special celebration for his birthday although secretly he does. Zelda has a surprise party planned for her husband, but when she, Georgie, Lucky, Dobie's dad, and Maynard all go into the kitchen to get the birthday cake, Dobie leaves thinking that no one wants to celebrate his birthday. He goes to the park where he is arrested for whacking *The Thinker* statue with a two-by-four believing it is the most significant thing he has done in his life. Everyone goes to the jail dressed in the outlandish outfits Maynard has given them from his world travels. After hearing the pleas from Dobie's family, the officer on duty decides to release him. The pilot ends with Dobie and Zelda having birthday cake together in bed, and Maynard playing drums in their attic.

Postscript

Some fans of *Dobie Gillis* commented that this pilot managed to erase any fond memories that they may have had of the original series. As with other Komack comedies, the cast of this pilot tended to yell their lines much to the boisterous delight of the studio audience. In some respects, it appears that the writers tried to fashion the pilot after *Welcome Back, Kotter*, with Dobie playing the Kotter part, his father, the Principal Woodman role from *Kotter*, and Maynard, Georgie, and Lucky (Lorenzo Lamas looking like Vinnie Barbarino) as the Sweathogs. Even though this pilot never resulted in a new *Dobie Gillis* series, another attempt was made in the 1980s to resurrect the comedy once more (see part 4, *Bring Me the Head of Dobie Gillis*).

Wojo

The focus of a special one-hour episode of *Barney Miller* titled "Wojo's Girl" featured Max Gail's character Detective Stanley "Wojo" Wojohowicz. This spin-off comedy would have concerned Wojo's life away from the 12th precinct.

Background

Noam Pitlik directed and Tony Sheehan and Danny Arnold scripted this episode that aired in January 1979. *Wojo* was not the first attempt by Danny Arnold to focus on the personal lives of detectives of the 12th precinct in Greenwich Village, New York City. As referenced above, the original pilot for *Barney Miller* and its first season dealt with Barney's family—wife Liz and their two kids—as well as with the activities at the police station. Arnold tried again in 1975 with the pilot for the *Miller* spin-off *Fish* featuring Abe Vigoda. Initially, it centered on Fish's life with his wife Bernice and daughter Beverly but was later re-worked to have Fish and his wife serve as house parents to a group of five foster kids.

The Pilot

Wojo's girlfriend Nancy (Darlene Parks) comes to the station to ask for the key to his apartment so she can move in. Wojo had met Nancy, a prostitute, in the park a few weeks earlier. She leaves in a huff after Wojo has second thoughts about letting her stay at his place. He then phones and leaves a message telling her that she can bring her things to his apartment.

The first half-hour of the two-part episode also dealt with a case involving Harriet Brower (Doris Roberts), whose husband wants to become a professional mercenary—not only for the money, but also to bring some meaning into his life.

In the second half of the one-hour episode, which takes place in Wojo's apartment, Nancy moves in and upsets Wojo's routine. He wants to know why Nancy became a call girl. She doesn't like to talk about it, but finally reveals that she got into the occupation gradually and, as most reformed prostitutes on TV say, she only went out with men she liked. Nancy goes to bed, while Wojo watches a basketball game on television and falls asleep on the couch. The next day, Nancy is upset and decides to move out. She departs, but then returns after Wojo leaves another message for her. He wants to take a second shot at living together. They agree to certain ground rules and then kiss.

Postscript

The pilot ranked thirteenth in the ratings for the week of January 31, 1979. However, ABC decided not to turn the pilot into a regular series. Supposedly, *Wojo* was to be the first of three one-hour pilot spin-offs from *Barney Miller* in 1979. The other two were to feature 12th precinct Detective Harris (Ron Glass) and then Detective Dietrich (Steve Landesberg).

Darlene Parks and Max Gail in the *Barney Miller* spin-off *Wojo*

As co-creator and producer of *Barney Miller*, Danny Arnold remarked at the time, "We'll explore their lives and see if they can lead to series."[51] However, plans for pilots featuring the characters played by Glass and Landesberg were apparently scrapped.

Young Love

Young Love, a back-door pilot that aired as part of *The Doris Day Show*, looked at the trials and tribulations of April and Peter, a young married couple played by Meredith Baxter and Michael Burns.

Background

The Doris Day Show premiered on CBS on September 24, 1968, and lasted until 1973. The series, produced by Day's company Arwin Productions, went through various format changes during its years on the air. Originally, Doris played a widow with two young sons who lived on a farm with her father. At the beginning of the comedy's second season, Doris found a position working at a magazine and commuted back and forth between the farm and the magazine's office in San Francisco. In the following season, Doris and her sons moved to an apartment in San Francisco. In the final season of the series, her sons disappeared altogether. It was in her apartment in San Francisco where the pilot for *Young Love* began.

Norman Tokar, who previously had directed several episodes of *The Donna Reed Show*, helmed this episode. Written by Bob Sand and Bruce Stertin, the pilot aired on March 15, 1971, as part of the third season of *The Doris Day Show*. What Bob Sand remembers most about the episode is that ". . . Doris Day and I watched the rough cut of the pilot together in a screening room at CBS–Radford, and that she said the word 'beautiful' a lot and cried into a Kleenex throughout the entire 22 minutes."[52]

The Pilot

April (Meredith Baxter), Doris's niece, knocks on her door late at night wanting to talk with her aunt about her marriage to Peter (Michael Burns). After dinner a few weeks earlier, April and Peter made love, and the next day, April went to her family doctor to see if she was pregnant. April then finds Peter to tell him that she thinks she is pregnant, and April's friend Dulcie (Brenda Sykes) holds a party to celebrate the news. At the party, Peter makes a remark that if April had a sense of rhythm, she wouldn't be pregnant. April asks him what he meant by the comment, and he says that it was just a joke. Her dad (Dick Van Patten) and mom (Gloria Lord) phone and say that Peter had spoken to her dad earlier about getting a job with him and dropping out of college. When April learns of this, she becomes upset. Her doctor subsequently stops by the apartment to inform the couple that April is not pregnant. She asks Peter if he really wanted the baby, and he says he didn't. April goes for a long walk and ends up at Doris's place. She realizes that she has to work out the problem for herself and returns to Peter. April asks him if he ever wants to have kids, and he replies in the affirmative.

Postscript

Writer Bob Sand remarked that the pilot looked like "a slam dunk" to become a series until just before the network said "no." If it had become a series, Norman Tokar, who created and directed the pilot, wanted Sand to write nine of the first thirteen episodes.

The two stars of *Young Love* took different career paths in later years. Meredith Baxter continued her acting career most notably starring as the mother on *Family Ties*, while Michael Burns eventually left acting to become a college professor. He retired as professor emeritus of history at Mount Holyoke College.

While the seventies were seen as the decade of ground-breaking comedies on the one hand and nostalgia-laced sitcoms on the other, the comedies of the eighties, mainly family and ensemble work comedies were somewhere in the middle between these two trends. NBC's demand for shows to add to its schedule seemed to be the biggest effect on 1980s sitcoms. At the beginning of the 1980s, third-place NBC had only two comedies on its fall 1980 schedule—*Diff'rent Strokes* and *The Facts of Life*—both from Norman Lear's production company.

PART 4

Proposed Sitcom Spin-offs and Sequels in the 1980s: Trying to Satisfy One Network's Demand

AS NOTED IN HIS BOOK *The Last Great Ride*, Brandon Tartikoff, who worked at NBC under both Fred Silverman and his successor Grant Tinker, originally joined the network as the director of comedy programs in the late seventies. When Tartikoff left NBC in the early nineties, the network had sixteen comedies, including *The Cosby Show*, *Family Ties*, *Cheers*, and *Night Court*. Despite producers pitching many comedy spin-off ideas to the network, as profiled in this part, NBC's rise to the top during the 1980s did not come from successful spin-offs but from new comedies—many created by alumni who had worked on the MTM and Lear sitcoms in the 1970s.

It is probably no coincidence that three of the four comedies in the original NBC Thursday night line-up of hits were created by alumni of MTM Enterprises. While Reinhold Weege, who had previously worked on *Barney Miller*, developed *Night Court*, Ed. Weinberger and Michael Leeson along with Bill Cosby himself created *The Cosby Show*. Weinberger and Leeson had both written for *The Mary Tyler Moore Show* and *Phyllis*. Gary David Goldberg, who had begun his career writing for the MTM-produced *The Bob Newhart Show* and *The Tony Randall Show*, came up with *Family Ties*, while *Cheers* was created by Glen and Les Charles who had scripted and produced *The Bob Newhart Show* as well as written for *The Mary Tyler Moore Show* and *Phyllis*. After Grant Tinker left MTM to become the President of NBC, MTM Enterprises devoted most of its resources to creating dramatic series for NBC such as *Hill Street Blues* and *St. Elsewhere* and not to developing new sitcoms.

Many of NBC's comedy hits during the 1980s attempted and, in a few cases, were successful in spinning off sitcoms during the decade. As mentioned below, *The Cosby Show* tried a back-door pilot starring singer Tony Orlando which was not picked up as a series, but it then had a successful spin-off, *A Different World*. *Family Ties* twice attempted to spin-off the Nick Moore character, Mallory's boyfriend on that series, while *Cheers* spun-off Carla's ex-husband in *The Tortellis* that quickly vanished after four months. *Cheers* would have much greater success in the next decade with the spin-off of *Frasier*. Also, *The Golden Girls*, created by Susan Harris, who had penned several episodes of *Maude*, had a popular spin-off called *Empty Nest*, which in turn attempted a spin-off involving the character of Laverne Todd from that series.

While the 1970s were very good to Norman Lear's production company with respect to the number of hit series, including spin-offs, that it produced, the 1980s were less successful for him. Of the thirty-seven proposed spin-offs described below, almost one-third came from series that were directly or indirectly developed by Lear's company. These included multiple attempts at spinning off comedies from *The Facts of Life* as well as single proposed spin-offs from series such as *One Day at a Time*, *Diff'rent Strokes*, and *The Jeffersons*. Even the few spin-offs produced by Lear's company that were picked up as a series did not do well. *Checking In*, a spin-off from *The Jeffersons* featuring their maid Florence, played by Marla Gibbs, ran for only four episodes, while *Gloria*, another spin-off from *All in the Family*, starring Sally Struthers as Archie Bunker's daughter now separated from her husband Mike, lasted for just one season. A sequel to *Sanford and Son* called simply *Sanford*, with Redd Foxx returning to his role as Fred Sanford, lasted for twenty-six episodes in the early 1980s.

In 1982, Norman Lear and his business partner at the time, Jerry Perenchio, purchased Avco Embassy Pictures and folded his production company T.A.T. Communications into Embassy Communications, Inc. Embassy Television, a division of Embassy Communications, produced sitcoms such as *Who's the Boss?* and *227*. Lear sold Embassy Communications to Coca-Cola in 1985 and was no longer involved in television production until the 1990s.

Through its comedies on NBC—*Diff-rent Strokes*, *The Facts of Life*, and *227*—Lear's production company tried several spin-offs profiled below to satisfy NBC's need for hit comedies, but none ever became a series. Mort Lachman, who helped to produce NBC's *Gimme a Break*, attempted the same thing through that series. Before forming his own production company, Lachman and Associates, Mort Lachman had scripted and produced several episodes of *All in the Family* as well as *Sanford* and *Archie Bunker's Place*.

Garry Marshall continued to produce situation comedies during the 1980s. He did have one short-lived spin-off that became a series. *Joanie Loves Chachi*, starring Erin Moran and Scott Baio from *Happy Days* moving to Chicago to pursue musical careers, lasted only for seventeen episodes before being canceled. Marshall attempted some other spin-offs from *Happy Days* and *Laverne & Shirley*, none of which became a series. Also, as with Norman Lear and Grant Tinker, writers and producers who had worked on the various comedies produced by Garry Marshall developed their own sitcoms and attempted spin-offs. For instance, William Bickley and Michael Warren, two producers and writers on *Happy Days*, created the mismatched buddy comedy *Perfect Strangers* and from that series, spun-off the popular *Family Matters* that initially focused on a black middle-class family, the Winslows, but soon came to feature almost exclusively Steve Urkel (Jaleel White), their nerdish neighbor who had a crush on one of the Winslow's daughters.

Of the thirty-seven proposed spin-offs profiled below, over half (twenty) were presented to NBC for a possible comedy series but none were picked up by that network.

The Academy

Set at Stone Military Academy in Peekskill, New York, *The Academy*, the male counterpart to *The Facts of Life*, centered on a group of mischievous cadets who were roommates—Buzz Ryan (Jimmy Baio), who had previously been in juvenile detention; overachiever, slightly overweight Alfred Webster (John P. Navin Jr.); African-American Chip Nelson (David Raynr sometimes billed as David Hubbard) whose mother was a famous singer, Paula Nelson; and Hank (Ben Marley) from a wealthy family. Other characters in the pilot included Major Tim Dorsey (David Ackroyd), the academy's headmaster and Cadet Corporal George Knight (Peter Frechette), his toady.

Background

This attempted spin-off was similar in intent to the proposed female imitations of *M*A*S*H* described in the Introduction. However, the

M*A*S*H imitations are not considered spin-offs for the purposes of this book since they did not air as episodes of *M*A*S*H*. *The Academy* is defined as a spin-off because it did air as part of *The Facts of Life* with characters from *Facts* appearing on *The Academy*. The boys on *The Academy* had a virtual one-to-one correspondence to the girls on *Facts*, with Buzz being like the Nancy McKeon character Jo, Alfred similar to Natalie, Nelson to Tootie, and Hank to Blair.

Scripted by *Facts of Life* writer-producer Jerry Mayer and directed by Asaad Kelada, who early in his career had helmed episodes of *Phyllis* and *Rhoda*, the first pilot aired on March 31, 1982. *The Academy* is unique in that two back-door pilots were produced. According to writer Jerry Mayer, NBC thought that the first pilot showed possibilities, but the network was not willing to green-light a series based on it and so asked for another pilot.[53] Written by Mayer and directed by Kelada, the second pilot titled "The Big Fight" aired later in 1982.

The First Pilot

Jo (Nancy McKeon) from *The Facts of Life* arranges for Blair (Lisa Whelchel) to have Buzz escort her to a military dance. Jo, Tootie (Kim Fields), and Natalie (Mindy Cohn) accompany Blair and Mrs. Garrett (Charlotte Rae) to the event. Buzz leaves Cadet Knight under the impression that he and Blair have had an ongoing relationship. But Knight finds out that Buzz just met Blair. Buzz informs Knight that he will prove that he didn't just recently become acquainted with Blair when he kisses her in the parking lot after the dance. To get her to the parking lot, Buzz says that he has to move Mrs. Garrett's car, and Blair accompanies him. Knight reports this to Major Dorsey as a potential infraction of the rules, and they, along with Mrs. Garrett, find the car, but Buzz and Blair aren't kissing. He is fixing the car's muffler. However, Blair later does give Buzz a good night kiss.

The Second Pilot

The second pilot saw the addition of Barbara Stock to the cast as Lieutenant Barbara Barton, a nurse. In the second pilot, Alfred attempts to impress Natalie by entering the Inter-Barracks Boxing Tournament. He wants to fight because his dad had boxed at West Point, and he expects his dad to see him in the tournament. His roommates agree to train him. However, they have Alfred eat too much; he gains weight and now must box opposite Mongo Moran (Bill Galligan) who is coached by Cadet Knight and had been a Golden Gloves champion. Alfred's dad calls Major Dorsey to say he won't be able to attend his son's match. When his roommates find out that Alfred will fight Moran, they try to convince Nurse Barton that Alfred is too sick to fight. Dorsey informs Alfred that his father won't be coming to the match, but Alfred decides to go through with it anyway. Hank and Buzz advise Mongo that he will need Alfred to tutor him in physics, and so Mongo may want to go easy on him. Mongo knocks him out anyway.

Postscript

After the second pilot, NBC ultimately decided to pass on turning *The Academy* into a series. Jimmy Baio, the cousin of actor Scott Baio, starred in another proposed spin-off in 1983 (see *Family Business* below).

Almost American (aka *Night School*)

Airing as an episode of *Diff'rent Strokes*, this potential spin-off featured Maureen McNamara as Catherine Armstrong, a young teacher who instructs foreign students preparing for their citizenship tests. Her students were a diverse group—Slovak Milosh Dubrowksi (Bob Ari), Chinese Ming Li Chung (Rosalind Chao), Hispanic Rudy (Richard Yniguez), and African-American Kwaine Botulo (Ernie Hudson). If it had become a series, presumably *Almost American* would have dealt with the lives of the students both in and away from the classroom.

Background

Scripted by Howard Leeds, Ben Starr, and Martin Cohan, all of whom had written other episodes of *Diff'rent Strokes* for Norman Lear's production company, Tandem Productions, and directed by Gerren Keith, the pilot aired April 1, 1981.

The Pilot

Milosh, an immigrant from Czechoslovakia, delivers a birthday cake to Mr. Drummond (Conrad Bain) for one of his friends. Arnold (Gary Coleman) is studying history because he got a D on a test, and Milosh is able to answer some of Arnold's history questions. Milosh then goes to his class taught by Ms. Armstrong. Detectives come to the class to question Ming Li, who had been a doctor in China, about a theft of drugs at the hospital where she works. Milosh tells the police he witnessed who took the drugs. The detectives take both him and Ming Li to the station for further questioning. Ms. Armstrong and Rudy, Milosh's roommate, are worried about the two. Milosh returns to class the next day and says that Ming Li is still in custody because the police didn't believe his story. Subsequently, the detectives come back to class with Ming Li. She is being released because the police say they further investigated Milosh's story and found that he was right about who took the drugs.

Postscript

Bob Ari, who played Milosh Dubrowski, indicated that *Almost American* was his very first TV audition and that his audition, callback, and getting the role all happened on the same day. During his first week of work on the pilot, he rehearsed and taped his scenes at the beginning and end of the episode with the cast of *Diff'rent Strokes*. He remarked that Gary Coleman, Todd Bridges, and Dana Plato (the child stars of *Diff'rent Strokes*) acted like the proverbial show biz kids ". . . who had too much thrust at them too soon."[54] During the second week, Ari and the other members of the *Almost American* cast rehearsed and taped the rest of the episode. According to Ari, the cast thought that NBC would inevitably turn the pilot into a series, but that never happened. After eight years in Hollywood, Ari returned to his native New York City and created a very thriving theatrical career.

Almost Home

This back-door pilot from *Webster* starred Mac Davis as a former country and western singer now taking care of five kids in a foster home with the help of Theo Gabler (Allyn Ann McLerie), the sister of his agent Charlie (Norman Fell).

Background

The pilot was written by Steve and Madeline Sunshine, who had done several episodes of ABC's *Webster*, and was directed by Joel Zwick. It aired on February 21, 1986. *Webster* starred diminutive Emmanuel Lewis as Webster Long who had been adopted by his godfather George Papadapolis (Alex Karras), a former football player and now a sportscaster, and his wife Katherine (Susan Clark), a consumer advocate, after Webster's parents had been killed in a car crash. Like *Webster*, *Almost Home* dealt with kids not living with their biological parents. The children in *Almost Home* were either waiting to be adopted or waiting to be reunited with their original parents.

The Pilot

Webster flies to visit Uncle Jake (Mac Davis), who went to school with his dad and George. The death of Jake's young son and subsequent divorce from his wife prompted him to change career paths and to begin working in a foster home. The foster kids include twins Mandy and Sandy (Robin and Shannon Lynch), preteen Michael (Larry O. Williams), young Sherman (Edan Gross), and PJ (Billy Lombardo), a preteen card shark. Jake learns that Sherman's mother (Faith Ford) is coming to take him home permanently. He argues with Theo about Sherman leaving and subsequently decides to go back on tour. The other kids ask Charlie to convince Jake to stay, and then Theo brings another young boy named Jack (Ben Ryan Ganger) to the home. Jake admits to Charlie that he is scared when the kids leave the home, but with prompting from the rest of the kids, young Jack asks Jake to stay.

Postscript

Commenting on the similarities between the character he played in the pilot and his real life, Mac Davis said, "I think he's going through a little midlife crisis, assessing his life and what he wants to do. I'm going through a change but not a crisis. I know what I want to do. I want to cut down on my road work, but not abandon it. After fifteen years of 250 days a year on the road, I'd like to stay at home more. This series will be a great way to do it. It's nice to come home and know your dogs aren't going to bite you."[55] Nevertheless, ABC never turned *Almost Home* into a series.

Almost Home represented actress Faith Ford's first appearance on a prime-time comedy. She would later star on such situation comedies as *Murphy Brown* and *Hope & Faith*.

The Art of Being Nick

In an attempted spin-off for Scott Valentine, the actor who played Mallory Keaton's boyfriend Nick Moore on *Family Ties*, twenty-four-year-old Nick moves in with his sister Marlene (Kristine Sutherland) and her young son Louis (John Daman) in an East Village apartment in New York City. The pilot also featured actress Julia Louis-Dreyfus as Marlene's

Scott Valentine as Nick Moore from *The Art of Being Nick*

co-worker. See *Taking it Home* below for the first attempted spin-off from *Family Ties*.

Background

Created and written by Bruce Helford and directed by Sam Weisman, the comedy pilot aired August 27, 1987. Director Sam Weisman recalls pushing for the casting of Julia Louis-Dreyfus as Nick's sister's co-worker.[56] *Family Ties* creator Gary David Goldberg backed him up since NBC did not want her. She went on to co-star on Goldberg's comedy *Day by Day* and then, of course, on *Seinfeld*. *Day by Day* has sometimes been mischaracterized as a spin-off from *Family Ties*. Both series were created by Goldberg, who got his first job writing episodes of *The Bob Newhart Show* for MTM Enterprises, but *Day by Day* was not a spin-off. However, Steven Keaton (Michael Gross) from *Family Ties* did make a crossover appearance in a November 1988 episode of *Day by Day* titled "Trading Places."

The Pilot

Nick's sister, Marlene, runs a bookstore called "The Hungry Mind" with Rachel Phillips (Julia Louis-Dreyfus) and is dating Bob (Ray Butkenica), her son's teacher. While he works on his art, Nick applies for a part-time job at his sister's bookstore. Rachel interviews and then hires him even though she says he is wrong for the job. But she is infatuated with Nick. After Marlene tells her son Louis that Bob proposed to her, Louis becomes depressed because he is afraid that his relationship with his mother will change. At school, Louis chains himself to his desk to protest a D he got on a test. Since Marlene isn't available, Nick goes to the school and manages to get Louis to unlock his chains. When Marlene arrives, she blames Nick for being a bad influence on Louis. That evening, Nick encourages Louis to confess that the real reason he chained himself to his desk was because he doesn't want his mom to marry. Louis explains this to his mother, and Marlene apologizes to Nick for blaming him.

Postscript

Even though *The Art of Being Nick* got big ratings finishing second for the week, NBC didn't pick up the series supposedly due to the network not wanting to lose the popular Nick character on *Family Ties*.

The Big Apple Blues

The Big Apples Blues, a season nine episode of *The Facts of Life*, had the Mindy Cohn character Natalie Green moving to New York City and living in an apartment with a group of other twentysomethings. The premise sounds a lot like the hit ensemble sitcom *Friends* that debuted about six years after the airing of this potential spin-off.

Background

Martha Williamson, at the time a writer for the NBC comedy *The Facts of Life* who later produced series such as *Touched by an Angel* and *Promised Land*, penned this episode. Directed by long-time *Facts* director John Bowab, the episode aired March 19, 1988.

The Pilot

Natalie thinks that her grades will be bad, and she may not graduate from college. Her friend Tootie suggests that Natalie accompany her to New York City. Natalie has a friend, Corey Daniels, who lives in SoHo, and the two decide to stay at her apartment. When they arrive, Natalie and Tootie discover that Corey found a job on a game show and moved to the West Coast. Tootie and Natalie meet Corey's roommates—Claire (Michelle Little), an artist and waitress; Nina (Terrah Smith), an African-American dancer and ballet teacher; Ben (Richard Grieco), an aspiring actor and waiter; and Scott (David Spade), a medical student. The roommates are looking for someone to take Corey's place so they don't have to pay extra rent money. Natalie, who is working on a story she hopes to submit to the *New Yorker* magazine, decides to stay and become one of the roommates.

One evening she has a run-in with Scott who reveals to her that he lost his first patient. Natalie empathizes, saying that her dad is a surgeon. The next day, when Natalie's purse is stolen, she decides to go back to Peekskill. The roommates encourage her to stay, but she wants to return to Peekskill to at least see what her grades are. She promises to come back to New York City in the future (i.e., if the spin-off is picked up as a series, which it wasn't).

Postscript

This pilot featured one of the first television appearances for David Spade who subsequently starred on *Saturday Night Live*, *Just Shoot Me!*, and *Rules of Engagement*. Richard Grieco, who played Ben in the pilot, later replaced Johnny Depp on *21 Jump Street* and then had his own spin-off series titled *Booker*.

Bring Me the Head of Dobie Gillis

This CBS movie brought back most of the original cast from *The Many Loves of Dobie Gillis* in yet another attempt to resurrect the Dobie character.

Background

Stanley Z. Cherry, who had helmed several episodes of the original series, directed this February 21, 1998, TV movie from a teleplay by Cherry, Deborah Zoe Dawson, and Victoria Johns based on a story by Max Shulman. It appears that Shulman attempted a comedy version of the play and the movie titled *The Visit*, written by Friedrich Darrenmatt about a wealthy woman who returns to her home town to take revenge on the man who impregnated her and left her when she was a teenager.

Dwayne Hickman, who played Dobie Gillis, produced the film. In talking about the sequel, Hickman said, "I think every actor would love to go back and reprise a series that was so good to him and to update the character that for so many years was a part of his life."[57]

The Pilot

Dobie is still married to Zelda and has a teenage son named Georgie, this time played by Scott Grimes. Dobie manages a grocery store, but the audience learns that he has also graduated from pharmacy school. His store is now called "Gillis Market and Pharmacy." The town council, which Dobie chairs, is concerned about the economic problems of the town where unemployment tops 60% because someone has been buying all the factories and then closing them. Dobie suggests buying back the factories by borrowing funds from his nemesis in high school, Chatsworth Osborne Jr., who now runs the town's bank. But Chatsworth won't lend the money.

Dobie's son Georgie is a "chip off the old block"—lusting after cute blonde high school student Bonnie (Lisa Wilcox) while being pursued by a short, dark-haired girl Chatsie (Tricia Leigh Fisher, Connie Stevens's daughter) who is Chatsworth's daughter. In the original series, Dobie desired Thalia Menninger while being pursued by Zelda.

Maynard arrives in town in a Rolls Royce dressed in top hat and tails. He reveals that he knows who is buying all the factories and says he has a big surprise for everyone.

Thalia Menninger, played by Connie Stevens, (Tuesday Weld portrayed Thalia in the original series) then arrives at the airport on Air Force One thanking the President for the lift. Maynard picks her up and calls her "boss." Thalia and Dobie visit their old high school, and she invites Dobie and Zelda to a town event she is planning.

Meanwhile, Georgie wants to play the male lead in a musical version of *Romeo and Juliet* written by Mr. Pomfrett (William Schallert who played the same role in the original series). Pomfrett taught Dobie and is still teaching at the high school. Georgie wants the role of Romeo because Bonnie is appearing as Juliet, but he doesn't know how to play the guitar which Romeo has to do in the production. He tries to bribe the school jock Earl (Mike Jolly), who has the part he wants, into pretending to break his leg so that Georgie can take over the lead after learning to play the guitar.

At Thalia's event, she says she is one of the richest widows in the world, but has never loved anyone other than Dobie. Furthermore, she says she will give every person in town $10,000 if Dobie divorces Zelda and marries her. Naturally, Dobie rejects the idea of divorcing Zelda. Thalia later appears on television to say how disappointed she is that Dobie won't get a divorce. She reveals that she is the one who purchased all the factories and says that she will give everyone $50,000 if something bad happens to Dobie. Separately, Dobie and Zelda try to discuss the issue with Thalia, but she refuses to retract her offer for Dobie's "head."

In the meantime, Georgie is becoming jealous of Bonnie and Earl performing together with Earl now having a sexual awakening. Earl quits the play when his performance begins to suffer from too much "rehearsing" with Bonnie. Georgie has now learned to play the guitar and gets Earl's part of Romeo.

After Dobie and Maynard crash the store's delivery truck because someone cut the brake lines and Maynard finds that the sheriff has already filled out Dobie's death certificate, Dobie decides to stay out of sight. He advises his son that he may not attend the play. He also tells his son that Chatsie is the woman for him, not Bonnie. Dobie ultimately attends the play in disguise, but everyone recognizes him anyway. Midway through the play, Bonnie quits when she realizes she will have to kiss Georgie. Chatsie takes over the role of Juliet. The lights go out in the auditorium, and the play is postponed until the next night.

Dobie decides to go for a walk by himself and is found dead the next day by a passerby. He had mixed a concoction that made him appear dead and had given Maynard the antidote. At the viewing, held in the grocery store, Thalia begins handing out $50,000 checks. Maynard accidentally breaks the vial containing the antidote, but Dobie wakes up anyway when he hears the cash register ring. He goes to the town's diner to reveal that he is alive and tells Thalia that he feels sorry for her and that she is mean and cruel on the inside despite being beautiful on the outside. After Dobie lectures the town about honesty, they tear up their checks.

In the end, Dobie sees Thalia off at the airport, and he and Zelda attend the conclusion of the *Romeo and Juliet* musical.

Postscript

Like the first pilot for a sequel to *Dobie Gillis* made in the 1970s, this one did not become a series either. If it had, the comedy would have played out on two levels—one centering on the grown-ups, Dobie, Zelda, and Maynard, and the other focusing on Georgie and his life as a teenager.

Carlton Your Doorman

This animated spin-off from Valerie Harper's sitcom *Rhoda* featured Carlton (voiced by Lorenzo Music), the never-seen doorman of Rhoda's apartment building, as he carried out his different duties working for his boss, Mr. Shaftman.

Background

According to Barton Dean who co-wrote the script with the voice of Carlton, Lorenzo Music, Grant Tinker suggested the idea of doing a spin-off of the Carlton character. Dean had the concept of Carlton as a slovenly, lanky, slope-shouldered Johnny Fever-type (Howard Hesseman from *WKRP in Cincinnati*) in his late twenties. Since Lorenzo Music, a short, balding, middle-aged man, looked nothing like Dean's concept, Dean and Music decided to do an animated show.

MTM and CBS liked the idea. The process of making an animated series is quite lengthy. For that reaszon, the network financed six back-up scripts so that if the spin-off became a series, they would be prepared to start animating more episodes. However, Mr. Dean does not recall the storylines of those scripts. *Carlton Your Doorman* aired on May 21, 1980.

The Pilot

Mrs. Shaftman (voiced by Lucille Meredith), the wife of Carlton's boss, wants Carlton to take her dog Pumpkin for a walk. What she really wants is to seduce Carlton, but he resists since she is his boss's wife. When Carlton sees an attractive girl jogging in the park, he and the dog jog along. But Pumpkin has a heart attack and dies. After having the dog buried in a pet cemetery, Carlton tries to find a look-a-like dog, but can't locate one. He doesn't know what to do and fears he'll be fired. As a last resort, he decides to have his cat Ringo made up to look like Pumpkin. However, after Mrs. Shaftman recognizes that Ringo is not Pumpkin, Carlton has no choice but to tell her the truth. Mrs. Shaftman wants Carlton fired, but Mr. Shaftman (voiced by Jack Somack) tells Carlton that he never liked Pumpkin anyway. He gives him $3 for walking the dog and the afternoon off.

In the pilot, viewers also see Carlton's mother (voiced by Lurene Tuttle) who appears as something like a "bag lady" trying to take care of her son by, for example, giving him one glove.

Postscript

Carlton Your Doorman, was probably ahead of its time—a rarity for spin-offs. Although networks, particularly ABC, had experimented with prime-time animated comedies for adults in the 1960s, most notably *The Flintstones*, it wouldn't be until the 1990s that this type of comedy made a real return to prime time. CBS had no idea what to do with *Carlton*, an animated show that contained sexual situations with a chronically-drunk lead character accidentally killing his boss's dog. The network sandwiched *Carlton Your Doorman* between a Bugs Bunny special and another show aimed at kids, and, since it did not do well in the ratings, the pilot did not turn into a series.

However, it did win an Emmy for best animated program. As Barton Dean points out, "It would be another 10 years before Lorenzo's boss on *Rhoda*, James L. Brooks… Sam Simon, the writer of one of our back-up scripts, and Matt Groening would bring prime-time animation back to life with *The Simpsons*."[58]

The Center

In the second proposed spin-off from NBC's *Gimme a Break!* (see *Max* and *The Last* Word for the others), Nell (Nell Carter) takes Grandpa Stanley (John Hoyt) to a senior center managed by Lilly (Gwen Verdon), a former exotic dancer, who has been married four times. Lilly likes Andy (Ray Walston), a widower who often visits the center. Papa Jack (Whitman Mayo), an ex- songwriter, also hangs out there. Combining nostalgia with funk in the pilot, the center becomes a meeting place for both seniors and teenagers.

Background

Gimme a Break! starred Nell Carter as the black housekeeper for the widowed police chief Carl Kanisky (Dolph Sweet) of Glen Lawn, California, and his three daughters—Katie (Kari Michelson), Julie (Lauri Hendler), and Samantha (Lara Jill Miller). Grandpa Stanley Kanisky (John Hoyt) came to live with the family during the sitcom's second season. Created by Mort Lachman and Sy Rosen, the comedy ran for six seasons on NBC.

Jeff Franklin, who previously worked on the Garry Marshall sitcoms *Angie* and *Laverne & Shirley* and subsequently created and produced *Full House* and *Hangin' with Mr. Cooper*, wrote *The Center*—a back-door pilot broadcast on April 19, 1984. John Bowab directed the episode. Franklin pitched the idea to NBC for a show about a place where feisty seniors interact with ethnically-diverse troubled teens. The network wanted to make the pilot for less money, and so they proposed shooting it as an episode of *Gimme a Break!* Doing this saved the producers of *Gimme a Break!* from writing and producing another episode, and they still got their license fees from NBC.

The Pilot

Lilly announces to the seniors that, since the youth center recently burned down, the recreation department has directed that the teen center be combined with the senior center much to the dismay of the old people. The senior center has scheduled a ballroom dance for Friday night, but the teens were planning to have their Boogie Funk-a-Thon that night. With the help of a committee, Lilly decides to combine both dances. Andy objects and tells Lilly that he's also rejecting her invitation for dinner at her place. One of the teens says he will get Lilly and Andy back together if a girl he likes agrees to dance with him Friday night. At the dance, the kids handcuff Lilly and Andy to each other until they make up. Andy confesses that he misses his late wife and feels he is cheating on her when he is with Lilly. Lilly says she feels the same about her late husband. After they both hug each other, the kids take off the handcuffs.

Postscript

About this potential spin-off, producer/writer Jeff Franklin remarked,

> I loved being able to re-unite Gwen Verdon with Ray Walston; they had not worked together since they starred in the movie musical *Damn Yankees* in 1958. When I was a little kid, my mother used to make me watch it and she would sing all the songs around

the house. Plus I was, and still am, a huge fan of *Fast Times at Ridgemont High* and *My Favorite Martian*, so I was thrilled to work with Ray Walston.... Whitman Mayo was famous for playing Grady on *Sanford and Son*, and I later wrote a special episode of *Full House* just so I could work with him again.⁵⁹

Disappointed that the network did not turn the pilot into a series, Mr. Franklin indicated that he really loved the concept of the pilot and the cast.

Charmed Lives

This attempted spin-off which aired as an episode of the Embassy Communications-produced comedy *Who's the Boss?* starred Fran Drescher as out-spoken model Joyce Columbus and Donna Dixon as reticent photographer Lauren Sullivan who eventually become roommates. *Charmed Lives* seemed like an updated, white-collar version of *Laverne & Shirley*.

Background

In *Who's the Boss?*, former second baseman for the St. Louis Cardinals, Tony Micelli (Tony Danza), a widower with a young daughter, went to work as a domestic for Angela Bower (Judith Light), a divorcee who headed her own advertising firm and had a young son. Directed by Asaad Kelada with a teleplay by Paul Haggis, the pilot aired May 13, 1986. *Charmed Lives*, the first of two proposed spin-offs from *Who's the Boss?*, never became a series like the other potential spin-off, *Mona* described below.

The Pilot

Angela Bower travels to San Francisco to work on an ad campaign for a pasta company owned by Frank Vionelli (John Randolph). She meets with Mickey Day (John Kapelos) of Mickey Day Public Relations and with Mr. Vionelli about having a Princess Vionelli to promote the company's products. Joyce Columbus, who has been selected to be Princess Vionelli, meets photographer Lauren Sullivan in the waiting room before seeing Vionelli. Lauren says that she has been waiting a very long time to see Mickey Day. Joyce replies that Lauren should just barge into Day's office and announce who she is. When she follows Joyce's advice, Frank Vionelli thinks she would be the ideal model for his products instead of Joyce. Later Joyce goes to see Lauren at the apartment the PR firm has picked for the photo shoot saying that since she didn't get the job, she is now homeless. When Joyce threatens to sue Vionelli, Frank fires Lauren and rehires Joyce. However, Lauren says she is going to stand up to Joyce. After Angela, Joyce, and Lauren discuss the situation, Angela suggests using both Lauren and Joyce as the "Vionelli Twins" for the company's commercials, and Lauren and Joyce plan to become roommates.

Donna Dixon and Fran Drescher as Lauren Sullivan and Joyce Columbus in *Charmed Lives*

Postscript

Donna Dixon did later reteam with Fran Drescher on an episode of Drescher's *The Nanny* about Fran Fine wanting to have a baby.

After writing for comedies like *Who's the Boss?*, *The Facts of Life*, and *Diff'rent Strokes*, Paul Haggis created and produced dramatic series such as *Due South* and later won Oscars for writing the screenplays for the films *Million Dollar Baby* and *Crash*.

The Coneheads

The Coneheads, an alien family, natives of the planet Remulak who came to Earth, had a most distinguishing feature—the tops of their heads were shaped like large cones. This parody of family comedies would have followed the adventures of husband Beldar, his wife Prymaat, and their daughter, Connie Conehead in this proposed animated spin-off based on the classic sketches from *Saturday Night Live*.

Background

The first Coneheads sketch, performed on the January 15, 1977, installment of *Saturday Night Live*, had Dan Ackroyd as father Beldar, Jane Curtin as mother Prymaat, and Laraine Newman as daughter Connie. The Coneheads have a very monotone speech pattern and use very technical language, for example, referring to food as "consumables" and to themselves as the "parental unit." No one meeting the Coneheads ever seemed to notice their monotone speech or the conical shape of their heads.

Directed by Arthur Rankin Jr. and Jules Bass from a script written by now-Senator Al Franken and his late writing partner, Tom Davis, both writers from *Saturday Night Live* at the time, this animated pilot first appeared on October 14, 1983, on NBC.

The Pilot

Prymaat (voiced by Jane Curtin) and Beldar Conehead (voiced by Dan Ackroyd) are sent to Earth to establish a refueling station for starships. They are supposed to land at the United Nations but instead splash down in the Hudson River and are chased by dogs to a trailer court where they are discovered by an elderly television repairman. They start repairing the broken TV sets he has and greatly increase his business with their quick turnaround.

Prymaat and Beldar Conehead with their neighbors—Barry and Cheryl Paisnor

Prymaat finds that she is pregnant and gives birth to daughter Connie (voiced by Laraine Newman). They attempt to contact their home planet without success. After six years, Connie starts school and is asked by her fellow students where she comes from. Her dad says "France." Prymaat and Beldar eventually get in touch with their home planet and inform the master that they weren't able to complete their mission. Their master says he will dispatch someone to rescue them, so they move to Parkwood Hills, New Jersey, and establish a starship landing site in their backyard. Beldar and Prymaat meet their new neighbors, Barry and Cheryl Paisnor. Beldar finally tells Connie, who is now a teenager, that they are from the planet Remulak and that they will soon return home, much to Connie's dismay. She is dating Ronnie, a boy she met at school. The master contacts them again and says that because of cutbacks, a star cruiser will not be arriving anytime soon, and so the Coneheads remain on planet earth.

Postscript

Because of the length of time it takes to produce an animated show, other Coneheads scripts were written in case the pilot became a series.

In one such script, written by Franken and Davis, titled "Atlantic City," Beldar is attempting to repair the Starcruiser in his back yard, but needs a custom-made part that could cost $100,000. The Paisnors invite the Coneheads for dessert after dinner and serve flaming cherries jubilee, which Beldar never saw before. He blows out the flames with such force that the dessert flies onto Barry. The Paisnors then suggest playing cards with the Coneheads even though Beldar and Prymaat know nothing about card playing. They play 21 which Beldar ends up winning due to his supreme mathematical skills. Later, the Paisnors invite Beldar and Prymaat to accompany them to Atlantic City on the weekend. Beldar would like to win big to purchase the custom-made part he needs. Meanwhile, back at home, Connie's boyfriend decides to throw a beer and pizza party when he sees the stockpiles the Coneheads have of these items. At the casino, Beldar wins big at blackjack, while the pit boss tries to get him drunk so he stops winning. When the drinks have no effect, the pit boss orders the Coneheads and the Paisnors to leave, and the couples are unceremoniously thrown into the Paisnor's car. When they approach the Conehead's house on the way back, they see police cars. A police officer says that the party Connie is having is creating a public disturbance. Drunken Barry rams his vehicle into a police car, and he and Connie's boyfriend both end up in jail.

In another script written for the proposed series titled "The Cave," Ronnie invites Connie to a party, but she wants to keep it a secret from her dad and so tells Ronnie to say they are going to the movies. When Beldar comes home after trying to teach their neighbor Cheryl to drive, Beldar asks Prymaat, "Now, what is for the evening mass consumption?" Prymaat replies: "Starch tubes covered in molten lactate extract of hooved mammals." To which Beldar says, "Ah! Macaroni and cheese. I will enjoy it."[60] They sit for dinner and consume mass quantities. Ronnie stops by for Connie. At the party, near the opening of a cave, the two decide to go into the cave to make out and, as often happens on comedies, they get lost. Prymaat and Beldar are worried when Connie doesn't come home. They contact Ronnie's dad and his friend Dog Man to find out where they are. While Ronnie's dad offers no help, Dog Man says that Ronnie and Connie were at a party at Pine Bluff Cave. They call the police who bring a rescue team to find the two teenagers. Hearing about the rescue on television, the Paisnors show up at the site, and Dog Man, Beldar, and Barry Paisnor go into the cave with the rescue team. Dog Man locates Ronnie and Connie, but Beldar and Barry become lost. The rescue team and Dog Man re-enter the cave where Dog Man is able to find the two.

The Dick Butkus Project

This potential spin-off centered on the relationship between the Kupkus family from the NBC comedy, *My Two Dads,* and former football player Ed Klawicki (Dick Butkus, who, in real life, was an ex-football player), the owner of a diner on that sitcom. Presumably, if it had become a series, this blended family spin-off would have dealt with the Ed Klawicki character romancing Karen Kupkus while helping her deal with her two teenage sons.

Background

Before DNA testing of paternity, NBC premiered a comedy in September 1987 about two young men who are given custody of a twelve-year-old girl after her mother dies. Called *My Two Dads*, the two men—Michael Taylor (Paul Reiser) an uptight financial advisor, and Joey Harris (Greg Evigan), an artist—had both dated the girl's mother thirteen years earlier and either one could have been the father. Judge Wilbur (Florence Stanley) awarded the two guys custody of Nicole (Staci Keanan). The judge also happened to own the apartment building in which Nicole and her two dads resided. Nicole had a boyfriend named Cory Kupkus (Giovonni Ribisi), and Ed Klawicki ran a diner on the ground floor of the building where Nicole lived.

Written by Michael Jacobs, the creator of *My Two Dads* and *Charles in Charge*, and directed by Matthew Diamond, the final episode of the first season of *My Two Dads* titled "Friends of the Family" which aired August 14, 1988, featured the characters of Klawicki, Cory Kupkus, his brother Roy Kupkus (Bradley Gregg), and their mother Karen (Lauren Tewes, who had played Julie on *The Love Boat*). According to Bradley Gregg who played Roy, the TV audience had a great, positive response to the Kupkus brothers after several episodes of *My Two Dad* had aired.[61] This prompted Michael Jacobs to do a pilot focused on the Kupkus family and the Dick Butkus character.

The Pilot

Cory's brother Roy waxes Joey's motorcycle, takes it for a spin, and ends up crashing it through the door of Ed's diner. Judge Wilbur, who happened to be in the diner and witnessed the accident, decides that Roy should work for Ed to pay for the cost of replacing the door. However, Roy wants his mother Karen to compensate Ed until he overhears that she has no additional money after paying for Cory to go to camp. He reluctantly takes the job as a bus boy in the diner where his friends give him a hard time. After Karen comes to the diner and meets Ed, Cory suggests that they all have dinner together. Roy doesn't want his mother to become involved with Ed since he is afraid that any new guy in his mother's life will leave like his dad did. Roy thinks his dad left the family because of him. From Cory, Ed learns about Roy and his father and tells Karen. Karen explains to Roy that his dad didn't leave because of him, but because he no longer loved her. Ed subsequently calls Karen and asks her out for dinner.

Postscript

A change in leadership at NBC at the time the pilot was made apparently doomed the chances of it being turned into a series.[62]

Giovanni Ribisi, who played Cory on *My Two Dads*, has had a lengthy career on television in series such as *The Wonder Years*, *Friends* (where he played Phoebe's half-brother), and *Dads*, as well as in movies like *Saving Private Ryan*, *Avatar*, and *Gangster Squad*.

The Eddie Mekka Project

This proposed spin-off from *Laverne & Shirley* (the Penny Marshall-Cindy Williams sitcom) aired on May 10, 1983, as the final first-run episode of that series. The episode titled "Here Today, Hair Tomorrow" featured the Eddie Mekka character Carmine "The Big Ragu" Rugosa along with Ben Powers as his roommate Rick—both aspiring Broadway actors.

Background

Another Garry Marshall-produced effort, Susan Lindner penned the script based on a story by her and Ken Sagoes. Tom Trbovich directed the episode.

The Pilot

Laverne's neighbor Rhonda Lee thinks that Carmine is going to kill himself since he had his gas and phone turned off in his apartment and has broken up with his girlfriend. At Phil's restaurant, Carmine announces that he is moving to New York City to become an actor. He visits Laverne, who is getting rid of her bed and buying a new waterbed, and asks her for $100 to help pay for his trip. She loans him the money she was saving for the new bed and ends up sleeping on a blow-up raft in a wading pool in her apartment. Carmine arrives in New York and goes to an audition for the musical *Hair* where he meets Rick West (Ben Powers, best known for playing Thelma Evans's boyfriend and then husband on *Good Times*), who is also auditioning. Rick is looking through the obituaries for someone who had lived in a rent-controlled apartment and asks Carmine to be his roommate. Rick and Carmine are called back for a second audition and both end up winning parts in *Hair*. Later Rick invites the cast to their one-room apartment for a party where Carmine performs "The Age of Aquarius" with the other cast members.

Postscript
This episode was seen as a possible continuation of *Laverne & Shirley* after Cindy Williams had quit the series the season before and Penny Marshall didn't want to remain on the comedy without her. One wonders if this proposed pilot had gone to series, would it have been titled *The Ragu and Rick* or simply *Carmine*?

Family Business

Family Business starred Lainie Kazan as Lucille Gribaldi, who inherited Gribaldi Construction after her husband had died. Lucille and her two sons, Salvatore (George Deloy) and Freddy (Jimmy Baio), struggle to maintain the business. Sal wants to be a professional baseball player and Freddy, a concert violinist. The sons are not all that interested in doing construction. The series would have explored Salvatore and Freddy's efforts at pursuing their dreams while working for a female boss.

Background
Written by Phil Doran and Douglas Arango and directed by Howard Storm, this episode of ABC's *Too Close for Comfort* aired on May 5, 1983. *Too Close for Comfort* starred Ted Knight from *The Mary Tyler Moore Show* as Ted Rush, a cartoonist, living with his wife Muriel (Nancy Dussault) in an apartment above the one occupied by his two young adult daughters.

Writers Doran and Arango had previously worked on the Norman Lear-produced series *All in the Family* and the short-lived *Hot L Baltimore* as well as on Redd Foxx's comeback vehicle *Sanford*.

The Pilot

When Muriel Rush suggests converting their attic into an apartment for her mother Iris after she is mugged, Henry hires the Gribaldi Construction Company to do the work. The project does not go well with the two guys breaking a window, cutting an antique chair in half, and dumping plaster powder on Muriel. Henry fires Freddy and Sal, but their mother pleads with him to reconsider. He says he will if she hires a foreman to supervise them. Lucille hires Donna Sullivan (Hilliary Bailey, who replaced Randi Oakes in this role), an attractive female, to supervise her boys, thinking that will keep them interested in the work. .When Donna finds that they installed the wrong heating ducts in the apartment and that it will not pass inspection, she wants both Freddy and Sal to rip them out and replace them. However, Freddy has a concert violin audition he needs to attend. Donna won't allow him, but Sal lets him go. Even though Freddy doesn't get the job with the Bay City Symphony, Sal is able to complete the work before the inspection. Sal then asks Donna out on a date to celebrate completion of the project, but Donna says she doesn't mix business with pleasure.

Postscript

Jimmy Baio, who played Freddy, felt that the basic idea of a family-run construction business with a female boss seemed to be a very thin concept with no clear idea of the direction a comedy based on the pilot would have gone.[63] Apparently, this is why ABC did not turn *Family Business* into a series.

Fenster Hall

This attempted spin-off from NBC's *Punky Brewster* involved the lives of foster kids at Fenster Hall, a facility for abandoned children, and the head case worker at the hall, Mike Fulton (T.K. Carter).

Background

The pilot, written by Rick Hawkins, Liz Sage, and Dave Duclon, the creator of *Punky Brewster,* and directed by Art Dielhenn, aired as a special one-hour episode of the *Punky* series on March 31, 1985. Duclon had previously worked on a number of Garry Marshall comedies including *The Odd Couple* and *Happy Days* as well as the Norman Lear spin-off *The Jeffersons.*

Part 4: Proposed Sitcom Spin-offs and Sequels in the 1980s • 121

According to writer Rick Hawkins, *Fenster Hall* would have been a series that followed a group of troubled but resilient orphaned boys and their inspiring mentor.[64] While *Punky Brewster* focused on foster parenting, the social worker as unsung hero was the driving force in the creation of *Fenster Hall*. Similar to a situation comedy version of the film *Boys Town*, the creators of *Fenster Hall* envisioned it to appeal to young male viewers to balance out the primarily female audience of *Punky*.

The Pilot

Someone breaks into Punky Brewster's (Soliel Moon Frye) room and steals her jewelry box. She follows the thief to his dumpy basement apartment where he reveals himself as a young kid named T.C. Fenestra (Billy Lombardo) living with Blade (James LeGros), a young tough who makes him steal in order to live with him. Punky invites T.C. to her place for dinner and asks Henry if he will adopt him. Henry says "no," but decides to take T.C. to Fenster Hall, a home for abandoned and neglected kids, where T.C. is introduced to Mike Fulton (T.K. Carter), the head caseworker, and Rita Sanchez (Rosanna DeSoto), Mike's boss and the administrator of the facility. Mike gets T.C. to talk by doing impressions and takes him to his room where he meets his roommates Dash (Benji Gregory), the youngest roommate; Lester (Morton Davis), nicknamed "Sugar" because he likes to box; Conan (B.J. Barie), who likes to eat; and Lyle (Gabriel Damon), the precocious one. Late that night, T.C. runs away back to Blade. Blade instructs him to go back to Fenster Hall to steal the money that Mike is planning to raise at an auction he is holding to purchase sports equipment for the kids.

At a gripe session, T.C. reveals that his mother died giving birth to him and that is why his dad abandoned him and why he is so mad all the time. While the boys are sleeping, Blade comes to Fenster Hall. T.C. says that he should forget about stealing the money from the auction, but Blade insists that T.C. take it. The auction raises a lot of money. T.C. walks away with the cash box saying he is taking it to Mike's office, but he really goes to his room where Blade finds him. T.C. has second thoughts about stealing the money and asks Blade to leave. Mike comes into the room and confronts Blade who pulls a knife on him. Blade steals the cash box, but leaves T.C. T.C. bonds with Mike and reveals he got the money out of the box before Blade took it.

Postscript

If *Fenster Hall* had become a series, the cast of *Punky Brewster* would have made crossover visits in the initial episodes of *Fenster* as well as during ratings sweeps weeks. When the pilot wasn't picked up, the character of Mike Fulton became a regular on *Punky Brewster* as Punky's fourth grade teacher beginning with the series' second season premiere. In the opening scene of "The K.O. Kid," Mike does a Howard Cosell impression to introduce boxer Marvin Hagler to Punky's class.

Flatfoots

Two bumbling Los Angeles police officers were the main characters in this proposed NBC series, a spin-off from *Here's Boomer*. Heading the cast in *Flatfoots* were John Reilly as Officer Frank Shackelford and Todd Susman as Officer Gabe Fortunato. Jason Bernard as Sgt. Lindsey Andrews, April Clough as Officer April Mikulanitz, Gary Epp as Officer Dave Heinrich, and Raymond Singer as Officer George Pesky rounded out the cast of characters. If picked up, the series would have focused on the escapades of Shackelford and Fortunato, characters that may have reminded some of Officers Toody and Muldoon from the 1960s comedy *Car 54, Where Are You?*

Background

Here's Boomer covered the adventures of Boomer, a mixed-breed stray dog, who wandered from town-to-town looking for food and solving people's problems. Written by Lowell Ganz and Art Silver and directed by Herbert Kenwith, the proposed spin-off aired on July 3, 1982. Ganz was a co-creator of *Laverne & Shirley* and *Joanie Loves Chachi* and also scripted episodes of *The Odd Couple* and *Happy Days* for Garry Marshall.

The Pilot

Specifics of the pilot's storyline are unavailable, but, in general, it deals with Boomer befriending Officers Shackelford and Fortunato who try to find a permanent home for him, while Boomer helps the officers arrest an affluent bookie.

Postscript

Lowell Ganz later helped to write the screenplays for the films *Splash*, *Parenthood*, and *A League of Their Own*, among others.

Gilligan's Island: The Second Generation
This proposed sequel would have featured the offspring of the original castaways from *Gilligan's Island* still stranded on the island.

Background

In the 1980s, Sherwood Schwartz came up with another idea for a *Gilligan's Island* sequel. He thought of producing a new television movie titled *Gilligan's Island: The Second Generation* which might have led to a syndicated comedy series.

The Concept

The pilot film would have centered on the sons and daughters of the original castaways along with the castaways themselves.[65] According to Bob Denver, his character was to wed Mary Ann, and they would have had a boy and a girl. The Professor would have married Ginger, and they also would have had a boy and a girl. The Howells were to adopt three children. All the kids then sail off to find an island.[66]

NBC's Brandon Tartikoff described the concept a little differently. As presented to him, the sequel was like a blend of *Gilligan's Island* and *The Day After*, a made-for-TV movie about a nuclear holocaust.[67] According to his account, Sherwood Schwartz had the idea that the castaways would hear a radio report announcing that nuclear bombs are exploding and the world will soon end. Gilligan, the Professor, Mary Ann, and Ginger decide to get married to repopulate the world. The second hour of the proposed pilot film would feature their offspring in love and discovering sex. The new generation of castaways learns from a guy on a fishing boat about the broadcast concerning the nuclear bombs really being a hoax. Apparently, the original castaways' radio batteries had gone dead immediately after the announcement several years earlier, so they never realized it was a hoax.

Postscript

No made-for-TV movie or new series ever resulted from this proposal. Bob Denver last portrayed Gilligan in a never-aired episode of the short-lived Bronson Pinchot comedy titled *Meego* that was canceled after six episodes. Meego was a 9,000 year-old alien who landed on Earth. In the never-broadcast episode seven, Meego attempts to call home and instead reaches three of the castaways—Gilligan, Mary Ann, and the Professor—still residing on the deserted island.

Jackee

This possible character spin-off from the comedy *227* involved Sandra Clark (Jackee Harry) moving to New York City to seek a new job. She finds new friends and eventually takes a job working at a health club.

Background

Sandra Clark was Mary Jenkins's (Marla Gibbs) sexy, single friend in the Embassy Communications-produced NBC comedy *227* about life in a black neighborhood of Washington DC. Michael G. Moye wrote and Tony Singletary directed the proposed spin-off. Moye had written for Norman Lear's spin-offs *Good Times* and *The Jeffersons* and would later co-create the comedy *Married… with Children*. *Jackee* aired on Thursday, May 11, 1989, on NBC right after *The Cosby Show* and ranked fifth for the week.

The Pilot

Sandra moves to the Big Apple thinking she is going to be head of the wardrobe department for Midway Productions. However, she soon discovers that Midway Productions produces porn films and so doesn't take the job. Her new neighbor Stephanie Potter (Debra Stricklin) suggests Sandra interview for an opening at the health club where Stephanie works as a manicurist. She mentions to Sandra that she will soon be marrying her boyfriend Rodger (Franc Luz) who does maintenance at the health club. Nathan Pollock (John Karlen), the manager of the health and fitness club "Sensations," hires Sandra as assistant manager despite her lack of experience after she shows an interest in boxing, of which he is a big fan.

Sandra discovers that Rodger is obtaining insider knowledge from the clients at the club about what stocks to invest in as well as having an affair with another woman behind Stephanie's back. She reveals this to Stephanie, but Stephanie doesn't believe her. Sandra asks Rodger to be honest with Stephanie, who overhears the conversation where he admits he is a liar and a cheat, and Rodger leaves.

Also, starring on the proposed spin-off were B'nard Lewis as Zoltan, a manicurist at the club who was very popular with the ladies; Dan Blom as Sven, the muscular, blonde juice bar attendant, and Margaret Smith as the club's receptionist.

Postscript

Commenting on why the pilot never became a series, Jackee Harry remarked, "Don't ask me why. It was very disappointing. To this day, I don't know why it wasn't picked up."[68] Harry later played the mother on the comedy *Sister, Sister*.

Jo's Cousins

Jo's Cousins, a third attempted spin-off from *The Facts of Life*, dealt with a widowed father raising three kids. This pilot focused on the Largo family consisting of Sal (Donnelly Rhodes), the dad; Pauli (John Mengatti) and Bud (D.W. Brown), his two sons; and Terry (Megan Fellows who subsequently portrayed Anne Shirley in *Anne of Green Gables* and its sequels), his fourteen-year-old tomboy daughter who worked in their garage with her father and brothers.

Background

Written by Linda Marsh and Margie Peters and directed by Asaad Kelada, this episode of *The Facts of Life* was broadcast on April 14, 1982. In addition to producing *Facts* for Norman Lear's company, Marsh and Peters had penned episodes of Lear's *One Day at a Time*.

The Pilot

Jo (Nancy McKeon) is visiting her cousins who live in Weehawken, New Jersey. Older brother Bud thinks his sister Terry should start seeing boys instead of just working at their gas station. When Pauli's friend Tony Valente (Grant Cramer) stops by, Terry wants to invite him to her birthday dinner that evening. She decides to wear a dress and asks Jo for make-up tips for which Jo needs to call Blair about for advice. When Tony sees Terry, he thinks she looks beautiful. However, father Sal is concerned and orders Tony to leave. Sal talks with his daughter and confesses that he doesn't know anything about raising teenage girls and says that she shouldn't work at the gas station anymore. But Terry wants to continue to both work at the station and be more feminine. Jo tells Terry that she should just be herself. In the end, Tony phones Terry.

Postscript

According to John Mengatti, who played Pauli on this back-door pilot, the show scored decent ratings, and NBC ordered nine more episodes for the 1982-83 TV season.[69] However, Norman Lear's production company wanted more money for the sitcom than the network wanted to pay, and so *Jo Cousin's* never materialized as a regular series.

Kat Mandu

One of the strangest premises for a comedy, *Kat Mandu* featured a character who doesn't say much as portrayed by actress Deborah Pratt, who originally played this character on an episode of *Happy Days*. In the pilot based on the character, mysterious Kat Mandu comes to the United States as a bodyguard for the exiled teenage heir to the throne of the Himalayan country of Pashimir along with his little sister. The siblings' adjustment to life in America would have been the focus of the series. In addition to Pratt, Vicki Lawrence, Victor Buono, and Alice Ghostley starred in the pilot.

Background

In the *Happy Days* episode "Fonzie Meets Kat" which aired September 25, 1979, the Fonz promises Father Delvecchio (Al Delvecchio's twin) that he will go one day without fighting when his former nemesis, Rico, a merchant seaman, shows up in Milwaukee. Rico provokes Fonzie to fight, but the Fonz resists. Kat Mandu, who is in Milwaukee with the merchant seaman, holds off Rico's guys until twenty-four hours have passed so that Fonzie can confront Rico. At the end of the episode, Kat stops at the Cunningham's house to return Joanie's purse. She informs Richie that she is from "where the strong winds emanate" which Richie's mother takes to mean that she is from Chicago.

David Ketchum, Tony DiMarco, and Jeffrey Ganz, all of whom had worked on various Garry Marshall-produced comedies, wrote the 1980 pilot based on the character from "Fonzie Meets Kat." Jeffrey Ganz, Lowell Ganz's brother, directed the never-aired pilot.

After auditioning, Garry Marshall thought that Deborah Pratt would be perfect for the lead in an action-adventure comedy he was developing. Pratt remarked, "Garry wrote a very fun script that was to be a direct spinoff from *Happy Days*, but Henry Winkler decided that enough spinoffs had come from *Happy Days* and wouldn't approve shooting the show. ... Dave Ketchum then wrote a short stand alone pilot which we shot. History tells it all, it never aired and it never went to series."[70]

The Pilot

Terrorists have taken over Pashimir and fourteen-year-old Prince Choy Ahmad Sindu (Alex Paez) and his seven-year-old sister, Yatzee Sindu (Sydney Penny) are rescued by Kat Mandu and taken to Fullerton, California, to live with Minnie Daniels (Alice Ghostley). Apparently, Minnie had volunteered to take in refugees. Her single daughter Brigit (Vicki

Lawrence) lives nearby and often visits her mom. Clark Henry (Paul Gale) from the U. S. State Department has been sent to unofficially meet the Prince. Kat asks Brigit, who is a professional photographer, to take a picture of the Prince and Princess to send to their home country to show that they are still alive. While Brigit is taking the photos, she and Kat engage in a conversation which is something new to the usually silent Kat:

> Brigit: "You fascinate me. We should talk. Maybe we'd have lunch sometime and have a conversation."
> Kat: "Conversation?"
> Brigit: "Yes, like, did you always live in Pashimir?"
> Kat: "No. I grew up in the jungle."
> Brigit: "Jungle. Uh, how did you learn to be a bodyguard?"
> Kat: "I studied the speed of the tiger and the grace of the panther."
> Brigit: "Silly me, I studied algebra."
> Kat: "I watched the animals protect their young. Is this a conversation?"
> Brigit: "Yes, you're doing fine."[71]

Clark warns Brigit that sending such a photo could be dangerous since it would alert the Prince's enemies. Suddenly, a man named Fouad (H.B. Haggerty) breaks into Brigit's photo studio in search of the Prince, and Kat subdues him.

Meanwhile, Clark informs the Prince that Arlo (Victor Buono) has been found. Arlo is the court elder who also comes to live with Minnie, the Prince, Yatzee, and Kat. The Prince asks Brigit to help him understand America and its customs.

Postscript

When contacted about *Kat Mandu* by this author, co-writer David Ketchum talked with Garry Marshall about the pilot. According to Ketchum, "Unfortunately those days at Paramount were filled with working long, insane hours. Garry had quite a few shows on the air and I'm sorry to say it's difficult for us to remember anything special from the Katmandu pilot…"[72]

In Deborah Pratt's opinion, "Kat Mandu was way ahead of its time." She went on to say, "Garry Marshall still owes me my break out starring role, and I will love him forever. He's a great mentor and a good friend."[73] Pratt subsequently wrote and produced the series *Quantum Leap*, which her husband at the time, Donald Bellisario had created.

The Last Word

This back-door pilot concerns two guys, Nicky (Harry Basil) and Tyler (Brian Backer), who run a restaurant together that was given to Nicky by his father, Mr. Pappalardo (Keuven Bar-Yotum).

Background

The Last Word, the third potential spin-off from *Gimme a Break* (see *Max* and *The Center* for the others) aired on May 10, 1986. The episode titled "The Purse Snatcher" was directed by Hal Cooper and scripted by Arthur Julian, a veteran comedy writer for series like *Maude*, *The Doris Day Show*, and *Hogan's Heroes*. According to comedian Harry Basil, then NBC entertainment head Brandon Tartikoff caught his act at the Comedy Store and signed him to a development contract. Tartikoff called Basil one night to help him make a birthday video for NBC President Grant Tinker.[74] Basil dressed as a page giving a tour of NBC and Grant Tinker's home to a group of Japanese tourists. At the end of the bit, Nell Carter came out of a closet with a vacuum singing "NBC, let's all be there." Tartikoff introduced Basil to Carter and told him that he was going to be in this proposed spin-off from *Gimme a Break*. The series writers asked him a lot of questions about growing up in a Greek family in New Jersey and came up with the Greek storyline for "The Purse Snatcher" episode. The writers left spots in the script for Basil to do impressions and improvise bits.

The Pilot

Nell (Nell Carter) and her best friend Addy Wilson (Telma Hopkins, former member of the singing group "Tony Orlando and Dawn") go for lunch at a new restaurant called "The Last Word." Addy receives a call from work and has to leave the restaurant before she and Nell have lunch. Nicky hooks Nell up with Steven Marken (Bennett Guillory) who is dining alone at the restaurant. After Steven leaves, Nell discovers that her purse is missing and concludes that Steven took it. When Steven returns to the restaurant for dinner, Nicky decides to set him up by enticing him with a purse holding all of the restaurant's daily earnings. After Tyler sees Steven leave, he finds that purse missing. Nell returns to the restaurant after hours to confess that she found her purse in her car. Nell feels sorry for the situation especially since Mr. Pappalardo fired Tyler over the most recent purse incident. At Nell's house, Nicky confronts his dad about Tyler's termination and proceeds to do imitations of Al Pacino and

Jerry Lewis, among others, to get Tyler's job back, but he is not successful. Nicky announces that he is quitting unless Tyler comes back, and his dad finally relents. Nell then tells Nicky's dad that Marken discovered the purse containing the day's cash receipts in his newspaper.

Postscript

Like the other potential spin-offs from *Gimme a Break!*, this back-door pilot never became a series. Harry Basil, who starred in *The Last Word*, also filmed another unsold spin-off pilot for NBC. See *Taking It Home* later in this part.

Late Bloomer

Late Bloomer featuring Lindsay Wagner, best known for her starring role in *The Bionic Woman*, aired as an installment of the CBS series *Kate & Allie*. Wagner played Julia Peterson, a former actress attempting to create a new life for herself in New York City. She lived in an apartment above her mother and dad.

Background

Kate & Allie starred Susan Saint James as Kate McArdle and Jane Curtain as Allie Lowell—two divorced mothers with kids who decided to share an apartment in New York in order to save money. The Reeves Entertainment Group and Mort Lachman and Associates, who were also behind the comedy *Gimme a Break!*, produced *Kate & Allie*. The *Late Bloomer* pilot aired in season three of *Kate & Allie* on May 12, 1986.

Bill Persky directed this episode written by Bob Randall, who had scripted several episodes of *Kate & Allie* as well as created a short-lived spin-off from that series called *Roxie* that starred Andrea Martin. Persky doesn't remember much about directing *Late Bloomer* except that Lindsay Wagner didn't have a great sense of humor.[75]

The Pilot

Julia Peterson holds cooking classes at night. During the day, she teaches college classes in acting and takes courses herself hoping to become a psychological therapist. Her mother Anna (Barbara Barrie) would like Julia to move in with her and Julia's dad Henry (Roger Bowen). Julia's best friend is Millie, played by actress Mercedes Reuhl, who later won an Oscar for Best Supporting Actress in *The Fisher King*.

The Susan Saint James character decides to take cooking classes from Julia when everyone complains about her lack of expertise in the kitchen. Kate is at Julia's apartment when Julia's ex-boyfriend Keith (Sam Freed), a director from Los Angeles, visits. He wants her to come back to Los Angeles with him and asks her to play a role in a new television series that he is directing. Julia says she will consider the offer. The next day, she learns that she is not doing well in her anatomy class and wonders if she should drop out of college and return to Los Angeles. In the end, she decides to stay in New York and continue building her life there.

Postscript

Sam Freed, who played Julia's ex-boyfriend on *Late Bloomer*, later got the role of Bob Barsky, Allie's boyfriend on *Kate & Allie*.

CBS ordered six episodes of *Late Bloomer* with filming to begin after the birth of Wagner's second child during summer 1986. Initially proposed as a midseason replacement during the 1986-87 season, the *Los Angeles Times* reported in November 1986 that the premise of the series had been changed to having Lindsay Wagner portray a woman in her thirties who gives up her law practice to become an artist.[76] CBS and Reeves Entertainment Group ultimately canceled the project before any additional episodes were made beyond the pilot because the network and the producers did not like the scripts that had been developed. *Late Bloomer* was Lindsay Wagner's first and, to date, only attempt at a situation comedy. Apparently, filming a comedy in front of a live studio audience was not Ms. Wagner's forte.

The Lisa Whelchel Project

A two-part story, titled "Beginning of the End" and "Beginning of the Beginning," served not only as the finale for *The Facts of Life* but also as a potential spin-off for the Lisa Whelchel character. In the finale, Blair Warner (Whelchel) learns that Eastland is closing, and so decides to buy and run the school herself.

Background

Veteran comedy writers Austin and Irma Kalish scripted and John Bowab directed the two episodes which were broadcast on April 30 and May 7, 1988. The Kalishes have written scripts for comedies ranging from *I Dream of Jeannie* and *My Favorite Martian* to *All in the Family*, *Good Times*, and *227*.

The Pilot

Blair's wealthy dad refuses to purchase the school with his money and suggests she use her grandmother's trust fund, which Blair had intended to use to start her own law firm. She buys the school with the trust fund and borrows money to keep the school going from Mr. Payne (Sal Viscuso), chairman of the school's board. When Blair discovers that the current headmaster is leaving the school, she becomes the new headmaster. She meets

Sam Behrens and Lisa Whelchel appearing on the series finale of *The Facts of Life*

Wes Mitchell (Sam Behrens), the handsome head of the science department, Miss Noreen Grisbee (Kathleen Freeman), the secretary to the headmaster, as well as Jennifer Cole (Mayim Bialik who subsequently appeared on *Blossom* and *The Big Bang Theory*), an underdeveloped female student, and Ashley Payne (Meredith Scott Lynn), the daughter of the chairman of the board. She also becomes acquainted with Adam (Seth Green of *Family Guy*, *Dads*) who initially dresses in drag to get into the school to meet girls. When the board says she needs to enroll more students to cover operating costs, Blair decides to admit boys at the school for the first time.

In the second part, Wes Mitchell advises Blair he is flunking Terry Rankin (Juliette Lewis, who later was nominated for an Oscar for her role in the 1991 film *Cape Fear*) in biology, which means she would have to be dismissed from the school. Blair asks Wes to give Terry a make-up test, but Terry decides to go to a bar with Ashley Payne and Sara Bellanger (Marissa Mendenhall) instead of studying for the test. Adam informs on them, and Blair goes to get them. She realizes that Terry has been messing up on purpose in order to be kicked out of school. Terry confides that her parents are divorcing and that's why she wants to go home. After talking with Blair, Terry decides to take the re-test.

Postscript

If the pilot had been picked up as a series, its title may have been *The Facts of Life: The Next Generation*. However, writer Irma Kalish said that they didn't think far enough ahead to come up with a title for the potential series.

According to Ms. Kalish, the inspiration for the Natalie spin-off (see *Big Apple Blues*) as well as the Blair spin-off came from NBC and from the desire of Mindy Cohn and Lisa Whelchel to further their careers. As to why neither of these pilots became a series, Ms. Kalish remarks, "Networks have their reasons, of which Reason knows nothing...."[77]

Max

Don Rickles appears as a deli owner named Max Green who befriends a young black girl in this attempted spin-off from *Gimme a Break!*, the Nell Carter comedy on NBC.

Background

Broadcast on April 28, 1983, Ted Bergman wrote the script for this episode titled "Nell and the Kid," which was directed by Oz Scott. According to Bergman, the idea for the pilot came directly from then-President of NBC, Fred Silverman, the "godfather" of spin-offs, who had commissioned a similar "button pusher"—a contrivance designed to push the audience's emotional buttons—titled *The Cop and the Kid*, starring Charles Durning as Officer Frank Murphy, an Irish cop who is assigned custody of a young, black streetwise orphan named Lucas (Tierre Turner) whom Murphy had caught shoplifting.[78] *The Cop and the Kid* had a three month run on NBC in late 1975 and early 1976.

The Pilot

Nell is shopping at Max Green's (Rickles) deli when a young black girl named Danny (LaShana Dendy) comes into the store, shoplifts some grocery items, and, while Max and Nell are talking, takes money from the cash register. After Max catches her with the groceries, Nell says she will pay for them. She takes Danny home where the girl confesses that she is an orphan living on the streets since her grandmother died three weeks earlier. Max comes to Nell's home after finding $200 missing from his cash register. He wants Danny arrested, but Nell convinces him to let Danny work at his store to repay the money. At the store, Danny disobeys Max, and they argue. Max later finds more items that she took from the deli. However, he forgives her.

Postscript

Bergman recalls Don Rickles as a very caring, considerate man, one of the warmest people he had ever met, unlike his onstage persona. After the initial table reading of the script, Rickles took Bergman aside, told him how much he liked the writing, and wanted him to promise to stay with the show if it became a series. However, Silverman passed on it. As to why, Bergman remarked "Sorry, I can't answer that. I'm plum out of tea leaves and chicken entrails."[79]

Max aired as the first of three possible spin-offs from *Gimme a Break!* The two others were *The Center* and *The Last Word*, which are described earlier in this part.

Mr. Bill's Real Life Adventures

A long-running sketch on *Saturday Night Live* centered on a clay figure named Mr. Bill, always involving himself in some outrageous situation causing him serious injury. This live-action farce based on the *SNL* sketches starred Peter Scolari as Mr. Bill, who lives in a very tiny house on Mr. Hand's property. He is married to Sally (Valerie Mahaffey) and has a young son, Billy Jr. (Christopher Burton), who dresses just like his dad in a red shirt, blue pants, and white belt and shoes. Mr. Bill's best friend from childhood, Sluggo (Michael McManus), a bully, is always injuring him. Sluggo resides next door in another tiny house with his wife (Lenore Kasdorf) and his daughter Junior (Hope Tibbetts), who acts a lot like her father.

Background

Initially titled *Meet Mr. Bill* and then *Oh No, It's Mr. Bill*, Mel Sherer and Steve Granat wrote the spin-off in 1986. According to Granat, Shelley Duval, a fan of the "Mr. Bill" skits on *Saturday Night Live,* got the idea of making a live-action series based on them.[80] Granat and Sherer's agent sent Duval and her producer, Bridget Terry, a sample of their work, and they were hired to do the pilot and two more scripts which were never produced. Jim Drake directed the pilot.

The Pilot

Involving a lot of cartoonish slapstick action, the pilot dealt with Mr. Bill wanting to go on a father-son kid scout jamboree with Billy Jr. only to find out that Billy hasn't been attending scout meetings and never took his test to become a badger scout because of his fear of failure. Bill tries to help his son prepare for the test by, for example, demonstrating how to get into a sleeping bag. Using a laundry bag, Bill gets stuck, is caught in an animal snare, rolls out to the curb, and is picked up as garbage. Later, Sluggo's daughter Junior informs Bill and his wife that Billy won't be coming back from his badger scout test because he became scared again and ran away. Sally calls the police to report Billy missing. Mrs. Sluggo stops by in a revealing outfit trying to seduce Mr. Bill and says that she saw Billy with her daughter. Mr. Bill and Sluggo begin searching for Billy and, naturally, become lost in the woods. In the meantime, Billy returns home and overhears his mother on the phone saying that his dad and Mr. Sluggo went looking for him. He goes to find them. Mr. Bill becomes stuck in quicksand, while a hungry Sluggo prepares to feast on him. Billy finds them just in time and, using a rope, helps his father escape from the quicksand. Mr. Bill tells his son that if he doesn't want to take the test for badger scout, he doesn't have to. In the end, Billy receives an award for rescuing his father and is made a badger scout.

Shelley Duval, the executive producer of this Showtime pilot, talks with the clay figure Mr. Bill at the end of the show and explains to kids watching how the special effects were done so that they don't think any of the actors were really in danger of being hurt. The end of the credits displayed the message "Look Out! For More Shows." However, no other episodes of *Mr. Bill's Real Life Adventures* ever appeared.

Postscript

As to why the pilot was not picked up as a series, Granat explains that,

> A lot of the edgy fun of the *SNL* segments was the crazy-kid-in-the playroom idea, which Mr. Bill's creator Walter Williams did so brilliantly with his falsetto voiceover of a child abusing his toys. It took the sweetness we usually associate with such play, and turned it on its head. It worked—as long as you knew it was a clay figure that was being beaten and flattened and torn apart. But to see that kind of thing happen to a live human elicits a different, more horrified, reaction from the viewer. So the initial problem may just have been the idea of doing it with live actors.
>
> On top of that, a lot of the violence that's built into the Mr. Bill concept had to be pulled back for television, which means even the diehard Mr. Bill fans who **wanted** to see a live Mr. Bill get pummeled and torn apart had nothing much to watch. And, of course, Mel and I never really solved the many script problems, so we take our fair share of the blame. Failure traditionally being an orphan, we hereby adopt it.[81]

Mr. Moe's

This potential spin-off from the syndicated comedy *She's the Sheriff* starred Karen Valentine, Jenilee Harrison, and Don Knotts all working in a beauty salon called "Mr. Moe's." Knotts played hairstylist Mr. Moe. The series would have explored the goings on of the employees and patrons of the salon.

Background

The pilot was broadcast February 13, 1988, as the "Hair" installment of *She's the Sheriff*. Written by Lawrence Hartstein and Richard H. Rossner, Russ Petranto directed the episode.

Starring Suzanne Somers as Hildy Granger, *She's the Sheriff* concerned a young wife and mother of two kids whose sheriff husband dies suddenly, and she becomes the sheriff of Lakes County, Nevada. Hildy's deputy, Max Rubin (George Wyner) never accepted the fact that she was made the sheriff instead of him.

The Pilot

Deputy Max Rubin is temporarily suspended from the force because of his antics. He takes a job at a trendy beauty salon in Reno, Nevada. Mr. Moe (Knotts) runs the salon with his partner Rosalind (Karen Valentine) and their assistant Grace (Jenilee Harrison). When Rosalind is offered a great position at another company in California, rather than struggle with the current business, she decides to take the new job, which will force Mr. Moe to close his salon. However, ultimately Rosalind changes her mind and stays in Reno so the salon can remain open.

Postscript

According to co-writer Richard Rossner who had previously worked on the comedies *Welcome Back, Kotter* and *Full House*, "... the show was terrible. It was a weak premise and the jokes in the script were not much better.... Lorimar wanted a spinoff. My partner, Lawrence Hartstein, and I were asked to write it. We wrote it. They shot it. And that was the end of it."[82]

Although not directly involved with this back-door pilot, the producer of *She's the Sheriff*, Mark Rothman, one of the creators of *Laverne & Shirley*, agrees that the pilot for *Mr. Moe's* was not that great.[83] Apparently, two versions of the pilot were made—one with the Max Rubin character and one without. The former version aired as an episode of *She's the Sheriff*; the latter version, shown to television stations at a NATPE convention as a possible first-run syndicated series, produced no enthusiasm from TV stations desiring to pick it up as a series.

Mona

At the end of season three of *Who's the Boss?*, Mona Robinson (Katherine Helmond), Angela Bower's mother, decides to visit her brother Cornelius Rockwell (James B. Sikking) who runs a hotel in New York City. The hotel staff includes Kitty McLaren (Susan Walters), the desk clerk; Don (Joe Regalbuto), the assistant manager; Packard (Paul Sand), the doorman; Tessie (Billie Bird), the head housekeeper; and Eddie (Robert Petkoff), the bellhop/waiter. The concept of the spin-off related to Mona staying at the hotel to help her brother run the establishment.

Background

Airing on May 12, 1987, Martin Cohan and Blake Hunter, the creators of *Who's the Boss?*, penned this episode directed by Asaad Kelala. *Mona* was the second proposed spin-off from *Who's the Boss?*; *Charmed Lives*, described above, being the first. In 1989, *Who's the Boss?* had another spin-off, *Living Dolls*, about four teenage girls aspiring to be models in New York City, that actually did become a series, but it lasted for only half a season on ABC.

The Pilot

The episode opens with a flashback to 1941 where young Cornelius and another boy are fighting, with young Mona breaking up the altercation and saying that her brother always aims for the stars. Back in present day, when she arrives in New York, Mona finds that the hotel Cornelius owns needs a lot of improvements and also that her brother invested her savings in the place. She invites the former owner, Jim Radcliffe (David Hedison) to her suite to try to get him to buy back the hotel. He refuses and threatens to foreclose on her brother since he is past due on his payments. Mona decides to restore the lobby to its former glory and give the staff new uniforms. She subsequently volunteers to work with her brother on fixing up the hotel.

Postscript

Katherine Helmond indicated that if *Mona* became a series, she would still appear on *Who's the Boss?* every three or four weeks. After the *Mona* pilot had aired, in the next episode of *Who's the Boss?*, titled "A Moving Episode," Tony moves into Mona's vacated apartment above the garage and decides to be a "swinging single." However, he tires of living alone, and Angela invites him back into the house. In the end, Mona returns to the apartment after having had an argument with her brother.

The Munsters' Revenge

This reunion movie, which also served as a pilot for a possible encore to the mid-1960s comedy, brought together the original cast of Fred Gwynne as Herman Munster, Al Lewis as Grandpa, and Yvonne DeCarlo as Herman's wife Lily. K.C. Martell replaced Butch Patrick as Eddie Munster, and Jo McDonnell portrayed Marilyn, the beautiful blonde cousin whom the rest of the Munsters considered ugly. Bob Hastings played Cousin Phantom (of the Opera), who visits the family for Halloween. If it had become a series, *The Munsters'* sequel would essentially have been the same as the original series, except filmed in color and with minor cast changes.

Background

The movie, penned by Arthur Alsberg and Don Nelson (Ozzie Nelson's brother) and directed by Don Weis, aired on NBC on February 27, 1981. To reprise their roles, both Fred Gwynne and Al Lewis demanded substantial pay increases over what they received when filming the original series. As Fred Gwynne commented to a writer, "I couldn't believe it! I couldn't believe that they were actually, that many years later, going to try to get the old men into those funny costumes again. Then I suddenly thought, well, if they want to, they're gonna pay."[84]

The Pilot

The Munsters visit a chamber of horrors wax museum and find models of themselves. The models turn out to be robots controlled by mad Dr. Diablo (Sid Ceasar) who wants to recapture the riches of the Nile since he believes he is a direct descendant of the Pharaohs. Diablo sends the robots out on rehearsal missions to scare people and steal their possessions in preparation for a bigger heist of Egyptian jewels. Mistaking Herman and Grandpa for the robots, the police arrest them, but the two escape and seek to clear their names. Glen Boyle (Peter Fox), a young police detective and son of the police Chief Harry Boyle (Herb Voland), is attracted to Marilyn Munster and investigates the case. Herman and Grandpa return to the museum after hours and see the manager activate the robots. They subsequently tell Glen what they witnessed, but, when the police descend on the museum, Diablo quickly replaces the robots with wax models. Later, Grandpa and Herman return to the museum and overhear Diablo's plan to steal the jewels from an Egyptian mummy exhibit on Halloween night. Herman and Grandpa fly to Transylvania to get Grandpa's life-generating potion to revive the mummy in the exhibit before the heist. At the exhibit on Halloween night, everyone is dressed in costumes, making it easy for the robots to steal the jewels. Grandpa gives the mummy the life-generating potion, but the dose is too much. The mummy comes to life as a young child. Herman then disguises himself as the mummy and attempts to strangle Diablo as he tries to steal the jewels with the police nearby to arrest Diablo and his assistants.

Postscript

In the movie, Fred Gwynne and Al Lewis act in many scenes like the comedy team of Laurel and Hardy with Gwynne playing the Laurel part and Lewis the Hardy role. Jo McDonnell Parker, who appeared as Marilyn in the film, doesn't recall any specific discussion of the movie being turned into a series. She does remember Fred Gwynne and Al Lewis being great fun to work with and always very kind to her. She recalls Gwynne very seriously relating a story about a New York actor who came to Hollywood for the pilot season one spring. The actor got an agent and rented a house in the Hollywood Hills with a pool. He went on auditions and got a few call backs, but hadn't booked anything yet. One sunny afternoon when he didn't have any appointments, he laid down on a deck chair by the pool with a book and fell asleep. When he woke up, he was seventy-two years old. McDonnell understood that this was Fred's cautionary tale about the "lure of the Siren City of Lost Angels!"[85] Jo McDonnell also recollects a story Herb Voland, who appeared as the police chief in the movie, told her. He indicated that the black glass skyscraper on Lankershim Boulevard on the Universal lot where filming of *The Munster's Revenge* occurred had been nicknamed "The Tower the Extras Built" because of the common perception among actors that Universal Studios had "nicked a dime or two out of each extra's pay packet every time they worked."[86]

Perhaps expecting giant ratings like the first *Gilligan's Island* reunion movie had received, NBC and Universal were disappointed. *The Munsters' Revenge* was slotted against CBS's umpteenth rerun of *The Wizard of Oz*, which won the time slot. While no series resulted starring the cast of *The Munster's Revenge*, beginning in 1988 a sequel to *The Munsters* did have a three-year run in syndication. Starring John Schuck as Herman, Lee Meriwether as Lily, and Howard Morton as Grandpa, *The Munsters Today* was based on the premise that the family had fallen asleep in 1966 when an accident occurred involving one of Grandpa's inventions and the Munsters reawaken in 1988.

Nick Derringer, PI

In this spin-off from *Hooperman*, which starred John Ritter as Detective Inspector Harry Hooperman, when a suspect at police headquarters attacks Hooperman, diminutive British private eye Nick Derringer (David Rappaport) saves him. Four-foot tall Nick's business motto was "No Case Too Small." If it had gone to series, *Nick Derringer, PI* would have explored the investigative exploits of its title character.

Background

Airing on May 4, 1988, Rick Kellard and Steven Bochco co-wrote this twenty-first episode of *Hooperman's* first season. Michael Zinberg directed the pilot. Bochco is better known for creating dramas such as *Hill Street Blues* while working at MTM than for his comedy series, most of which didn't last very long, like *Public Morals* and the animated *Capitol Critters*. Bochco had cast actor David Rappaport in two October 1987 episodes of *LA Law* ("The Wizard of Odds" and "Cannon of Ethics") where Rappaport played crafty attorney Hamilton Schuyler whose tactics were ethically questionable. This appearance by Rappaport led to Bochco and Kellard creating the Nick Derringer character for the actor. Kellard described Derringer as "a motormouth, a charmer and a natty dresser… Women find Nick Derringer irresistible."[87]

The Pilot

Nick reveals to Hooperman that he is tracking murderer Ernie Sadler who is involved with drug dealing and prostitution. Through an intermediary, Nick has arranged to purchase cocaine from Ernie and then capture him. The San Francisco police department decides to tail Derringer. When Hooperman goes to Nick's hotel, he discovers that Derringer hasn't paid his hotel bill. Nick sneaks out as part of a group of kids. After Derringer advises Hooperman that the cocaine deal is about to go down, Hooperman and his captain go to the bar where the purchase is to take place. Nick confronts Sadler and beats him up as the other police officers take care of Sadler's henchmen. However, they don't find any cocaine. The police interrogate Ernie's mule, an attractive female, whom it is discovered is Nick's wife. Nick subsequently reveals that there was no big drug deal; he just wanted to get his wife back, but, in the end, he is not successful.

Postscript

On the first season finale of *Hooperman*, Rappaport guest starred again as Nick Derringer in an episode about Harry Hooperman's surprise birthday party. *Hooperman* itself lasted for only two seasons. Apparently suffering from depression, David Rappaport took his own life and died on May 2, 1990.

The Parkers

The first potential spin-off from *The Facts of Life*, *The Parkers*, also known as *Brian and Sylvia*, explored interracial marriage through the experiences of Sylvia Parker (Rosanne Katon), an African-American television news anchor in Buffalo, and her husband Brian (Richard Dean Anderson before he became Angus McGyver), the director of a youth center who coached a boys hockey team. Brian, born in Buffalo, had been on the 1976 U.S. hockey team in the Olympics. Also in the pilot were Ja'net DuBois as Sylvia's mother Edna, and Anthony Holland as Ray, the manager of the television station where Sylvia worked.

Background

Norman Lear had dealt with the subject of interracial marriage before with supporting characters Helen and Tom Willis as an interracial couple on *The Jeffersons*. However, *The Parkers* was the first attempt to make this subject the central premise of a comedy. Airing March 25, 1981, John Bowab directed this installment of *The Facts of Life* from a script written by Jack Elinson.

Who would have thought that a comedy that ran on NBC from 1979 to 1988 and was never in the top twenty of the highest rated shows (its highest ranking was 24th during the 1981-82 and 1983-84 seasons) would be the launching pad for more potential spin-offs than any other situation comedy? As described above in this part, in addition to *The Parkers*, *The Facts of Life* had four other proposed spin-offs—*The Academy*, *The Big Apple Blues*, the Lisa Whelchel project, and *Jo's Cousins*.

The Pilot

Tootie (Kim Fields) and Natalie (Mindy Cohn) from *The Facts of Life* are visiting Brian and Sylvia, who is Tootie's aunt. Sylvia has just informed Brian of her job offer for a position in New York City, but Brian doesn't want to leave his home town or his job at the center. Sylvia invites Tootie and Natalie to go to the television station with her and Brian, whom she is interviewing on her newscast. During the interview, Brian tells Sylvia that he will move to New York City with her, but Sylvia argues with him about his commitment to the kids of Buffalo. In the end, she changes her mind about accepting the new position because she feels Brian would be miserable leaving Buffalo.

Postscript

Upon reviewing the pilot, *Variety* stated, "The key to a future might be its likeable cast regulars, but at best its chance of survival would seem to be as an 8:30 runningmate for a stronger sitcom—a commodity in scarce supply at NBC-TV at the moment."[88] The network decided against turning *The Parkers* into a series.

A Piece of the Pie/Carlos and Chuck

A Piece of the Pie, a proposed spin-off from *The Jeffersons,* centered on two men, a Latino and an Anglo, running a bakery in Miami.

Background

In one of Norman Lear's few attempts at a back-door pilot, he initially conceived *A Piece of the Pie* as an episode of *The Jeffersons*. Lear asked Luis Santeiro and Julio Vera to write the script for *A Piece of the Pie* in February 1983. Santeiro had previously created the series *Que Pasa, USA?* for PBS, the first bilingual comedy, which followed the struggles of a Cuban-American family living in Little Havana, Miami, as they adapt to life in America.

The Script

The script had George and Louise Jefferson traveling to Miami for a dry cleaners' convention. George is organizing a big event at the convention, but there is a hotel workers' strike. He and Louise end up in Little Havana where Carlos runs a Cuban bakery with Chuck, an Anglo. George and Louise wander into the bakery while sightseeing. Carlos learns of George's problem and, eager to expand the business, makes a deal with him to cater the event. However, Chuck feels that Carlos has promised more than he can deliver.

Postscript

Later simply titled *Carlos and Chuck*, the script was rewritten to focus more on the personal conflict between the two characters. However, in March 1983, Lear dropped the idea of a *Jeffersons* spin-off episode and just wanted the writers to focus on the Carlos and Chuck characters. The title changed again to *Thicker than Water,* and the storyline had Frankie and Robin, Carlos and Chuck's son and daughter, wanting to marry. Lear then decided to add another character to the pilot script—a young immigrant from Cuba named Lenin who had come to the United States in hopes of becoming the "first Capitalist Lenin." The title of the script changed once more to *Yankee Doodle Cuban.*

In 1984, the project was dropped altogether. However, the head of CBS at the time decided to give Santiero and Vera another chance at developing a Latino comedy called *Only in Miami,* but this script, like the ones described above, never got off the ground.

Lear did subsequently develop a new Latino comedy with stand-up comedian Paul Rodriguez titled *A.K.A Pablo* which aired for six episodes in spring 1984. Rodriguez played a rising TV comedian whose ethnic humor did not always sit well with his family.

Schneider

This attempted spin-off from *One Day at a Time* starred Pat Harrington Jr. as Dwayne Schneider, the building superintendent taking care of his nephew and niece in Florida.

Background

Bonnie Franklin starred as Ann Romano, a divorcée with two teenage daughters, Julie (Mackenzie Phillips) and Barbara (Valerie Bertinelli), living in an apartment building in Indianapolis in the Norman Lear-produced series *One Day at a Time.* By the series' ninth and final season, Ann Romano had remarried, as had her two now grown-up daughters, and she had taken a job in Paris. The spin-off, featuring the Dwayne Schneider character, aired on May 28, 1984, as the final installment of *One Day at a Time.* Noam Pitlik directed the episode titled "Another Man's Shoes" from a script by *One Day's* writers and producers, Dick Bensfield and Perry Grant.

The Pilot

Schneider learns, after his brother passes away, that someone needs to take care of Keith (Corey Feldman in an early television appearance) and Lori (Natalie Klinger), his nephew and niece, and so he flies to Morgan Beach, Florida. When he arrives, Schneider discovers the kids living over a diner run by Jackie Cahill (Candy Azzara), whose mother Zorina (Ruth Kobart) is a fortune teller with a booth next to the diner. Schneider intends to take his niece and nephew to live with their Aunt Martha, but then is made aware that the aunt has been arrested for embezzling church funds. He has to decide whether or not to take the kids back to Indianapolis with him. They, of course, want to stay in their apartment, and Jackie needs a maintenance man to repair things around the building. Everyone tries to persuade Schneider to move there, and, in the end, he decides to stay in Florida.

Other characters hanging out at Jackie's diner included a mime named Bernard (Bob Griffard); Mr. Tuller (Bill Zuckert), a retired locksmith; Cassie (Darian Mathias), a taxi bike driver; and Clifford (William Jones aka J. Bill Jones), the resident hunk.

Postscript

According to Harrington, he didn't really like the premise for the proposed series. However, he went on to say that "I didn't mind the idea of a spinoff. I wouldn't have minded doing another series about the Schneider character."[89]

Taking It Home

This first potential spin-off from *Family Ties* starred the Nick Moore character played by Scott Valentine. *The Art of Being Nick*, profiled at the beginning of this part, was the second such attempt. In *Taking It Home*, Nick works in his family's toy business while pursuing his aspirations to be a serious artist.

Background

Scott Valentine joined *Family Ties* in October 1985 as Mallory Keaton's (Justine Bateman) boyfriend, an environmental artist, which really meant that he made things out of trash. *Family Ties* revolved around liberal Elyse (Meredith Baxter) and Steve (Michael Gross) Keaton raising three kids including conservative Alex (Michael J. Fox). Created by Gary David Goldberg, *Family Ties* had kind of the reverse premise of Norman

Lear's *All in the Family*. While Valentine's character's last name on *Family Ties* had been "Moore," his name became "Morelli" for this spin-off, also known as *All the Way Home*. The pilot, written by *Family Ties* scribes Ruth Bennett and Susan Seeger and directed by Sam Weisman, aired September 12, 1986.

The Pilot

Nick Morelli returns to Detroit to live with his sister Kitty DeLuca (Natalija Nogulich) and his Italian grandfather Papa Joe Morelli (Herschel Bernardi) after his father's death. Nick helps out with Morelli Toys, the family's business, but finds himself torn between the business and his artistic ambitions. Other characters in the pilot were Ray Baker as Kitty's husband Johnny; Summer Phoenix (Joaquin Phoenix's sister and currently the wife of Casey Afleck) as Franny, their daughter; and Lola (Liz Torres) as Papa Joe's cousin. Sheila (Lisa Jane Persky) and Gino (Harry Basil) were Lola's kids.

Postscript

Reminiscing about making this pilot, Natalija Nogulich indicated that she enjoyed working with Gary David Goldberg. She learned so much about relaxing into the situation and dialogue to make it realistic. Nogulich had been in a play at the South Coast Repertory Theatre when the director of the pilot, Sam Weisman, asked if she had ever played an Italian and if she had an agent he could contact to bring her in for an audition. "I went to audition in Gary's office at Paramount the next day, and that evening I went before the network and I had booked my first pilot."[90] Later Nogulich appeared on Gary David Goldberg's *Brooklyn Bridge* as Aunt Miriam.

In the middle of taping *The Last Word*, the proposed spin-off from *Gimme a Break*, described earlier in this part, NBC asked Harry Basil to audition for *Taking It Home*.[93] Goldberg loved Basil's audition, and there was almost a guarantee that *Taking It Home* would become a series. The pilot ranked thirtieth for the week. However, a few weeks before NBC firmed up its fall schedule, Herschel Bernardi died of a massive heart attack, and the pilot was shelved.

Supposedly after *Taking It Home*, the Nick Morelli character appeared in another pilot working in a day care center for juvenile delinquents. However, no details about the title or specific storyline of that pilot could be found.

That's My Mama Now!

This sequel to *That's My Mama* starred Ted Lange as attorney Clarence "Junior" Russell, with Theresa Merritt as Mama playing his secretary.

Background

With the success of the first-run syndicated version of *What's Happening Now!*, a sequel to the ABC comedy *What's Happening*, Columbia Pictures Television attempted the same thing with *That's My Mama* which had centered on Clifton Curtis (Clifton Davis), a young, single barber living and working in Washington DC, who had inherited his shop after his father died. He lived with his mother, "Mama" Eloise Curtis (Theresa Merritt) who, as with many mothers, wanted her son to marry like his sister Tracy (Lynne Moody and then Joan Pringle) had done. Tracy had married engineer Leonard Taylor (Lisle Wilson). Other characters on *That's My Mama* included Clifton's friend Earl Chambers (Teddy Wilson) and Junior (Ted Lange), a street philosopher.

Since the star of *That's My Mama*, Clifton Davis, had already contracted to star in *Amen* with Sherman Hemsley from *The Jeffersons*, the producers of *That's My Mama Now!* decided to focus on the Ted Lange character, Junior, from the original series. Initially, the proposed sequel was to be called *That's My Grandma*.

The Pilot

As described in Lee Goldberg's book, *Television Series Revivals*, Clarence "Junior" Russell is now a lawyer and has turned the former Curtis barbershop into his storefront law office. "Mama" Curtis begins work as Clarence's secretary. Her daughter Tracy (played by Daphne Maxwell) and her husband Leonard return along with their children. Clarence also has an investigator working for him—Deuce (Timothy Stock).

Postscript

Advertisements to local stations said: "The feeling's still the same around Mama's place. Plenty of laughter. Lots of love. And a houseful of good times. Who says you can't go home to Mama?" Apparently a lot of TV stations declined to go home to Mama. While a pilot was produced in 1986 with the series intended to be syndicated beginning September 1987, not enough stations signed on to turn *That's My Mama Now!* into a series.

The Tony Orlando Show

This back-door pilot from *The Cosby Show* starred singer Tony Orlando as Tony Castillo, the director of a community center, whose staff included Chester (David Langston Smyrl), the reception desk clerk, and Selena Cruz (Ada Maris), the center's counselor who had fallen in love with Tony.

Background

On *The Cosby Show*, Bill Cosby played Cliff Huxtable, a New York City obstetrician, married to Claire (Phylicia Rashad), a legal aid attorney. Together they were raising five children—Sandra (Sabrina Le Beauf), Denise (Lisa Bonet), Theo (Malcolm-Jamal Warner), Vanessa (Tempest Bledsoe), and Rudy (Keshia Knight Pulliam). The Tony Orlando spin-off, also known as *The Center*, aired May 2, 1985. Emily Tracy wrote and Jay Sandrich directed the episode titled "Mr. Quiet." According to Marcy Carsey, one of the producers of *The Cosby Show*, Bill admired Tony Orlando, and the producers found him wonderful to work with.[92]

The Pilot

Dr. Huxtable is teaching pregnant women about weight gain at the local community center. Theo (Malcolm-Jamal Warner) finds Enrique (Alexis Cruz), a young boy who has been beaten up by other kids. He brings him to the center to be examined by his dad. Tony Castillo tries to bond with Enrique, but the boy doesn't want to talk much. Later, Enrique's mother (Pearl Tama) comes to the center to take her son home and says that Enrique has been quiet ever since his policeman father was shot and killed in the line of duty. He finds it difficult to talk with strangers. Enrique leaves the center and says he may come back, or he may not.

Postscript

In talking about this potential spin-off, Orlando remarked that:

The dress rehearsal was phenomenal, so much so that Marcy Carsey, the producer, came running backstage to congratulate me. But when it came to the actual show, Bill (Cosby) changed the script. It was a change for the better, but I'm sorry to say that I wasn't quick enough… I was so uptight that I started forgetting the new material. Bill had to feed me the lines.

When the show wrapped, I overheard Warren Littlefield, the head of NBC, tell Bill to get me some acting lessons... The network turned down a spin-off, and it's no wonder. I've watched it several times over the years, and even with the mellowing effect of time, my performance stunk, then and now.[91]

The Cosby Show producers had better luck with the spin-off *A Different World*, which initially featured the character of Denise Huxtable attending fictional Hillman College, an all-black institution that her mother and dad had attended. Denise enrolled in Hillman at the beginning of the third season of *The Cosby Show*. When *A Different World* premiered in September 1987, she had become a sophomore. Lisa Bonet left *A Different World* at the end of its first year, but the series continued for another five seasons.

Three Apartments

In this proposed sequel to *The Ropers*, Stanley and Helen Roper move back to their old building where they manage three apartments each occupied by characters from *Three's Company*, *Too Close for Comfort*, and *Three's a Crowd*, the sequel to *Three's Company*.

Background

Stanley and Helen Roper (Norman Fell and Audra Lindley) were the lead characters in *The Ropers*, a spin-off from *Three's Company* that lasted one and a half seasons on ABC from March 1979 to May 1980. Stanley Roper had sold the apartment building where the roommates from *Three's Company* lived and bought a condominium next to realtor Jeffrey Brookes (Jeffrey Tambor) and his wife Anne (Patricia McCormack).

D. L. Taffner Ltd. wanted to produce *Three Apartments*, which was intended to be syndicated to local stations as a replacement for *The Ted Knight Show*. Knight's self-titled comedy ran in syndication for twenty-two episodes before the death of Ted Knight in August 1986. Apparently, *The Ropers* in syndication had good ratings. D. L. Taffner Ltd. came up with the idea to combine the twenty-six *Roper* episodes with forty-four episodes of *Three Apartments* that would be made over two years, so a total of seventy episodes could be used as a strip by local television stations beginning in 1989.[94]

The Concept

The premise of the attempted spin-off dealt with Stanley Roper selling the condo town house where he and his wife lived during the brief run of *The Ropers* and moving back to his old apartment building. The three apartments in the Ropers's building were to be used to feature characters who had appeared on the Taffner-produced comedies *Three's Company*, *Too Close for Comfort* and *Three's a Crowd*. In addition to the characters on those comedies played by John Ritter, Don Knotts, Joyce DeWitt, Jim J. Bullock, Nancy Dussault, and Robert Mandan, the character of Chrissy Snow might have re-appeared although played by an actress other than Suzanne Somers, who had left *Three's Company* during its run in a contract dispute. Taffner still owned the rights to the Snow character, but had no interest in having Somers reprise that role.

Postscript

Offered to local stations at the January 1987 NATPE convention, *Three Apartments* did not generate enough interest among TV stations to turn it into a syndicated series, and so the project was dropped. It is not known if a pilot was ever made for *Three Apartments*

*W*A*L*T*E*R*

Gary Burghoff, as Walter "Radar" O'Reilly from *M*A*S*H*, starred on this spin-off attempt. The producers must have thought that putting meaningless asterisks in the character's first name would be a hint to viewers that the show was based on a *M*A*S*H* character. O'Reilly played a cop patrolling the streets of St. Louis during the fifties in the pilot.

Background

Corporal Radar O'Reilly had left *M*A*S*H* at the beginning of its eighth season in a two-part episode titled "Good-Bye Radar" where he leaves the war zone and returns to his home town in Iowa. Radar reappeared on two episodes of *AfterMASH*, an unsuccessful spin-off from *M*A*S*H*, which foreshadowed the *W*A*L*T*E*R* pilot. *AfterMASH* featured the characters of Colonel Potter (Harry Morgan), Max Klinger (Jamie Farr), and Father Mulcahy (William Christopher) from *M*A*S*H*. Gary Burghoff had a cameo appearance on the January 16, 1984, episode of *AfterMASH*, while, at his wedding rehearsal, reading a letter Klinger had sent him about recent events in his life. In the following week's episode, the Potters, Klingers and Father Mulcahy are getting ready to leave for Radar's wedding when Radar appears at the Potters' doorstep. He has left his own wedding after hearing that Sandy, his bride-to-be, had slept with a good friend. Sandy subsequently appears in her wedding dress to explain to Radar what really happened. After discovering the truth, the couple reconciles, and Father Mulcahy performs their wedding ceremony.

Originally titled *Radar* and then *W*A*L*T*E*R*, Bill Bixby directed the pilot from a teleplay by Everett Greenbaum, Bob Schiller, and Bob Weiskopf based on a story by Schiller, Weiskopf, and Michael Zinberg. Greenbaum had scripted episodes of *The Andy Griffith Show* and *M*A*S*H*; Schiller and Weiskopf had worked on *I Love Lucy* as well as on *Maude*, *All in the Family*, and *Archie Bunker's Place*. *W*A*L*T*E*R* aired on July 17, 1984, on CBS in the Eastern and Central time zones. It wasn't shown in the rest of the United States because of network coverage of the 1984 Democratic National Convention.

The Pilot

After being unable to make a go of his family's farm and after marrying his girlfriend Sandy, Radar and his new wife head to Missouri to start a new life. En route to their honeymoon, Sandy deserts Walter when she falls in love with a garage mechanic. Walter struggles on to St. Louis where he becomes a rookie cop.

Appearing in the pilot with Burghoff were Ray Butkenica as Wendell Mikeljohn, his cousin, roommate, and police partner; Noble Willingham as Sgt. Sowell, their superior; Lyman Ward as Sgt. Bigelow; and Victoria Jackson as Victoria Peterson, Walter's friend who works at the soda fountain in a drug store. The setting was 1950s St. Louis.

While O'Reilly and Mikeljohn are making their rounds, newsman Clete Roberts is appearing on television interviewing former members of the 4077th. Clete Roberts, a real-life broadcast journalist, had served as a war correspondent in World War II and Korea and had appeared on a memorable 1976 episode of *M*A*S*H* interviewing members of the 4077th. Walter explains to Clete that he would still like to buy back his farm some day and that his mother is living in Davenport, Iowa, with her sister. He had met Victoria Peterson after his wife left him a note about leaving with another man. Walter was depressed and asked Victoria for some sleeping pills, but she cheered him up. While giving autographs after the television interview to people viewing TV through a store front window, Walter and Wendell's wallets are stolen. The two officers later see the kid who they think took their wallets. The boy explains to Walter that he was stealing to support him and his grandma. Instead of arresting him, Walter befriends the boy.

Postscript

According to *Variety*, "The pilot managed to capture fleetingly the unique child-like innocence of O'Reilly... , but his escapades as a police recruit in St. Louis in 1954 had an exceedingly flat, old-hat flavor."[95] The broadcast of *W*A*L*T*E*R* ranked 33rd for the week, and CBS declined to move forward with a series.

We the People

Red Buttons and Ron Glass starred in "The Audit," episode sixteen of the second season of the Marla Gibbs's comedy *227* in what could be termed a "pre-pilot." "The Audit" was taped February 20, 1987, the day before it aired, to include references to current events. If the episode had been successful, a regular pilot would have been made, and the series would have been called *We the People* about patrons of a diner discussing topical issues.

Background

Gerren Keith directed "The Audit" from a script written by Ron Bloomberg. According to Bloomberg, he had been pitching a topical comedy series to the networks for years.[96] With the assistance of Glenn Padnick, a vice president of Norman Lear's company, which originally produced *227* before the company was sold to Coca-Cola, the two proposed a topical comedy to NBC executive Brandon Tartikoff. Tartikoff indicated that he would let them demonstrate their pilot idea within an episode of *227*. The cast was informed that topical portions of the script wouldn't be given to them until right before taping.

In addition to "The Audit," *227* had another potential spin-off, *Jackee*, profiled earlier in this part.

The Pre-Pilot

Mary Jenkins (Marla Gibbs) and her husband Lester (Hal Williams) go to an IRS audit, being particularly concerned about a deduction they took for a party they held for Lester's business associates. Before the meeting with the IRS, Lester and Mary have coffee in a diner run by Toots

(Buttons) and his wife Cindy (Louise Troy). Customers in the diner include Perry (David Leisure), a stockbroker; Leonard (Rick Ducomman), and Chris (James Lashly) who discuss politics along with Robert Stone (Glass). Stone talks about a recent Supreme Court decision that requires employers to grant pregnant women maternity leaves. He says that getting pregnant is a vacation. Mary strongly disagrees, and the two get into an argument. Later, at the audit, Lester and Mary discover that Stone is the IRS official examining their tax return. He questions the deduction for the business party, and Mary has to retrieve, from the diner's trash, a list of the party's attendees she wrote on a napkin. Sandra (Jackee Harry) visits the diner, talks with Cindy, and then goes to the IRS office to meet Stone since the two are dating. Sandra is able to back up Lester and Mary's claim about the business party, and Stone lets them off the hook.

Postscript

If the series had been sold, episodes would have revolved around topical conversations at Toots's dinner with Red Buttons as the star and Ron Glass having a recurring role. However, apparently a slow news week impacted the script for this episode, and nothing really controversial was covered during this installment of *227*.

New broadcast networks that started or grew during the 1990s like Fox, UPN, and the WB as well as cable channels would provide additional outlets for potential comedy spin-offs during that decade. The 1990s would see fewer attempted spin-offs and a lesser number of spin-offs that became series compared to the 1970s and 1980s. Despite this, two of the longest-running comedy spin-offs would debut in the 1990s.

PART 5

Proposed Sitcom Spin-offs and Sequels in the 1990s: Not Your Typical Fare

THE NINETIES BEGAN with two of the most popular spin-offs in television history. *The Simpsons*, a spin-off from *The Tracey Ullman Show*, actually premiered in December 1989. Developed by Matt Groening, Sam Simon, and James L. Brooks from *The Mary Tyler Moore Show*, *The Simpsons* became the longest running comedy on television and paved the way for other adult animated fare on Fox, MTV, and Adult Swim. *Frasier*, a spin-off from *Cheers*, became the other hit spin-off of the decade. It was created by David Angell, Peter Casey, and David Lee, all of whom had written and produced *Cheers* and *Wings* before *Frasier*. Angell sold his first TV script for an episode of *Archie Bunker's Place*, while Casey and Lee had both worked on *The Jeffersons*. One other spin-off during the 1990s, *The Parkers* (not to be confused with the proposed *The Facts of Life* spin-off profiled in part 4), which emanated from the UPN comedy *Moesha* and featured Moesha's best friend Kim (Countess Vaughn James) and her single mother played by Mo'Nique, was the only other sitcom that had anywhere near a successful run, lasting for five seasons on UPN beginning in 1999.

The other spin-offs and sequels that were picked up as series during the decade lasted barely a season. *Top of the Heap* from *Married... with Children* ran for six episodes in 1991. A year later its own spin-off, *Vinnie & Bobby*, aired for seven episodes. *Women of the House*, a spin-off of the Suzanne Sugarbaker character from *Designing Women*, had a brief run in 1995. *Buddies*, a back-door pilot starring Dave Chappelle and Christopher Gartin, which began on *Home Improvement*, aired only four episodes in 1996 before it disappeared.

Sequels did not do much better. *Golden Palace*, a sequel to the *Golden Girls* without Bea Arthur, the *New Get Smart*, *Billy*, a sequel to *Head of the Class*, and *Saved by the Bell: The College Years* all vanished quickly from the air after a single season or less. *The New WKRP from Cincinnati*, a syndicated sequel to the original series, did last for two seasons.

The spin-off and sequel efforts described in this part did have many unique features. Three proposed spin-offs to the comedy *Charles in Charge*, which starred *Happy Days* alumnus Scott Baio, represented the first and, to date, only attempts to turn character spin-offs into back-door pilots by having the character from the original series play a lookalike relative in the proposed spin-off. Also, the first attempt to make a network series sequel from a comedy that originally aired on a cable channel occurred during the decade as did a proposal for a spin-off from the very popular *Seinfeld* that eventually became a series on the web. While MTM had tried in the prior decade to turn a character, Carlton, the doorman, on a live-action comedy into an animated series, the reverse was attempted in the 1990s with the idea to make Krusty the Clown from *The Simpsons* into a live-action sitcom. However, perhaps the most unique idea for a spin-off came from the star of *Roseanne*, who proposed a spin-off based on an episode of her series involving two husbands raising a daughter—the real "My Two Dads."

The nineties also saw a unique approach to sequels by trying to save short-lived series through changing their premise and deleting some of their characters. While some have termed these attempts "reboots," they bore many similarities to "sequels" as the term is used in this book, since the same actors played the same roles in a slightly revised situation. However, unlike traditional sequels where the producers rely on viewers' fond memories of the original series to try to make the sequel a success, for the three sequels described in this part, the producers probably wanted the audience to forget the original series that spawned them.

Almost Family

Who knew that Charles's mother (Ellen Travolta) from *Charles in Charge* had a lookalike sister named Sally who ran a car wash that she had received in a divorce settlement with her ex-husband Vincent? Sally (Travolta), the main character in this proposed *Charles in Charge* spin-off, had a staff of five working at her business. Her employees included Arthur Stigley (Jack Bannon, Travolta's real-life husband), a former stockbroker who had lost all his money when convicted of insider trading and who tends the waiting room for the car wash; Tyrone Sampson (Billy "Sly" Williams), a black dude who washes cars and whom Sally is always blaming when customers complain; Bobby Nijinski (Rodney Eastman), a young tough who also washes cars; Lewis "Spiderman" Barch (Jeff Davis), the third car washer and a former hippie; and Penny Hennesy (Crystal Carson). Also, young Emily Perdue (Molly Orr), a nursery school student, stops by the car wash every day after school until her mother is done working.

Background
Like the other *Charles in Charge* spin-offs (see *The Lost Resort* and *Fair Exchange* in this part), Kathy and Bill Greer wrote and Scott Baio directed this pilot broadcast on October 20, 1990. Also, like these other spin-offs, the regular character from *Charles in Charge* played a look-alike but different character in the pilot from the character they portrayed on the series.

Charles in Charge focused on a college student who worked as a male nanny for a busy couple. Willie Aames played Charles's not-so-bright best friend, Buddy Lembeck. In the syndicated version of the series, Charles took care of the three Powell kids—Jamie (Nicole Eggert), Sarah (Josie Davis), and Adam (Alexander Polinsky).

The Pilot
When his mother doesn't mail her sister's birthday gift to her on time, Charles has to deliver it in person. Upon arriving, Sally describes her financial troubles with her car wash business. She announces to her employees that she has to let everyone go. The employees meet and decide to stay even if Sally can't pay them. They promise to give her the tips they receive to help with her rent. Arthur subsequently discovers that Sally's ex-husband kept money from her and that she has paid too much in income taxes. She will be receiving a sizeable refund and so doesn't have to close the car wash after all.

Postscript
According to Mitchell Bank, one of the producers of *Charles in Charge*, Scott Baio wanted to give Ellen Travolta a shot at her own series, but the producers thought that her character on *Charles in Charge* wasn't strong enough to spin off so they went with another character for her to play.[97]

The Chatterbox

The Fran Drescher series *The Nanny* gave rise to a potential spin-off called *The Chatterbox* about a hair salon run by Mr. Anthony (Patrick Cassidy) who has a thirteen-year-old son, Mimo (J.D. Daniels). Claude (Edward Hibbert), the stereotypical gay hair stylist, and Kim (Lauren Tom), the Chinese manicurist, are part of Mr. Anthony's staff. If *The Chatterbox* had been picked up as a series, presumably it would have followed the interactions among the salon's employees and with their customers.

Background

Veteran sitcom director Lee Shallat Chemel helmed this pilot written by Fran Drescher, Peter Marc Jacobson, Robert Sternin, and Prudence Fraser from a story by Fran Drescher and Peter Marc Jacobson (Drescher's then real-life husband). Drescher and Jacobson had also created *The Nanny*, in which Fran Fine (Drescher) became the governess for the three children of Broadway producer Maxwell Sheffield (Charles Shaughnessy) after showing up at Mr. Sheffield's door selling cosmetics, but being mistaken as an applicant for the vacant nanny position. *The Chatterbox*, episode twenty-five of the second season of *The Nanny*, aired on May 15, 1995.

The Pilot

One of the children nanny Fran Fine (Fran Drescher) cares for, Maggie Sheffield, has an appointment at the Chatterbox to have her hair done for her sweet-sixteen party. While waiting for Maggie, Fran meets Mary Ruth (Tracy Nelson), who had unsuccessfully auditioned for Mr. Sheffield. Fran asks Mary Ruth to accompany her to the Chatterbox since they have a job opening. Sylvia, Fran's mother, and Yetta, Fran's grandmother, are having their hair done at the salon as well. Sylvia wants the open position for a shampoo girl, but Mr. Anthony selects Mary Ruth. While trying to help Mr. Anthony's son, Mimo, who has a cut on his head, Mary Ruth finds a picture of his mother. She wants Mr. Anthony to consider that his son misses his mother, but Mr. Anthony doesn't like her interfering in his personal life. He fires her but reconsiders when Mimo says he wants to keep the picture of his mom.

Postscript

Patrick Cassidy, who played Mr. Anthony, didn't think he would get the part when he auditioned since he was Irish from California and the character was an Italian from Flushing, New York.[98] However, he worked on his accent, and much to his surprise, Peter Marc Jacobson cast him. Cassidy remarked that the pilot never became a series because CBS couldn't figure out what the show would be without Fran Drescher appearing on it. "...Fran's involvement made the network think it was just another episode of *The Nanny*, as opposed to its own show about these characters from Flushing who work at a hair salon."[99]

Both Patrick Cassidy and Tracy Nelson came from acting families. Cassidy's mother is Shirley Jones; his father was actor Jack Cassidy. Actor/producer Shaun Cassidy is his brother, while actor/singer David Cassidy is his half-brother. Tracy Nelson is the daughter of singer/actor Rick Nelson and the granddaughter of Harriet and Ozzie Nelson.

Clarissa Now

Before she starred in *Sabrina, The Teenage Witch* and *Melissa & Joey*, Melissa Joan Hart had the lead role on the Nickelodeon channel situation comedy titled *Clarissa Explains It All* as Clarissa Darling, a fourteen-year-old high school student who lives with her parents and younger brother. Shortly after *Clarissa Explains It All* ended, a proposed sequel, titled *Clarissa Now*, featured Hart working as an intern at a New York City newspaper.

Background

John Whitesell, who began his career directing daytime soaps in the 1980s, helmed this 1995 pilot. Terri Minsky did the teleplay from a story written by her and Mitchell Kriegman, who had created *Clarissa Explains It All*.

Foreshadowing the proposed sequel, in the final episode of *Clarissa Explains It All* called "The Last Clarissa," Melissa Joan Hart's character thinks her future is all planned out with her attending the College of Cincinnati's School of Journalism. However, the editor for the local newspaper she is currently writing for notifies her that, based on an article of hers that he submitted, Clarissa has been awarded a one-year internship at the *New York Daily Post*. After discussing it with her parents, Clarissa decides to go to New York City instead of to journalism school in Cincinnati.

In the sequel effort, instead of working for the *New York Daily Post*, Clarissa finds a job as an intern at the *New York Star Chronicle*.

The Pilot

Clarissa is the assistant to renowned columnist Hugh Hamilton (Robert Klein) whose office looks as messy as Oscar Madison's bedroom in *The Odd Couple*. Other staff at the paper include city editor Porter Russell (Lisa Gay Hamilton), owner/publisher Lillian Banyon (Marian Seldes), and young Spencer Armstrong (Chris Coburn), a reporter trainee.

Hamilton has to come up with a story for his next column. He wants nothing to do with Clarissa, but nevertheless, she tries to find a story for him. All the story ideas she suggests Hamilton already knows about, and he orders her out of his office. He decides to write about Clarissa and her naiveté about New York City. The publisher congratulates Clarissa on re-igniting Hamilton's fire. Hamilton invites Clarissa into his office and says he wants her to be his assistant.

Postscript

Commenting on *Clarissa Now*, Melissa Joan Hart thought "…it was a fun show… but it skewed a lot older because it was a different time. CBS was very much an older-demographic network back then. They tried to age the show up a little bit, but the thing is, the 'Clarissa' audience was so young and hip. I just think it didn't work. It's not what people wanted to see."[100]

In an interview with the *Huffington Post*, Mitchell Kriegman, who helped to develop the sequel, said about the pilot that:

> I think it was too early for the show to be true to its form. It was a funny situation because I had written a lot of drafts, I had cast it, I had started building the set and everything and I just think they weren't ready—which is really funny when you look at "Modern Family" and everything else out there—but they [CBS] weren't ready for her to talk to the camera and have fantasies. And I was like, "Well, what do you mean? That's how she expresses herself! That's how this show cuts itself above other shows!" And there was one exec that said something that I'll never forget. He said, "Network audiences can't handle that postmodern sensibility." And look at everything on TV now. That's so not true.[101]

In summing up *Clarissa Now*, Hart indicated, "After production wrapped, Mitchell and I felt that we didn't have as much freedom on a network as we did on cable to keep it going the way we liked. I think fans would have been disappointed if it went to air."[102]

Daddio

This attempted spin-off from the UPN comedy *Malcolm & Eddie* looked at fatherhood from the perspective of a stay-at-home dad. Rapper Coolio starred as Troy Jensen, a building contractor, who has three children—Rome (Christian Copelin), Cairo (Orlando Brown), and Geneva (Jazz Raycole)—with his wife Vina (Vanessa Bell Calloway). While his spouse is a nurse, Troy works from home and takes care of the kids. Troy employs Duke (Alimi Ballard) and Earl Gibson (Rawle Lewis) as his construction workers.

Background

Directed by Malcolm-Jamal Warner, who co-starred on *Malcolm & Eddie*, and written by David Duclon, Gary Menteer, Stephen Langford, and Meg DeLoatch, this pilot was broadcast on May 4, 1999. Malcolm (Warner), the serious one, and Eddie (Eddie Griffin), the more free-spirited part of the duo, were roommates on *Malcolm & Eddie*, which ran for four seasons on the United Paramount Network (UPN), a precursor to the CW.

The Pilot

Malcolm and Eddie are opening a branch of their Fifty/Fifty Club in Chicago. They travel to the Windy City to see Troy, who has submitted a bid for designing their new club. When they arrive at his home, Troy is dealing with various problems involving his kids. His daughter has had a bad dye job done on her hair by a friend; his youngest son Rome has gotten his head stuck between two posts in the stair rail; and his older son Cairo gave away the family dog because he felt that taking care of the dog was too much work. Malcolm is able to free Rome's head from the stair rail, while Troy counsels his daughter about her hair and threatens to send Cairo to military school unless he retrieves the family pet. Malcolm and Eddie want Troy to lower his bid on their project because they think that it is too high. However, Troy says that he gave them an honest price which is guaranteed, and so they give him the job.

Postscript

Artes Leon Levy Jr., better known as Coolio, continued to act on such television series as *Charmed* and *Robbery Homicide Division* as well as in movies in between his performing engagements after *Daddio* failed to become a series.

Enemies

This pilot, a parody of the long-running hit NBC sitcom *Friends*, starred Matt Borlenghi as Tom, Nicole Eggert as his girlfriend Shannon, Terri Ivens as Maria, Tom's half-sister, and Chris Young as Jackson, Tom's unemployed friend, who all live in the same apartment. *Enemies* came from the people who produced the long-running Fox comedy *Married... with Children*.

Background

The Bundy family—Al (Ed O'Neill), a clerk at a shoe store, his lazy wife Peg (Katey Sagal), and his two kids, promiscuous Kelly (Christina Applegate) and conniving Bud (David Faustino)—was the focus of *Married... with Children*, which had been created by Michael Moye and Ron Leavitt. Both had worked on comedies like *The Jeffersons* and *Silver Spoons* while at Embassy Television. *Married... with Children* had one spin-off that became a short-lived series called *Top of the Heap* featuring Joseph Bologna as a scheming father who wanted his son, played by Matt LeBlanc, to marry rich. In addition to *Top of the Heap*, *Married... with Children* also had two attempted spin-offs that were never turned into a series—*Enemies* and, profiled later in this part, *Radio Free Trumaine*.

Helmed by long-time *Married... with Children* director Gerry Cohen and written by Richard Gurman, Stacie Lipp, and Russell Marcus, *Enemies* aired on April 14, 1996. According to Gurman, who had previously worked on *227*, *The Facts of Life*, and *Diff'rent Strokes*, "*Enemies* was simple: If *Married... with Children* was the anti-*Cosby*, then *Enemies* would be the anti-*Friends*.... We wanted to show what it's really like to live with people, *Married* style. There was nothing deeper than that and we really felt we could pick up the backlash of people who were tired of *Friends*. And even if you weren't tired of *Friends*, we hoped people could still appreciate seeing something with edge and satire."[103]

The Pilot

Bud, Kelly, and Al Bundy are watching *Friends* on television with Kelly the only one who really likes the show. A delivery guy named Tom (Borlenghi) drops off some packages at the Bundy house and chats up Kelly. Later Tom comes home to his girlfriend Shannon (Eggert) who has been stalking him to find out what women he has been seeing. Tom and Shannon argue over womanizing. She walks out on him, and Tom goes out with Kelly Bundy. Tom and Kelly end up at George's diner. George

Part 5: Proposed Sitcom Spin-offs and Sequels in the 1990s • 161

(Phil Lewis), the cook, employs a scatter-brained waitress named Keiko (Melissa Chan). Shannon, with a wealthy guy named Henry (Alan Thicke), comes into the diner. To make each other jealous, each couple goes into the diner's bathrooms to pretend they are having sex. Tom crashes through the wall separating the bathrooms and kisses Shannon. Kelly and Henry then go on a date together.

Postscript

Richard Gurman remarked that he wasn't sure why this spin-off didn't move forward. At the time of *Enemies*, the head of Fox, John Matoyan, wanted to make the network more like CBS, and *Enemies* never fit into that mold. Gurman also mentioned that the pilot probably didn't test well for Fox in their pilot pick-up process.[104]

Fair Exchange

Not to be confused with the sixty-minute comedy from the 1960s with the same title, in this third potential spin-off from *Charles in Charge*, Nicole Eggert stars as Amanda, a teen who has to contend with her parents, siblings, and a foreign exchange student in this proposed family sitcom.

Background

Directed by Scott Baio and written by Bill and Kathy Greer, this November 3, 1990, pilot, like the other two (see *Almost Family* and *The Lost Resort*) featured a character from *Charles in Charge* playing a look-alike relative. As with Ellen Travolta's character in *Almost Family*, the producers of *Charles in Charge* agreed that Nicole Eggert's character was not strong enough to support a show, and so they created her cousin Amanda as the center of a possible spin-off.

The Pilot

Sarah Powell (Josie Davis), one of the kids Charles cares for, goes to Albuquerque to visit her cousin, Amanda Colfax, who looks remarkably like Sarah's sister Jamie. Amanda has a younger sister, Melanie (Olivia Burnette), and a brother, Michael (Michael Manasseri), who all live with their parents Elaine (Cecilie Hart) and Steve (David Graf). The family has just arranged for a foreign exchange student from Romania, Nikki Kovacs (Ivan Geuron) to stay with them. Nikki discovers that the family ordinarily does not eat its meals together. He also finds that each of the kids has a problem that they should discuss with their parents. Michael wants a new pair of high-top shoes; Amanda would like to date a boy from Mexico, but is not sure how her parents will react; and Melanie is upset because her best friend is hanging out with another girl.

Nikki suggests that they talk to their parents at dinner about their problems and that he will prepare the meal. However, Elaine and Steve do not have time for dinner; they have a charity event to attend. Nikki overhears Amanda blame him for the dinner fiasco and says he should go back to Romania. Sarah calls Charles for advice, and he says that Nikki should talk to Elaine. Nikki requests that Elaine and Steve stay for dinner because their kids have problems that they need to discuss with them.

The parents ultimately decide to have dinner with their offspring. For Melanie's problem, dad Steve suggests that she invite both her friend and the other girl to a party to get to know them better. Steve recommends that Michael work Saturdays in his office to earn money for the new shoes he wants. After Amanda says she wants to date Danny Martinez, her father says she needs to make her own decision about dating him. He and her mother will not interfere.

Postscript

After *Fair Exchange* failed to become a series, Nicole Eggert starred in the *Married... with Children* proposed spin-off *Enemies* and then went on to various roles in television and films. Probably the most successful of the actors who played the Colfax siblings has been Olivia Burnette who starred on *The Torkelsons* and more recently on *Sons of Anarchy*.

Goin' for Mine

Actress Tichina Arnold, who played Gina Waters's friend and secretary, Pam James, on the Martin Lawrence comedy, *Martin*, starred on her own spin-off pilot working for a record company.

Background

Scripted by Kenny Buford, a writer and producer of *Martin*. Gerren Keith, who began directing TV comedies in the 1970s, helmed this episode which aired in April 1997. In *Martin*, Lawrence played Martin Payne, a wise-cracking radio talk show host, whose girlfriend Gina Waters (Tisha Campbell), worked as a marketing executive.

The Pilot

Pam James is terminated from her job at the advertising agency. Martin and his buddies Tommy (Thomas Mikal Ford) and Cole (Carl Anthony Payne II) stop by her apartment along with their friend from high school Trey Foster (Dondre T. Whitfield), who works at *Keep It Real Records* as an artists and repertoire (A & R) representative responsible for talent scouting and overseeing the development of recording talent. After Trey mentions to Pam an opening for another A & R person at the company, she visits Trey's workplace hoping to get the position. KR Records is owned by Sterling Sweets (Phil Morris). On staff, in addition to Trey, are Donna (Jenna von Dy), the receptionist; Clyde, the messenger who is Sweets's nephew; and Tony (Billy Gallo), the creative director who fancies himself a ladies' man. When Trey shows up late for work, Sweets demands that he locate some new singing talent or lose his job. Pam tells Trey that she may be able to assist him in finding some talent if he helps her get the A & R position. Back at her apartment, Dante, an assistant from her former job, delivers the rest of Pam's things from her old office. He begins to play the piano and sing. Impressed with his singing, Pam invites him to a showcase for new talent that she is putting together for Trey. That night, Dante fails to show at the scheduled time, and Trey's boss Sterling Sweets makes an unexpected appearance. Dante finally shows up, but is nervous to perform in front of an audience. Pam begins to sing with him which calms him. Sweets is impressed with Dante's talent, and, as a result, he offers Pam the A & R position.

Postscript

As with many other potential spin-offs described in this book (for example, the pilots from *Charles in Charge* and *Green Acres*), *Goin' for Mine* aired in the final season of *Martin* in hopes that it would become a series leading to, among other things, continued employment for the crew that produced *Martin*. Like other such attempts in the final season of a long-running series, that didn't happen.

Harlan and Merleen

Married couple Dr. Harlan Ellridge (Charles Durning) and his wife Merleen (Ann Wedgeworth) are at the center of this potential spin-off from *Evening Shade*. The premise had Merleen deciding to open their home to single pregnant women which her husband would care for.

Background

First titled *It's Never Too Late* and then *The Second Time Around*, this pilot aired in two installments on July 12 and 19, 1993. The two-parter was written by Burt Reynolds and James Hampton and directed by Reynolds. On *Evening Shade*, Burt Reynolds played Wood Newton, a former pro-football player who returns to his home town of Evening Shade, Arkansas, to coach the losing high school football team.

The Pilot

When pregnant as a teenager, Merleen had to give up her baby. She doesn't want this to happen to other women, and so she places an ad in the newspaper for pregnant women who are alone with no place to go. Three pregnant women respond to the ad—Frances "Frankie" Mosea (Leah Remini), Sherilee Croft (Rose Kristin), and Carmen Louisa (Maria Canals). Frankie worked as a magician's assistant before she got too big for her costume and the box for sawing her in half. Carmen, from Miami by way of Cuba, became pregnant after marrying a wealthy man whose family didn't approve of the marriage, and so she ran away. Sherilee wanted to be a Dallas Cowboy cheerleader. However, she had a daughter, April (Janna Michaels) by a football player she had met and then became pregnant again. Since he was not very nice, she wanted to get away from him. Harlan helps with the delivery of Carmen's baby, a daughter she names Harleena.

Postscript

The first installment of *Harlan and Merleen* ranked 32nd in the ratings; the second part ranked 42nd. Burt Reynolds had hoped that if *Harlan and Merleen* became a series it would follow *Evening Shade* on Mondays at 8:30 p.m. on CBS. Ossie Davis, who played Ponder Blue, the owner of Ponder Blue's Barbecue Villa restaurant on *Evening Shade*, was set to appear on both series as his character.

The Jackie Chiles Show

This much discussed spin-off attempt from *Seinfeld* would have starred Phil Morris as Jackie Chiles, a parody of real-life attorney Johnnie Cochran. Chiles imitated Cochran's distinctive speaking style, known for using four adjectives in a row, usually ending with the word "outrageous."

Background

The character of Jackie Chiles first appeared in season seven of *Seinfeld* on an episode titled "The Maestro," where Kramer burns himself in a movie theater with a cup of coffee he is holding between his legs while trying to climb over the legs of another moviegoer. The coffee company offers Kramer free coffee from all their stores which he quickly accepts before the company executive has even finished describing the offer or mentioned any money—much to the dismay of Jackie Chiles.

Variety reported in July 1999 that Castle Rock TV, the production company for *Seinfeld*, was in the early stages of developing *The Jackie Chiles Show* spin-off.[105] Phil Morris had revealed plans for the new series during a Television Critics Association panel, and Jerry Seinfeld and Larry David had given their approval for the project. Both were supposedly to be executive producers of the spin-off.

The Concept

In the proposed spin-off, Chiles is to be the only black attorney in an otherwise all-white law firm. Morris remarked that his character would work in "a very austere white law firm, and sparks will fly. Jackie needs to be in constant conflict." [106]

Postscript

At the time of the proposal, NBC claimed no knowledge of a possible series. The project never got off the ground. However, Morris brought the character back in TV commercials as well as in episodes for Will Ferrell's *Funny or Die* website. In one webisode, the character of Jackie Chiles does a commercial advertising his services telling people he will watch out for them and to call 1-555-4-Jackie. In another, he talks about the internet and social media and warns people to safeguard themselves from the loonies. But he forgets his password for Netflix and asks his assistant, who is also his cameraman, for help. In two of the episodes, Jackie talks about his famous friends—Tiger Woods and Barack Obama. Jackie claims that Obama used to work for him as a paralegal during a summer while in college and that he did an excellent job on his laundry. Concerning Woods, Jackie says that everyone cheats and, to illustrate the point, when a colleague comes into his office to remind Jackie to be on time for a meeting, Jackie mentions how the colleague cheats on his wife, at golf, etc., while filming of another Chiles's commercial continues. In a fifth episode about how Jackie Chiles knows television, he says that he knows what he likes, but bemoans the fact that he doesn't see shows with other than token black characters. He also suggests that he could have been Ally McBeal.

Krusty the Clown

This proposed spin-off would have featured the acerbic Krusty the Clown character from the long-running comedy *The Simpsons*. Unlike *The Simpsons*, the *Krusty* situation comedy was conceived as a live-action series focusing on Krusty in Hollywood hosting a talk show.

Background

Krusty the Clown first appeared on one of *The Simpsons* short episodes on the Fox network comedy/variety series *The Tracey Ullman Show*, which James L. Brooks, co-creator of *The Mary Tyler Moore Show*, and Sam Simon, who had helped to script and produce *Taxi* and *Cheers*, had written and produced.

Krusty, who has his own popular local television show in Springfield on channel 6, looks like Homer Simpson in clown make-up. Born on the Lower East Side of Springfield, Herschel Shmoikel Pinchas Yeruscham Krustofski aka Krusty the Clown became Bart Simpson's favorite television character.

Matt Groening (the creator of *The Simpsons*) and Michael Weithorn tried to develop a spin-off of the Krusty the Clown character in 1994. According to Weithorn, "Matt and I worked on it for about 6 months, did a lot of research on ways to give an animation-type feel to live action footage. We had a million notes on the series and even much of a pilot script in rough form, but finally it became clear that James L. Brooks (who had left 20th for Sony a year or two before, acrimoniously) had no interest whatsoever in seeing 20th [Century Fox] profit more from the Simpsons and killed the whole thing." [107]

The Concept

Dan Castellaneta, who voices Homer Simpson and Krusty among other characters on *The Simpsons*, would have portrayed Krusty, who has moved from Springfield to Los Angeles to host a late-night talk show for the Fox network. Krusty lives in a house on stilts with beavers gnawing their way through the support structure. The president of Fox, who viewers were never to see, would appear via Skype on the huge television monitors located in every room of Krusty's home anytime he wanted. Supposedly, the tone of the spin-off would have been very dark with Krusty in a very hostile world.

Postscript

No live-action pilot of the proposed spin-off resulted from the concept. Groening would later create the science fiction animated series *Futurama* about Philip J. Fry, a pizza guy from New York City who is accidentally frozen in 1999 and thawed out one thousand years later. Michael Weithorn subsequently developed the long-running comedy *The King of Queens*.

Laverne Todd Show

Park Overall in her role as Laverne Todd would have appeared in this 1993 spin-off from *Empty Nest*. In the pilot script, Laverne marries and moves to her new spouse's home town where she butts heads with his ex-wife and kids.

Background

Empty Nest starred Richard Mulligan as Dr. Harry Weston, a widower with three adult daughters. At work, Nurse Laverne Todd (Overall) assisted Dr. Weston. Gary Jacobs, a writer and producer for *Empty Nest*, penned the script for the spin-off titled "Scenes from a Marriage." However, a pilot never resulted from the script.

The Script

Laverne marries a trucker named Tom and moves to Florida where his two kids, Becky and Joey, live. Liz, Tom's ex-wife, meets Laverne when she comes for her monthly child support payment. Liz says that she will bring their kids by the next day, ruining Laverne's honeymoon plans.

The next morning, Becky, Tom's daughter, a begrudging teenager, and Tom's son, the pleasant Joey, arrive. Becky ignores Laverne and is not enthusiastic about spending the day with her. She picks a fight with Laverne, who wants to set her straight, but Tom doesn't support his new wife. This leads to an argument between Tom and Laverne, and, when they return to their living room, they discover that Becky has left.

Laverne later finds Becky at the mall with her friends. Becky's friends leave after Laverne threatens them with a Taser that she doesn't really have. She talks Becky into a kind of working relationship between

Park Overall who starred as nurse Laverne Todd on *Empty Nest*

the two of them, making Becky smile in the process, although she won't admit it. Later, Tom apologizes for his argument with Laverne, and they make up.

Postscript

According to Gary Jacobs, the pilot was never shot because of difficulties casting the husband's role.[108] Robert Urich, set to play Laverne's husband on the spin-off, instead decided to appear as the love interest on the ill-fated Faye Dunaway sitcom *It Had to be You*.

The Lost Resort

Willie Ames, Buddy on *Charles in Charge*, starred in this potential spin-off from that series as his look-alike cousin Dudley helping to run a hotel in Hawaii. The series would have dealt with the escapades of Dudley and another young assistant manager, Mitch Hunt (Jeff Bennett) as they interact with guests and girls at the Hawaiian resort.

Background

During the final season of *Charles in Charge*, three potential spin-offs were piloted. *The Lost Resort*, the first of the three, aired September 1, 1990. The other two, *Almost Family* and *Fair Exchange*, were profiled earlier in this part. As noted, all three of the spin-off episodes were directed by Scott Baio and written by Kathy and Bill Greer.

The Pilot

One of Charles's professors has a brother who manages a hotel in Hawaii that needs a college student as assistant manager. Charles asks Buddy if he can fill the spot, but Buddy can't go because he has a hot date. Buddy calls his cousin Dudley Kranz, who lives in California and is studying hotel management, and asks him to fly to Hawaii. However, not knowing that Buddy's cousin is taking the position, Charles also flies to Hawaii to help out. When he arrives, Dudley, played by Willie Ames with his hair dyed blonde, says that Charles can stay with Mitchell Hunt (Bennett) and him. Mitch, like Dudley, is also an assistant manager. Other characters on the spin-off included Karl Higler (Dick Gautier) as the manager, and Tippi Brewster (Susan Jennifer Sullivan) as the desk clerk.

Mitch and Dudley are turned on by the beautiful bikini-clad girls who enter the lobby from the beach which leads to conversations like this:

> Dudley: "Mitchell, we've died and gone to Heaven!"
> Mitch: "No Dudley, we've lived and gone to Hell. We can look but we can't touch. If Mr. Higler catches us even thinking about touching, he'll cut off our… benefits!"

Mitch and Dudley try to save a man, Leonard Burley (Brian Backer), who wants to jump off the fifth floor ledge because his girlfriend has left him. Burley is in the same room that Henry Horton, the owner of the hotel, wants to occupy during his pending visit. Also, a human fly (Frank Ferrante) is scaling the hotel. Dudley gets Tippi to talk Leonard out of jumping, and he calls the press about the human fly saying that the fly is there to honor Mr. Horton's sense of adventure. Naturally, Mr. Horton congratulates Dudley's manager, Mr. Higler, for thinking of the stunt.

Postscript

With respect to this potential Willie Ames spin-off, Ames apparently didn't want his character of Buddy on *Charles in Charge* to be his legacy. He wanted to play a different character, hence the creation of his cousin Dudley.

The Mighty Quinns

A sequel of sorts to the short-lived 1993 Faye Dunaway comedy, *It Had to Be You*, *The Mighty Quinns* starred Robert Urich as Mitch Quinn, a widower raising three boys—oldest son David (Justin Whalin), middle son Christopher (Will Estes), and youngest son Sebastian (Justin Jon Ross).

Background

A fall 1993 comedy on CBS, titled *It Had to Be You*, featured Faye Dunaway as twice-divorced book publisher Laura Scofield, who falls in love with a widowed carpenter Mitch Quinn (Robert Urich). The Urich character has been a widower for about four years, ever since his wife Jenny had passed away. Eve Parkin (Robin Bartlett) was Laura's assistant. Set in Boston, CBS canceled the comedy after only four episodes had aired.

After the demise of *It Had to be You*, a pilot, featuring all of the characters except for Faye Dunaway's character, was made focusing on the Mitch Quinn character and his sons in a 1990s version of *My Three Sons*. Robert Urich, Robin Bartlett, Will Estes, Justin Whalin, and Justin Jon Ross were brought back to star in the project called *The Mighty Quinns*. Andrew Nicholls and Darrell Vickers, who developed *It Had to Be You*, wrote the pilot.

The Pilot

The pilot for *The Mighty Quinns*, titled "Family Night," starts with the oldest son David doing laundry and his brothers, Chris and Sebastian, completing a dating questionnaire for their dad who has been out of town for awhile working on a construction project. This leads to dialogue such as,

> Chris: "I always wondered when exactly does clothing become laundry? It's like, when does lettuce become salad?"
> David: "You know Chris, that's funny because I always wondered when exactly an idiot becomes a moron?"

Not knowing how to answer all the questions on the dating questionnaire, Chris and Sebastian indicate that their dad is seven feet tall, weighs 100 pounds, and has had forty-three romantic partners.

When Mitch returns from his trip, he is concerned that his kids don't have time to talk with him, and he doesn't know who they are dating or what they are doing in school. He finds the completed questionnaire and thinks that David filled it out. Mitch decides to take his sons fishing to reconnect with them, but they all have other plans and leave him alone.

At Quinn Carpentry, Mitch's secretary is Eve (apparently having left Laura's employ who is never mentioned in the pilot). Eve advises Mitch that boys like his sons do not really want to talk with their parents. But Mitch decides to have a "family night" with cocoa and board games. They all begin playing Scrabble. However, the kids start yelling at each other when Chris knocks over a mug of cocoa and David says he is tired of cleaning up after his brothers. Mitch talks with David about him trying to fill in for his late mother and asks him about the dating questionnaire. Chris and Sebastian reveal they filled out the form as a favor for their dad. The next day, the kids decide to go fishing with their dad, and they find a date for him who likes fishing.

Postscript

According to Andrew Nicholls, he and his writing partner referred to this project as "the Done-Away-With-Faye show." Apparently, no one at the network let Dunaway know that the series was going ahead without her. She had to read the news in the trades. After learning of the cancelation of *It Had to Be You* and the planned sequel, *The Mighty Quinns*,

Dunaway said, "If the series comes back without me, I may even watch it. I still adore Bob Urich."[109] Ultimately, CBS decided against turning *The Mighty Quinns* into a series.

Radio Free Trumaine

Radio Free Trumaine involved three college students—Oliver Cole (Eric Dane, later Dr. Mark "McSteamy" Sloan on *Grey's Anatomy*), Mark Campbell (Andrew Kavovit), and April Adams (Keri Russell, who subsequently starred on *Felicity*). They all worked at Trumaine University's FM radio station, WHIP (FM 106.2), in this potential spin-off from *Married...with Children*.

Background

The pilot aired as the twenty-sixth episode of season nine of *Married...with Children* on May 5, 1995. Directed by Gerry Cohen, Richard Gurman and Stacie Lipp penned the planned spin-off. Gurman's fascination with radio in general and college radio in particular led to the idea for *Radio Free Trumaine*. "This was the pre-Facebook era and I felt that a college radio station was a great form of social networking and that the characters who would be attracted to working there would be good sitcom characters.... Also, with Bud (Bundy) being in college, it felt like an organic way to do a spinoff."[110]

The Pilot

Bud (David Faustino) is dating April Adams, a student at the school who also works as an intern at Marcy D'Arcy's (Amanda Bearse) bank. He asks April to the university's Spring Formal and wins a free limo ride from Oliver and Mark to take April and him to the dance. Nickolai Pushkin, a soccer player at the school, also likes April and wants to go steady with her. Meanwhile, Oliver and Mark are planning to interview Steve Rhoades (David Garrison), Marcy's ex-husband and former *Married...with Children* regular, who is the new dean at the university. He gives them pre-planned questions to ask him. However, during the interview, the two guys ask Dean Rhoades how he so quickly went from being the University President's chauffeur to Dean, and they reveal that he has incriminating photos of the President with the school's mascot. For this, Rhoades kicks them off the air and out of school. Marcy drops by the radio station and encourages the guys to protest their dismissal by taking over the station. While they are doing this, April talks with Bud and Nickolai about her feelings for each of them, and Mark broadcasts the conversation live over the air calling it "Hot Talk with April." Callers advise April who to go steady with—Bud or Nickolai. April decides to find herself by working at the station, while dozens of students turn out to demonstrate against Rhoades's dismissal of Mark and Oliver. In response to the demonstration, Dean Rhoades allows Mark and Oliver back in the school and a return to the airwaves.

Postscript

As indicated earlier about *Enemies,* the other attempted spin-off from *Married...with Children,* the head of Fox at the time, John Matoyan, felt that *Radio Free Trumaine* didn't fit into his plans for the network and, like *Enemies,* this pilot didn't test well.

Related by Birth

In this non-traditional sequel to the short-lived comedy *Sibs,* two single sisters, Audie (Margaret Colin) and Lily (Jami Gertz), attempt to build their relationship living next to one another. Others in the cast included Warren Morris, an accountant (Dan Castellaneta, the voice of Homer Simpson), who previously worked for the third sister, Nora, but is in love with Audie; Michael Brickman (Mark Nassar), Audie's new boss; and Henry (Grayson McCouch), Lily's assistant in her catering business.

Background

Sibs starred Marsha Mason as Nora Ruscio, the oldest of three sisters, who was married to Howie (Alex Rocco). Her sisters Audie and Lily would always bring their problems for Nora to help solve. *Sibs* had been created by Heidi Perlman (Rhea Perlman's sister) and produced by her, James L. Brooks, and Sam Simon, who had all worked together on *The Tracey Ullman Show.* A year after the cancelation of *Sibs,* Perlman proposed the sequel *Related by Birth* to ABC. Former actor Will MacKenzie directed the pilot broadcast on July 2, 1994.

The Pilot

Audie is out of work and desperate for a job, so she updates her resume showing a college degree and other untruths. Michael Brickman, a venture capitalist who made his money selling earthquake survival kits,

Jami Gertz, who played Lily on *Sibs* and *Related by Birth*, later starred on *Still Standing* and *The Neighbors*

hires her based on her updated resume for $50,000 a year as his assistant. He assigns her the task of getting him a new accountant to audit his books to avoid potential IRS problems. Lil suggests that Audie hire neurotic Warren Morris, Audie's former boyfriend who still loves her, for the position. He accepts and does an excellent job auditing Brickman's accounts. Audie then confesses to Brickman that she is a failed realtor and lied on her resume. Brickman likes how she handled her first assignment and decides to keep her. Meanwhile, Lil, a caterer working out of her small apartment with her young assistant Henry, needs a bigger place for her business. She wants to move into the apartment across the hall from Audie, but is afraid to ask her if it would be all right. She finally works up the courage to explain to her sister what she wants. Audie, thankful to Lil for suggesting Warren and advising her to tell the truth to Brickman about her resume, says she would love Lil to live next door.

Postscript

ABC decided not to turn *Related by Birth* into a series. Creator Heidi Perlman had better luck as one of the producers of the *Cheers* spin-off *Frasier*.

Roseanne's Gay Family Project

This proposed spin-off from *Roseanne* centered on two men, Richard and Rolf, married to each other, who take care of Richard's teenage daughter.

Background

Roseanne Barr had the idea for a comedy based on an episode of her show about Leon Carp (Martin Mull) marrying his boyfriend Scott (Fred Willard). The episode was originally titled "The Bride Wore Boxers," but apparently the producer did not get the reference to the film noir classic *The Bride Wore Black*, and so the title became "December Bride," also the title of a 1950s sitcom starring Spring Byington.[111]

The storyline of the episode had Roseanne meeting Scott at the diner where she worked and learning that he will be marrying Leon, who had bailed on the marriage ceremony five years ago. She volunteers to plan their wedding while they are in Minneapolis for pre-marital counseling. Roseanne decides to have an over-the-top gay wedding with male strippers and Liza Minnelli and Judy Garland impersonators at the reception. When Leon sees what Roseanne has done, he calls off the wedding. Roseanne then locks him in the bathroom. After Leon's mother (June Lockhart) and Reverend Crosley (Norm Crosby) show up for the nuptials, Roseanne releases Leon from the bathroom. Leon says he is not ready for marriage because he is not prepared for a permanent relationship. He announces that he is not really gay, but, after kissing Roseanne, he admits he is gay and goes ahead with the ceremony. As the two men kiss, Sharon (Mariel Hemingway), who had kissed Roseanne in a controversial 1994, episode shows up, sits down behind Roseanne, and stares lovingly at her. In the final scene, comedian Milton Berle, dressed in drag, catches the wedding bouquet.

Penned by *Roseanne* writer and producer, William Lucas Walker. Gail Mancuso, who began her career directing *Roseanne*, helmed this episode. Roseanne Barr thought that the characters of Leon and Scott could headline their own sitcom with an interracial, inter-generational gay couple played by Don Knotts and RuPaul as the co-stars.

The Proposal

As William Lucas Walker described the proposal for this gay family sitcom spin-off:

> On September 21, 1995, I was summoned by Roseanne (she summoned people) to her trailer (the only time I was invited there during four years of employ). I was told to drop whatever I was doing (helping to prepare whatever script would have been next up that season) and come up with a treatment for a "gay family sitcom" that would be spun off the characters based on Leon and Scott… For reasons I cannot recall… in the treatment the characters are not named Leon and Scott, but Richard and Rolf.
>
> The only specifics that I recall Roseanne asking for were that RuPaul and Don Knotts would co-star, playing an interracial, cross-generational couple, with Knotts as RuPaul's sugar daddy. And that Richard and Rolf be raising a child together.[112]

In the treatment written by Walker, Richard has recently moved from Lanford, Illinois, to New York after he married Rolf, who is an award-winning Broadway costume designer known as the "Queen of the Bugle Bead." Rolf Willows and Richard Martin had met twenty years earlier on the dinner theater circuit where, as so often happens, a simple inseam measurement developed into a torrid love affair.

Other characters envisioned for the spin-off included Cathryn Constantine, Richard's ex-wife, whom he had also met on the dinner theater circuit and had married when he found she was pregnant. The marriage ended when she discovered that not only was Richard seeing men, but, even worse, letting the men wear her clothes. Navida Martin, Richard's sixteen-year-old daughter from the marriage, whose mother starred in Broadway musical comedies, wanted to live with her dad and Rolf.

Richard and Rolf's upstairs neighbor is Tiffany Diamond (RuPaul), a poor black man from Georgia, who at nineteen had put on a wig and a dress and changed his name from Willy Barksdale to Tiffany Diamond. Tiffany moved to New York and became a Rockette, but had her career cut short when one of the other Rockettes caught him in the bathroom tucking his genitals so as not to show a bulge. Tiffany now writes an advice column for a gay magazine and has a loving and financial relationship with her benefactor, Rodney Jefferson Pruitt III (Don Knotts), an heir to a large plumbing supply company. Rodney is, so to speak, nuts for Tiffany.

Finally, there is Jupiter Smith, Navida's best friend, who just might be a lesbian and may have to live with the Martin-Willows given her parent's objections to her sexual orientation.

According to Walker, in the first proposed episode, Navida moves in with Richard and Rolf after a fight with her mother. Navida is actually closer to Rolf than to her dad, and Rolf is proud of the fact that he played a crucial role in her conception. She would never have been born if Richard hadn't fled Rolf's apartment after a lover's quarrel, gotten drunk, and slept with Cathryn out of spite. Cathryn is jealous of this arrangement.[113]

As a wedding gift, Rolf backed Richard's dream of opening a Midwestern themed restaurant in SoHo which has become quite a success.

Postscript

Walker also came up with ideas for other episodes for the proposed series, such as:

Navida bringing her new boyfriend home. He is very handsome and Richard has to tell her that the boy is probably gay. However, Richard is touched that Navida wanted a guy just like dad.

Jupiter develops a crush on a woman from the professional golfing tour and wants to quit school to follow the woman around the country. Richard and Rolf have to make her realize the importance of completing school first.

A drag queen friend of Tiffany's dies from hair-peroxide poisoning, and Richard and Rolf help in throwing a drag-queen benefit to raise money for the funeral. At the last minute, the drag-queen's family, who know their son only as Roscoe, shows up.

Kind of outrageous for a network situation comedy, ABC did not accept the idea because it believed that a comedy about a gay couple could not be sustained.[114]

The Young Americans

In this proposed sequel to the Margaret Cho comedy, *All-American Girl*, Margaret Kim moves out of her parents' place and into an apartment with three single guys and lands a job as the assistant to the assistant to the Associate Vice President of a record company. In addition to Cho, the potential sequel also featured Amy Hill, who played Cho's grandmother on the original series, continuing to appear as the same character in the pilot.

Background

The pilot aired on March 15, 1995, as the final episode of *All-American Girl*. In *All-American Girl*, Margaret lived with her parents, grandmother, and two brothers while working at a department store's cosmetics counter. Her mother wanted her to be a very traditional Korean young woman, while Margaret wished to be fully assimilated to American life. Written by Aline Brosh and Jeff Kahn and directed by Arlene Sanford, the proposed *Friends*-like sequel featured Andrew Lowry as Jimmy, Deidrich Bader as Spencer, a law student, and Sam Seder as Phil, a security guard—all roommates of Margaret.

The Pilot

Margaret is waiting for word on whether she got the job as an assistant at Bleach Records. However, phone service in her apartment has been cut off for non-payment. She and Phil go to the phone company to pay the bill, but find they owe a large amount in late fees. Phil decides to concoct a medical excuse for Margaret as to why she couldn't pay the bill to get the late fees removed. Not knowing Phil already went to see the phone company lady played by Vicki Lawrence, Margaret visits her with another excuse. Seeing through the ruse, the phone company demands payment or the late fees will double. Margaret persuades Phil to sell concert tickets he has in order to get the money to cover the late fees. In the end, Phil informs her that the record company called and that she got the job.

Postscript

Mariska Hargitay (*Law and Order SVU*), billed as a special guest star in this episode, played Jane, a bartender at the Goat's Head where the guys hung out, and to whom Phil was attracted. Disney, who produced *All-American Girl*, said that the idea of the pilot gave ABC the option of either renewing the original series or going with the new series. The network declined to do either.

While comedy spin-offs declined dramatically in numbers during the 1990s, they would decrease further in the new century, at least among ABC, CBS, and NBC. The major sources of spin-offs during the 2000s were cable channels, in particular the rise of cable outlets like Nickelodeon and the Disney Channel, as the TV viewing audience became more fragmented with choices from hundreds of network and cable channels.

PART 6

Proposed Sitcom Spin-offs and Sequels in the 2000s: Spin-offs for a New Generation

MOST POTENTIAL SPIN-OFFS during the current century have emanated from two sources—Nickelodeon and The Disney Channel, both aimed at tweens and teens. Some were attempted live action spin-offs like *Arwin!* and *Gibby*. Others were animated comedies such as *The Carmichaels* and *The Patakis*. The 2000s also saw the development of one of the most talked about but never seen spin-off efforts—the live-action *Monsignor Martinez* from the animated series *King of the Hill*.

Launched in 1979, Nickelodeon became a dominant cable channel for kids in the 1990s and early 2000s with animated series like *Doug*, *Rugrats*, and *The Ren & Stimpy Show*, and with comedy series produced primarily by former *Head of the Class* actor Dan Schneider. Schneider developed such hits for Nickelodeon as *The Amanda Show*, *Drake & Josh*, *Zoey 101*, *iCarly* and *Victorious*. As noted in Part 5, one of the first hit teen comedies on Nickelodeon was *Clarissa Explains It All* featuring Melissa Joan Hart.

In the early 2000s, with its transition to a basic cable channel, the Disney Channel phased out most of its reality and dramatic series and increasingly relied on situation comedies as well as animated series. *Lizzie McGuire*, starring Hilary Duff, centered on middle-school student Lizzie dealing with studying, family, and boys. *That's So Raven* about fifteen-year-old Raven Baxter, who had premonitions of the near future, premiered in 2003 and became one of the channel's biggest hits, spawning a spin-off, *Cory in the House*, that had Raven's brother moving with his dad to the White House when the father became head chef there while his mother attended law school and his sister Raven enrolled in college. Likewise, the Disney comedy *The Suite Life of Zack and Cody*, about twins living in a hotel where their mother sang in the establishment's lounge, gave rise to a sequel, *The Suite Life on Deck*, in which Zack and Cody enrolled in a semester-at-sea aboard a ship.

Other cable channels such as TBS and TV Land still produced what could now be termed "old-fashioned" spin-offs. *Tyler Perry's House of Payne* gave rise to *Meet the Browns*, and TV Land's *Hot in Cleveland* had a back-door pilot for *The Soul Man* that became a series on that channel. The relatively small television network UPN, which later merged with the WB to form the CW, scheduled a spin-off of *Girlfriends* called *The Game*, about the wives of pro-football players, as well as a spin-off of *One on One*, a comedy about a divorced sportscaster becoming responsible for raising his teenage daughter. The *One on One* spin-off titled *Cuts* centered on mismatched managers of a hair salon. Fox as well had an animated spin-off of the *Family Guy* character named Cleveland Brown in *The Cleveland Show*.

However, even with the trend away from spin-offs of CBS, ABC, and NBC network comedies, there were a few exceptions. Mary Tyler Moore and Valerie Harper, as described below, attempted a sequel featuring the characters each played on *The Mary Tyler Moore Show* and *Rhoda*. The very popular comedy *Friends* had a spin-off *Joey* centering on the Joey Tribbiani (Matt LeBlanc) character. A major disappointment, *Joey* lasted for only one and a half seasons.

Arwin!

Arwin Q. Hawkhauser (Brian Stepanek), the handyman at the Hotel Tipton where Zack and Cody Martin (Dylan and Cole Sprouse) and their mother lived on *The Suite Life of Zack and Cody*, is the central character in this proposed spin-off for the Disney Channel.

Background

Nerdish, awkward, balding, bespectacled Arwin first appeared on the sixth episode of *The Suite Life* during its first season. Carey Martin (Kim Rhodes), the twin's mother, receives a bouquet of flowers with a poem from a secret admirer. Zack and Cody try to find out who their mom's admirer is. While having Arwin take the parental control off a video game they want to play, the twins discover that he wrote the poem to their mother.

Pamela Eells wrote and Richard Correll directed the 2007 *Arwin!* spin-off, originally titled *Housebroken*. Both Eells and Correll worked on the *Suite Life* series.

The Pilot

In the never-aired pilot, Arwin decides to move out of his mother's house and live with his sister-in-law to help her take care of her three kids—Alexa (Selena Gomez), scholarly Lidia (Jasmine Villegas), and young son Jason (Logan Grove). They all live in a highly automated house protected by EDNA (Electronic Domestic Networking Appliance) that Arwin's sister-in-law's company developed. Klutzy Arwin adds a lot of slapstick to the proceedings by, for example, turbo-charging the kitchen table so that it spins around so fast that it throws Jason into Arwin's arms.

Alexa, pretending to be studying at her best friend Summer's (Samantha Drake) house, sneaks out at night to attend a party to meet a boy. Arwin goes to bring her home before her mother (Nia Peeples) arrives back from a business trip. When the mother finds out what Alexa did, she grounds her.

Postscript

Selena Gomez would have better luck starring as Alex Russo in the Disney Channel's *Wizards of Waverly Place*. Gomez played a teen with magical abilities living with two other siblings with the same capabilities.

The Carmichaels

This potential animated spin-off features the Carmichaels, a black family who lives across from Tommy Pickles's family of Nickelodeon's *Rugrats* fame. The mother, Lucy Carmichael, is an over-achiever, having gone to medical school, lecturing at the Cordon Bleu, and receiving a commercial pilot's license. Her husband Randy writes scripts for the television series *The Dummy Bears*. They have four kids—Buster, who is into sports; Alisa, their teenage daughter; Edwin, the intellectual; and three-and-a-half-year-old Susie who quickly bonds with Tommy Pickles. *The Carmichaels* centers on Susie and her family as they move from California to Atlanta, Georgia, where the rest of the Carmichaels' relatives lived.

Background

Directed by Anthony Bell and written by Lisa D. Hall, Jill Gorey, and Barbara Herndon, the pilot aired in December 2001.

The Pilot

In a "Rugrats Kwanza," the Carmichaels receive a visit from their great Aunt T who drops by to celebrate Kwanza which the Carmichaels had never done before. Susie feels that she isn't as great as her siblings since they all have trophies or awards for something. She wants to do something important to earn a trophy and decides to make Aunt T a Kwanza gift, but it doesn't turn out well. Aunt T explains to Susie that greatness doesn't have anything to do with winning awards. She shows the Rugrats her scrap book and says that not all great people get their pictures in the papers. Aunt T reminisces about when she and her husband Charles stopped to help Martin Luther King fix his car so he could make his "I Have a Dream" speech in Washington DC, and about when she gave her daughter Lucy the money to attend medical school. She says that Susie has her whole life to discover how great she is.

Postscript

Nicktoons decided against doing the spin-off series and instead opted to keep the Carmichaels in California to incorporate them into *Preschool Daze* and *All Grown Up*. These two sequels to *Rugrats* took the characters to pre-school and then into their tween and teen years.

The Farm

Dwight Schrute (Rainn Wilson), the somewhat arrogant assistant manager on *The Office*, is the focus of this spin-off effort from that series.

Background

Phil Lieberstein, a former writer for the animated series *King of the Hill*, wrote and directed the pilot, a version of which aired as an episode of *The Office* on March 14, 2013.

The Pilot

Dwight's Aunt Shirley has died, and he attends her funeral along with his brother Jeb (Thomas Middleditch) and sister Fannie (Majandra Delfino). Jeb is a pot farmer, and Fannie is a budding poet who has a nine-year-old, somewhat nerdy son named Cameron Whitman (Blake Garrett). Dwight's cousins Mose (Michael Schur) and Zeke (Matt L. Jones), who work on the aunt's beet farm, also attend the funeral. Dwight's great uncle, Heinrich Manhiem (Tom Bower), a former member of the German National Socialist Party, apparently came

Dwight Schrute (Rainn Wilson) was the lead character on *The Farm* spin-off

to the United States to escape the war. As he explained, "I was just a kid. I didn't know what a Nazi was. I just knew if you said something bad about the Jews you got more pudding. I didn't hate anybody. I just loved pudding."[115]

In a videotaped will, Aunt Shirley (Mary Gillis) leaves her large beet farm and inn to Dwight and his siblings provided they live there. Dwight's brother and sister are not so sure they want to stay, but he talks them into giving it a try for a few days to see what it is like. In the end, they decide to remain with Dwight managing the place. Heinrich thought that his sister Shirley should have left the farm to him and is not pleased when it is revealed that she wanted Dwight, Jeb, and Fannie to run the farm. In fact, he vows to kill Dwight.

Also, a black family, the Haskins, are staying at the bed and breakfast on the farm. The Haskins, whom Dwight confuses with the Huxtables from *The Cosby Show*, arrive during Aunt Shirley's wake, and Dwight, his brother, and sister give them a tour of the place.

Postscript

The pilot was edited to make it seem more like a regular episode of *The Office* when it aired. The scenes involving Dwight's uncle and the Haskins family were deleted and a subplot involving Todd Packer (David Koechner) returning to the office to supposedly make amends for his past misdeeds was added. During his apology, he makes rude remarks to the staff, hence they do not believe he is sincere. However, he brings gourmet cupcakes for everyone to show he is serious about his apology. Pam (Jenna Fischer) warns everyone that they should not eat the cupcakes since she feels that, by consuming them, they would show Packer's apology was sufficient. When Packer leaves, everyone, except Pam, eats their cupcake. Packer reveals to the camera that the cupcakes were spiked with laxatives, drugs, and other ingredients as revenge for previous tricks the office staff had pulled on him. Next day, everyone except Pam is reeling from the effects of eating the cupcakes.

As to why NBC failed to pick up *The Farm* as a series, AVClub.com states it best, "... *The Farm* was deemed to singular and too special for the more inclusive, multiple-cameras-and humorous-perspective-on-parenting future of NBC."[116] As of this writing, viewers are still waiting for NBC to launch a successful broad-based comedy.

Gibby

This spin-off attempt from the Nickelodeon series *iCarly* features Noah Munck as Gibby Gibson who had been a friend of Carly Shay's. In the proposed series, Gibby works at a recreation center and helps some nerdy middle-school students.

Background

In 2012, Dan Schneider, who created *iCarly*, announced that Nickelodeon had given the go-ahead for a pilot spin-off from that series to be called *Gibby*. Schneider has a track record of spinning off actors from one of his creations to another. For example, *The Amanda Show*, a sketch-comedy series starring Amanda Bynes, featured Drake Bell and Josh Peck who went on to star in *Drake & Josh* about two step brothers learning to live together. Miranda Cosgrove, who played Drake's little sister Megan on that series, starred on *iCarly*. Premiering on September 8, 2007, *iCarly*, a teen comedy, revolved around Carly Shay (Miranda Cosgrove), who created her own show on the internet with her best friends Sam Puckett (Jeanette McCurdy) and Freddie Benson (Nathan Kress).

The Pilot

The pilot opens in Mr. Waggit's (Paul Tigue) classroom where Waggit has been bitten on the butt by Gibby's pet ferret which Gibby brought to school. Chaos ensues. As part of Gibby's punishment, he's required to work in the school cafeteria and, in the course of that work, he stands up for four nerdish middle-school kids when they are bullied. The four middle-schoolers are played by Parker Bolek, Duson Brown, Adam Dorfman, and Kalama Epstein. They start following him around, and he brings them to where he works—The Bixby, a recreation center for kids to hang out, play games, and take classes. He tries to toughen them up by playing a game of dodge ball with them on a trampoline. Juliana Long Tyron played Sierra, the manager of The Bixby, whom Gibby has a crush on.[117]

Postscript

While *Gibby* never became a series, storylines for episodes beyond the pilot were apparently developed which included Gibby searching for one of his missing protégés, Winston (Duson Brown), before a tornado hits; becoming infatuated with a new girl at The Bixby; trying to catch a local thief; and losing his pet wild goose. Noah Munck's brother Ethan would have appeared on the spin-off series as Guppy Gibson.

Goin' Hollywood

In this spin-off effort from *That's So Raven*, Ally Parker (Alyson Stoner), star of her own television show, seeks to live the normal life of a tween.

Background

In the third season of Disney's *That's So Raven*, a back-door pilot aired on November 4, 2005, titled *Goin' Hollywood*. The pilot, also known as *I Know Lindy*, was directed by Richard Correll and written by Dennis Rinsler and Marc Warren.

The Pilot

Cory (Kyle Massey), Raven's brother, learns that he has won a part on his favorite television show, *Better Days*—a series set in the 1950s starring tween Ally Parker (Alyson Stoner) as Lindy Hopper, "America's Sweetheart." *Better Days* was obviously a spoof of the long-running comedy *Happy Days*. The Baxter family goes to Hollywood for Cory's television debut as a delivery boy with one word to say—"delivery." In the episode of *Better Days* in which Cory has a cameo, teen heartthrob Justin Banks (Dylon Patton) is to kiss Ally's character, Lindy. Meanwhile, Ally wants to live a normal life and attend public school much to the dismay of the director of her series, Dava (Jackee Harry). Ally's cousin Carly (Allie Grant) accompanies her to Valleywood Junior High School where she runs into the popular girls clique led by Chrissy Collins (Skyler Samuels). She also meets Arvin Barrington, the school activities coordinator who wants her to appear in a school talent show. He suggests a dance off between Ally and Chrissy. When Ally does her dance, she falls off the stage and injures her nose and so is afraid to kiss Justin on the next episode of her TV show. During the filming of the episode, Cory forgets his one word of dialogue, while Ally is hesitant to kiss Justin. The director re-stages the scene with Cory showing up with his delivery right before the kiss. This time he performs his dialogue correctly, and while the camera is on him, Ally's cousin Carly, dressed like Ally's character, stands in for her and kisses Justin.

Postscript

While *Goin' Hollywood* never became a series, the concept of a child star trying to have a normal life did become the basis of another hit Disney Channel comedy—*Hannah Montana*.

Mary and Rhoda

This potential sequel to *The Mary Tyler Moore Show* and its spin-off *Rhoda* updated the lives of Mary Richards and Rhoda Morgenstern including their efforts to get back into the work force while adjusting to their grown daughters' needs.

Background

First CBS and then ABC were approached about doing a reunion series with Mary Tyler Moore and Valerie Harper playing their characters from their original sitcoms and showing how they were doing twenty-five years after viewers last saw them. CBS turned down the offer for the sequel, but ABC initially gave the go ahead for thirteen episodes as a possible midseason replacement during the 1998-99 TV season. The comedy reportedly would have shown Mary and Rhoda as two friends who had lost touch with each other, but then are reunited as widows each with a daughter named for their old friend. However, agreement among the principals couldn't be reached on a version of the pilot script they all liked. ABC decided to make a TV movie version of the Mary and Rhoda sequel and gauge viewer re-

Valerie Harper, Cloris Leachman, and Mary Tyler Moore from the original
The Mary Tyler Moore Show

action to determine whether to pursue a series. By this time, MTM Enterprises no longer existed. Through a series of takeovers, the shows they produced had been absorbed by 20th Century Fox Television.

Written by Katie Ford, directed by Barnet Kellman, and executive produced by Mary Tyler Moore for 20Th Century Fox, the movie aired in February 2000. None of the original producers or writers from *The Mary Tyler Moore Show* were involved in this project.

The Pilot

As Mary Richards Cronin, Moore appears as a widow whose politician husband has just died in a rock climbing accident. She has a daughter in college named Rose (Joie Lenz) who is an English major. After working at WJM in Minneapolis, Mary had been a news producer for ABC but decided to quit that job to be a full-time mother. Rhoda Morgenstern Rousseau has just gone through her second divorce, this time from a philandering Frenchman with whom she also had a daughter, Meredith (Marisa Ryan), who is constantly at odds with her mother because of the divorce. Rhoda is now a professional photographer having come back from Paris to surprise her daughter who is majoring in pre-med. Mary has just returned from Europe where she was vacationing after the death of her husband. Mary's daughter suggests that Mary get in touch with Rhoda. They had lost contact after Rhoda's second marriage because Mary really didn't like Rhoda's new husband.

Rhoda and Mary finally run into each other in front of Mary's New York City apartment building. Mary invites Rhoda to move into her apartment since her daughter is no longer living there. Similar to what Phyllis Lindstrom discovered when her husband died in the *Phyllis* spin-off, Mary learns from her attorney that her late husband lost all their money, and so she decides to get back into the work force. Eventually, she lands a job as a news segment producer for WNYT-TV in New York City. Mary finds that she got the job because of her age so that the head of the news division could demote a female news anchor of about the same age who then couldn't sue him for age discrimination. Meanwhile, Rhoda becomes the assistant to a vain photographer who treats her as a lowly gofer getting his coffee and running errands for him.

Mary's daughter wants to quit school and become a stand-up comedian, while Rhoda's daughter doesn't like her mother interfering in her life. At work, Mary and the recently demoted news anchor do a story about the family of a gang member who killed another boy. She doesn't like the way the news anchor edits the story to sensationalize it and so decides to re-edit the story to make it more poignant. When her boss refuses to view the re-edited story, Mary goes ahead anyway and puts it on the air. Meanwhile, Rhoda decides to leave New York because she is not getting along with her daughter and doesn't like her photographer's assistant job. Mary talks her out of leaving. Rhoda reconciles with her daughter, and her boss gives her expanded duties as his assistant. After her story airs, Mary is fired by her boss for not following his instructions. He apparently didn't like spunk. But she convinces him to rehire her. Rose decides to continue her comedy career, but attend college at the same time.

Postscript
Even though the movie scored respectable ratings when it aired, the ratings were not spectacular enough for ABC to move forward with a series given the challenges the network had experienced in developing the project.

Monsignor Martinez

The character of Monsignor Martinez appeared on a Spanish-language soap opera titled *Los Dias y Las Noches de Monsignor Martinez* that the Hill family from Fox's *King of the Hill* sometimes watched on television. This Mexican soap opera was to *King of the Hill* as the Krusty the Clown show is to *The Simpsons*—a show within a show. Argentinean actor Ivo Cutzarida starred as the Monsignor Martinez character in this never-aired live-action pilot.

Background
Under the guise of a Catholic priest, Monsignor Martinez fought criminal elements in Mexico often dispatching his adversaries with the phrase "Vaya con Dios" ("Go with God"). The 2001 pilot, titled "In the Beginning," was written by the creator of *King of the Hill*, Mike Judge, who directed the pilot, and by Greg Daniels and Jim Dauterive. The following description of the pilot is taken from a script dated March 26, 2001 provided to this author by actor Adam Vernier who had a role in the pilot.

The Pilot
On the surface, Monsignor Martinez is a priest who engages in violent behavior against drug lords. The Monsignor is really a member of the "Juanajuatenos"—a secret religious order located in Mexico which has no

affiliation with the Catholic Church. One hundred years earlier, crime was rampant in Juanajuateno and the citizens turned to the priests for help since the police and government were corrupt. One priest decided to fight the corruption and so gave birth to Los Juanajuatenos. Because they killed bad people, the Catholic Church ex-communicated the members of the order.

Monsignor Martinez is at a mission in Mexico with his favorite altar boy, Amador, and a young nun named Graziela (Sophia Santi) who is struggling with her "earthly desires." A drug kingpin named Cuaderno (Rene Rivera) comes to Monsignor Martinez for confession. He wants to be the king of all the drug lords and is striving to expand his operations to San Diego. Martinez draws a gun from his robes and puts it against the screen of the confessional at Cuaderno's ear level. Cuaderno draws his gun and places it at the Monsignor's mouth level. Both fire at the same time but, as luck would have it, miss each other. A gun battle ensues. Amador takes cover behind a statue, but the statue topples over in the hail of bullets, mortally wounding him. Cuaderno flees. Martinez vows to hunt him down in San Diego.

The Monsignor flies to the city where thirty-year-old John Smith (David Herman), who works for Mansack and Gold Investment Group, has been ordered by his boss, Warren Mansack, to pick Martinez up at the airport. The Juanajuatenos represent 40 percent of the brokerage house's revenue. While waiting for Smith, a boy named Tony (Franco Velez) asks Martinez to help him saying that a couple nearby, Ted (Michael McCafferty) and Dawn (Dana Case), are not really his parents. Martinez sees a brick of white powder poking out of Tony's bag. The Monsignor punches Ted in the stomach. Dawn grabs the brick of cocaine and fires a gun at Martinez and Tony. While Tony hides, Martinez and the couple each commandeer baggage jeeps. The Monsignor chases them on to the tarmac where Ted and Dawn end up in the path of a DC-11 and are sucked into the jet's engines.

John Smith arrives to pick up Martinez who volunteers to take Tony home to his mother. Driving to the mother's house, Martinez confiscates the cocaine from Tony's bag. Arriving at the house, Smith has a cell phone conversation with his boss about Martinez:

> John Smith: "He's making me drive him around with a big bag of cocaine!"
> Mansack: "That could be zinc powder. The 'Wah-jah-nah-joes' have a huge zinc mine in Mexico. They supply companies who make sun block and acne medicine."
> John Smith: "He does have very good skin."

At Tony's house, a mailman walks past Smith's car to the mail slot on the front door. When Martinez hears a squeak as the slot opens, he fires his gun at the door, and the mailman flees. The Monsignor tells John that Cuaderno is a man of many disguises and that he could have been dressed as the mailman.

After the Monsignor and Smith leave the boy with his mother, she becomes angry when she doesn't find the cocaine in Tony's bag and exclaims that Cuaderno will kill her and Tony. The mother has Smith's business card to track him down.

As Smith and Martinez are driving to the brokerage firm, the Monsignor tells John about Cuaderno, who turns out not only to be a drug lord, but also had ravished Martinez's ex-wife. After having sex with Cuaderno, Martinez's ex-wife joined a convent in Las Vegas, while Martinez joined the Juanajuatenos. Arriving at Mansack and Gold, Smith and Martinez find Tony's mother waiting for them. She pulls a gun demanding the cocaine and takes the two as hostages in the trunk of her car. Heading to the Mexican border, the Monsignor finds a bullet in the car trunk and makes it discharge through the car's tail light just as the vehicle approaches the border. Smith and Martinez are freed, and the mother arrested. Martinez offers a border security guard money for the mother's car, and he and Smith take off for Tijuana, the location of one of Cuaderno's strip clubs.

Arriving at the club, Martinez and Smith find some inebriated American frat boys, several locals, a few Mexican thugs, and a DJ. There is also a skinny stripper dancing to the music. One of the frat boys, upon spotting the Monsignor, yells out: "Hey, Priest. Pray for this chick's boobs to get bigger!" Another frat boy wants to make Martinez drink a bottle of booze. He tries to poor liquor down the Monsignor's throat, while the first frat boy attempts to hold Martinez's head back. The Monsignor whips around and puts the second frat boy in a choke hold and kicks the first guy unconscious. Martinez asks the second boy in the choke hold to pray with him. The guy repeats after the Monsignor: "Forgive my foolish debauchery… And please don't let Monsignor Martinez catch me in a naked club again because he will hunt me down—yea, even in my Mother's house—and kill me." The terrified boys beat a hasty retreat.

The Monsignor then demands to know where Cuaderno is. Cuaderno enters from the back of the club. Martinez shows him the brick of cocaine which he retrieved from Tony's mother. Cuaderno has taken Tony from his mother. Tony reveals that he is an orphan and that the woman was not really his mom. Cuaderno says that Tony works for him as a mule and that Graziela works for him as well. Graziela appears and opens her nun's habit to show a stripper's outfit and two 9 mm guns in her holsters. She shoots one of Cuaderno's henchmen and tosses a gun to Martinez who takes aim at Cuaderno. Graziela and the Monsignor engage in a fierce gun battle with Cuaderno and his men.

Martinez and Cuaderno finally face off against each other and pull the triggers of their guns at the same time only to find that both are empty. Tony gets a bullet clip from one of the dead henchmen. Both the Monsignor and Cuaderno ask Tony to throw the clip to them. He tosses it to Martinez as Cuaderno flees out the back door into an alley. Martinez runs after him but sees only a cat holding a mouse. He notices that the mouse has a matchbook from the Flamenco Hotel in Las Vegas in its teeth.

In the end, the Monsignor makes Tony his new altar boy. He anoints Smith as a Juanajuateno, and they, including Graziela, all head to Las Vegas on the trail of Cuaderno and perhaps also to see Martinez's ex-wife at a convent in that city.

According to Rene Rivera, his character was constantly changing identities to carry on his drug-invested, criminal life like when Cuaderno dressed as a mailman outside Tony's mother's house.

Postscript

David Herman indicated that the reason Fox did not pick up *Monsignor Martinez* was because of fear about the reaction of viewers to a series showing a priest running around shooting people.[118] Rene Rivera agrees with Herman that the pilot was too controversial at the time, although he heard that Fox went into the eleventh hour trying to decide if it should become a series.[119]

Mystik Spiral

This potential animated spin-off from MTV's *Daria* centered on the rock band Mystik Spiral, which included Trent Lane, the brother of Daria Morgendorffer's best friend Jane. Trent, who has a scraggily goatee and three rings on each ear, is a guitarist and lead singer in the group. The other members of the band include Jess, the handsome lead guitarist, Nick, the bassist who is more talented than he thinks he is and is in love with Charlotte, a ballad singer, and Max, the drummer with a shaved head who, to try to get sympathy for the group, often pretends he has only one arm.

Trent Lane, the lead singer of Mystik Spiral

Background

Glenn Eichler, the writer and producer of *Daria*, who went on to write for the *Colbert Report*, penned the pilot script in 2001. However, no pilot resulted from the script. *Daria* was itself a spin-off from *Beavis and Butthead* and ran on MTV from 1997 to 2002

The Script

Mystik Spiral is playing at a grunge club in Lawndale to an audience of seven that includes Max's brother Mark. Trent is singing the band's signature tune, "Incontinent Love:"

> Now you say that maybe
> We'd be better off as friends

Our love's become a soggy thing
That needs to wear Depends!
Incontinent love!
Incontinent love!
Drowning the dragon of our dreams!

Every time I call you
You don't have time to speak
When I ask you why, you say
Our love has sprung a leak!
Incontinent love!
Incontinent love!
Watering the turnip of our dreams!

After the show, Trent suggests that maybe the group should split up because they are not making it. However, Max's brother, who liked their performance, suggests that the town of Lawndale may not be hip enough for the group. He invites them to move to Mirage, an artist's colony, and live in a house he owns there. The guys jump at the offer and prepare to move. Nick decides it is time to break up with his girlfriend Charlotte.

When the group arrives at Mark's house, they find it in total disrepair—broken windows, plumbing not working, dangling railing, and rats. Despite the conditions, they move in. The next day the group auditions for various club owners. They aren't offered that much money to perform and decide to practice more so at least all the members can start and stop a number at the same time.

Later, they go to another audition at Cowbane, owned by hippie Cubby who has an attractive daughter named Tulip. Tulip and Cubby like their performance, but offer the group only $50 to perform like the other club owners had done even though they said the group sucked. Cubby decides to sweeten the offer by giving them 1.5% of the door as a bonus.

When Mystik Spiral arrives back home, Charlotte is waiting for Nick, and they decide to get back together. Charlotte has moved to an apartment in Mirage.

At their first performance at Cowbane, only eight people, including Charlotte, show up to hear them. But the group considers this a good sign since it is one more person than they played for at their last gig.

Postscript

The MTV Animation Unit shut down in 2001, which is the reason the *Mystik Spiral* pilot was not made.

The Patakis

Helga Patakis, her family, and friends are the focus of this potential spin-off from *Hey Arnold!*, conceived as a series for Nick at Nite. *The Patakis* takes place about five years after *Hey Arnold!* when Helga is fifteen.

Background

Hey Arnold!, another animated series on Nickelodeon, featured nine-year-old Arnold, with blonde frizzy hair and a football-shaped head, who lived with his grandparents in a boarding house whose other residents were a cross-section of immigrants from Eastern Europe and Southeast Asia. Helga Patakis, one of Arnold's friends and secretly in love with him, had blonde pigtails, wore a pink bow in her hair, had a uni-brow, and was perpetually grumpy.

Craig Bartlett and Michelle Lamoreaux wrote the pilot script in 2000. Bartlett developed *Hey Arnold!* and is married to Lisa Groening, the sister of Matt Groening who created *The Simpsons*.

The Script

Helga, a budding author, constantly writes letters to Arnold, who has moved away. However, she never mails the letters but simply files them. Her perfect sister, Olga, who had attended Bennington, has returned home from college and is pursuing a career in acting in way, way off-Broadway shows. Helga's blowhard dad, Big Bob, continues to run his beeper empire. The only things he seems to care about are getting rich, football, golf, alien abduction conspiracies, his cars, and Olga's collection of awards.[120] Helga's mom, Miriam, is still lame-brained and doesn't see anything particularly interesting in her future. She drinks too much and is considering a twelve-step rehab program.

Postscript

Nickelodeon felt the pilot script was "too dark" for their audience. The series was then offered to MTV who passed on it as well since they thought the show would be too similar to *Daria*.

What's Stevie Thinking?

This attempted spin-off from *Lizzie McGuire* focuses on Stevie Sanchez, the younger sister of Lizzie's best friend Miranda. Stevie (Selena Gomez) often feels like an outsider in her own family. The series would have focused on Stevie as she adjusts to life with her sister and parents in a new city.

Background

Scripted by *Lizzie McGuire* writer Terri Minsky and directed by Howard Deutch, this 2005 spin-off pilot titled *What's Stevie Thinking?* is also known as *Stevie Sanchez*. As with *Lizzie McGuire*, Stevie's thoughts are illustrated by an animated alter ego.

The Pilot

Moving from California to New York, the Sanchezes begin a new life. Stevie is twelve, while her older sister Miranda, who is in a band, is sixteen, and they both face the challenges of attending new schools and meeting new friends. The series planned to focus on the relationship between Miranda and Stephanie ("Stevie") and their parents Edward (Armando Molina) and Daniella (Dyana Ortelli).

Postscript

This project would have been the Disney Channel's first effort at depicting a Latino family. But after test audiences showed little interest in the pilot, it never became a series. According to Stan Rogow, the executive producer of the pilot, Terri Minsky wrote a wonderful and emotional script, but Disney didn't think there was enough comedy in it.[121]

Witchright Hall

From *Sabrina, The Teenage Witch*, Sabrina Spellman's (Melissa Joan Hart) trouble-making cousin Amanda (Emily Hart) enrolls in Witchright Hall, a school for unruly witches in the mortal realm.

Background

Broadcast on April 6, 2001, Bruce Ferber and Molly Sims wrote and Kenneth Koch directed the pilot. According to Ferber, every year Viacom Productions would pitch a proposed spin-off of *Sabrina, the Teenage*

Witch.¹²² As with virtually all back-door pilots, *Witchright Hall* was shot as an episode of *Sabrina* in order to use the series budget to cover costs. The production company loved Sabrina's talking cat, and so they thought *Witchright Hall* should have a talking dog.

An episode of *Sabrina* titled "A Halloween Story," which aired during the first season of that series, introduced the Amanda character. In that episode, Sabrina is invited to a Halloween party given by a boy at school to whom she is attracted, but Sabrina's aunts insist that she go with them to the other realm which witches inhabit. Sabrina's Aunt Marigold is throwing a party and exchanging gifts. At the party, Sabrina meets her young cousin, Marigold's daughter Amanda, a spoiled brat who puts everyone she doesn't like in a jar. Because Sabrina wouldn't color with her, she magically places Sabrina in a jar, but Sabrina's aunts free her. At the end, when Amanda gets on her mother's nerves, Marigold puts Amanda in a jar.

The Pilot

Amanda is sent to live in the mortal realm for a year with Sabrina and her aunts because she is not adapting well to her mother's nineteenth husband. The Spellmans decide to enroll Amanda in a school called Witchright Hall, which helps unruly witches adapt to the mortal world. The school's headmaster, James Hexton (Charles Shaughnessy), has a son, Sean (Thad Luckinbill), who causes trouble by, for instance, putting all the girls in the neighborhood under a spell to make them fall in love with him. Robin Davis (Jane Sibbett) is the school director.

Sabrina takes Amanda to Witchright Hall where a talking dog is the physical education teacher. Amanda meets the other students and sits in on an ethics class taught by the headmaster. Hexton tells the group that they need more than magic to survive in the mortal realm; they need to experience human emotions. Sabrina says that Amanda could find stability at the school, but Amanda is initially turned down for admission because Hexton feels she is not that troubled. However, when he sees her cry after learning she wouldn't be admitted, he changes his mind and accepts her.

Postscript

Because the WB was starting to go in a different direction with their shows, *Witchright Hall* never became a series.

The Xtacles

This animated spin-off from the series *Frisky Dingo* dealt with a private freelance army formed by a billionaire superhero and its lack of direction after its leader has been abducted by aliens. The army takes on random missions from the President of the United States, but proves to be hopelessly inept. The characters include Jack Taggart (voiced by Marshall Bell), the leader of the Xtacles who is just as incompetent as the army he leads and who likes to rush to conclusions that are always wrong; A.L.E.X (Rachel Harris), the holographic avatar for the Xtacle's flying aircraft carrier's computer; Chase Fountain (Michael Ian Black), a member of the Xtacles who is attracted to A.L.E.X's hologram; Joseph Bigsby (Matthew Stanton), a naïve member of the Xtacles who mans the bridge of the carrier Xcalibur; Stan (Stuart Culpepper), the President of the United States who has to rely on the Xtacles for help since all other heroes are retired or cannot be reached; and Mr. Ford, a black man living rent-free in the Xcaliber's reactor room because his house had mistakenly been destroyed by the Xtacles.

Background

Frisky Dingo, the series from which *The Xtacles* emanated, dealt with the conflict between superhero Awesome X, alias billionaire Xander Crews, and the super-villain, Killface. Created by Adam Reed and Matt Thompson for Adult Swim, the series ran for two seasons on that cable channel. Unlike many of the other potential spin-offs described in this book, *The Xtacles* actually had two episodes produced which aired on November 9, 2008.

The Two Episodes

The first episode, titled "Operation: Mountain Punch," involved the Xcalibur smashing through the peaks of the Rocky Mountains since Taggart received no orders to change course. The President then calls on the Xtacles to investigate who is destroying the Rocky Mountains. Taggart, never one to assume responsibility for anything, blames Yeti terrorists for the destruction. He kills one of his crew who looks like a Yeti and considers his mission accomplished.

The second episode, titled "Operation: Murderous Conclusions" involves the President asking the Xtacles to find out who sodomized his new statue. Taggart blames a made-up criminal he calls Rape Ape. Since no file exists for Rape Ape, the Xtacles move to the next file, Rapier Ape, a retired ape swordsman. A massacre occurs at the restaurant where Rapier

Ape is employed, and Rapier Ape is beaten for the violation of the statue. However, it turns out that there really is a Rape Ape who rapes the President's new statue—go figure.

Postscript

The spin-off would have become a regular animated series, but then Adult Swim decided not to produce any more episodes and the production company behind *Frisky Dingo* and *The Xtacles*, 70/30 Productions, went out of business.

As Josef Adalian states in an article titled "Why the Sitcom Spinoff Isn't Coming Back," the increasing fragmentation of the television audience and the relative lack of highly-rated and broad-based sitcoms makes it unlikely viewers will see a return to the Golden Age of Spin-offs as in the 1970s and, to a certain extent, the 1980s.[123] *Modern Family* and *The Big Bang Theory* are the most popular situation comedies thus far in the second decade of the twenty-first century. There is always concern among producers and network chiefs that spinning off characters from these comedies might endanger the popularity of the original series. However, there does appear to be a market for niche comedy spin-offs, particularly those directed at kids, as the recent popularity of *Girl Meets World* on the Disney Channel, a spin-off of the ABC comedy *Boy Meets World,* may attest.

Appendix

Proposed Spin-offs and Sequels Listed by TV Series that Spawned Them

Proposed Sequels

All-American Girl: *Young Americans*
Clarissa Explains It All: *Clarissa Now*
Father Knows Best: *Father Knows Best Reunion*
Gilligan's Island: *The Castaways on Gilligan's Island* and *Gilligan's Island: The Second Generation*
It Had to be You: *The Mighty Quinns*
The Many Loves of Dobie Gillis: *Whatever Happened to Dobie Gillis?* and *Bring Me the Head of Dobie Gillis*
The Mary Tyler Moore Show: *Mary and Rhoda*
The Munsters: *The Munsters' Revenge*
My Friend Irma: *My Wife Irma*
My Little Margie: *Margie's Little Margie*
Sibs: *Related by Birth*
The Ropers: *Three Apartments*
That's My Mama: *That's My Mama Now!*

Proposed Spin-offs

The Andy Griffith Show: *Goober and the Trucker's Paradise*
The Ann Sothern Show: *Always April* and *Pandora*
Barney Miller: *Wojo*
The Brady Bunch: *Kelly's Kids*

The Bob Cummings Show: *Chuck Goes to College*
Charles in Charge: *The Lost Resort*, *Almost Family*, and *Fair Exchange*
Chico and the Man: *Della and Son*
The Cosby Show: *The Tony Orlando Show*
The Courtship of Eddie's Father: *We Love Annie*
The Danny Thomas Show: *The Jack Carter Show*, *The Pat Buttram Show*, and *The Two Musketeers*
Daria: *Mystik Spiral*
Diff'rent Strokes: *Almost American*
The Donna Reed Show: *Aloha, Kimi*, *Wide Open Spaces*, and *The Roberta Sherwood Show*
The Doris Day Show: *Young Love*
Empty Nest: *The Laverne Todd Show*
The Facts of Life: *The Parkers*, *The Academy*, *Jo's Cousins*, *The Big Apple Blues*, and the Lisa Whelchel Project
Family Ties: *Taking It Home* and *The Art of Being Nick*
Frisky Dingo: *The Xtacles*
The George Burns and Gracie Allen Show: *The Plumber and His Daughters*
Gimme a Break!: *Max*, *The Center*, and *The Last Word*
Green Acres: *Pam* and *The Blonde*
Happy Days: *Potsie and Ralph and Maxine*, *Pinky Tuscadero*, and *Kat Mandu*
Here's Boomer: *Flatfoots*
Here's Lucy: *The Lucie Arnaz Show*
Hey Arnold!: *The Patakis*
Hooperman: *Nick Derringer, PI*
iCarly: *Gibby*
I Love Lucy: *The Mertzes*
The Jeffersons: *A Piece of the Pie!*
Kate & Allie: *Late Bloomer*
King of the Hill: *Monsignor Martinez*
Laredo: *Thataway*
Laverne & Shirley: *Lenny & Squiggy in the Army* and the Eddie Mekka Project
Lizzie McGuire: *What's Stevie Thinking?*
The Love Boat: *Bo and Sam*
*M*A*S*H*: *W*A*L*T*E*R*

Malcolm & Eddie: Daddio
The Many Loves of Dobie Gillis: Zelda
Married… with Children: *Radio Free Trumaine* and *Enemies*
Martin: Goin' for Mine
The Mary Tyler Moore Show: The Councilman
McKeever and the Colonel: *Shape Up Sergeant* and *Munroe*
Mister Ed: *The Bill Bendix Show*, *Emmy Lou*, and *Moko and Tatti from Outer Space*
Mr. Adams and Eve: Teenage Idol
My Three Sons: After the Honeymoon
My Two Dads: The Dick Butkus Project
The Nanny: The Chatterbox
The New Andy Williams Show: Barney and Me
The Office: The Farm
On the Rocks: The Rita Moreno Show
One Day at a Time: Schneider
Punky Brewster: Fenster Hall
Rhoda: Carlton Your Doorman
The Rifleman: Which Way'd They Go?
The Rockford Files: Jersey Bounce
Roseanne: Roseanne's Gay Family Project
Rugrats: The Carmichaels
Sabrina, The Teenage Witch: Witchright Hall
Saturday Night Live: *The Coneheads* and *Mr. Bill's Real Life Adventures*
Seinfeld: The Jackie Chiles Show
She's the Sheriff: Mr. Moe's
The Simpsons: Krusty the Clown
The Suite Life of Zack and Cody: Arwin!
That's So Raven: Goin' Hollywood
Too Close for Comfort: Family Business
227: *We the People* and *Jackee*
Wagon Train: Wagon Train's "Prairie Hillbillies" Spin-off
Webster: Almost Home
Welcome Back, Kotter: Horshack
Who's the Boss?: *Charmed Lives* and *Mona*

Endnotes

1. Neil Wilkes, "'Joey' Spinoff 'Killed' 'Will & Grace' Spinoff," digitspy.com, February 18, 2010, retrieved April 4, 2014.

2. Quoted in Sally Bedell, *Up the Tube: Prime Time TV and the Silverman Years*, New York: The Viking Press, 1981, 82.

3. Carl Kleinschmitt, Private communication with author, May 23, 2013.

4. Garry Marshall with Lori Marshall, *My Happy Days in Hollywood: A Memoir*, New York: Crown Publishing, 2012, 76.

5. Jeffrey Silver, Private communication with author, January 17, 2015.

6. Coyne Steven Sanders and Tom Gilbert, *Desilu: The Story of Lucille Ball and Desi Arnaz*, New York: William Morrow and Company, Inc., 1993, 153.

7. Rob Edelman and Audrey Kuperberg, *Meet the Mertzes: The Life Stories of I Love Lucy's Other Couple*, Los Angeles: Renaissance Books: 1999, 159.

8. "Marie Wilson, Alias 'My Friend Irma' About to Commit Some Sort of Bigamy," *Panama City News-Herald*, July 19, 1954.

9. "Burns (& Allen) Refuses to Get Stampeded," *Variety*, May 17, 1957.

10. Quoted in the author's *George Burns Television Productions*, Jefferson, North Carolina: McFarland & Company, Inc. 2014, 53.

11. Wally George, "Strictly off the Record," *Los Angeles Times*, March 8, 1958.

12. Sheldon Leonard, *And the Show Goes On: Broadway and Hollywood Adventures*, New York: Proscenium Inc., 1994, 109.

13. Tony Owen, Letter to Al Schneider, November 1, 1961.

14. Susan Silo, Private communication with author, December 17, 2012.

15. Noanna Dix Feldman, Private communication with author, February 25, 2014.

16. Norman Paul and William Burns, "Moko the Martian," Draft script, October 28, 1963.

17. Pat Carroll, Private communication with author, October 15, 2013.

18. Ann B. Davis, Private communication with author, February 21, 2013.

19. Chad Stuart and Jeremy Clyde Official Website, chadandjeremy.net, retrieved May 19, 2013.

20. "Hillbilly Comedy as 'Wagon Train' Spinoff," *Variety*, January 29, 1963.

21. James Rosin, *Wagon Train: The Television Series*, Totowa, New Jersey: Lightning Press, 2008, 46.

22. Sheila James Kuehl, Private communication with author, December 15, 2012.

23. Grant Tinker with Bud Rukeyser, *Tinker in Television: From General Sarnoff to General Electric*, New York: Simon and Schuster, 1994, 97.

24. Jennifer Keishin Armstrong, *Mary and Lou and Rhoda and Ted and All the Brilliant Minds Who Made The Mary Tyler Moore Show a Classic*, New York: Simon and Schuster, 2013, 276.

25. Bedell, *Up the Tube*, 127.

26. Dave Kaufman, "On All Channels," *Variety*, June 29, 1971.

27. Mark Christensen and Cameron Stauth, *The Sweeps: Behind the Scenes in Network TV*, New York: William Morrow and Company, Inc., 1984, 132.

28. Philip Charles MacKenzie, Private communication with author, May 26, 2013.

29. Sherwood Schwartz, *Inside Gilligan's Island: From Creation to Syndication*, Jefferson, North Carolina: McFarland and Company, Inc., 1988, 236.

30. Arnold Margolin, Private communication with author, October 31, 2014.

31. Jerry Ross, Private communication with author, January 3, 2015.

32. Army Archerd, "Just for Variety," *Variety*, April 18, 1977.

33. Elinor Donahue, Private communication with author, December 1, 2014.

34. Rich Eustis, Private communication with author, December 10, 2013.

35. Robert Pegg, *Comical Co-Stars of Television: From Ed Norton to Kramer*, Jefferson, North Carolina: McFarland & Company, 2002, 204.

36. Rich Eustis, Private communication.

37. Jerry Rannow, Private communication with author, June 10, 2013.

38. Ibid.

39. Pegg, *Comical Co-Stars*, 251.

40. "TV Followup," *Variety*, December 19, 1979.

41. Marley Brant, *Happier Days: Paramount Television's Classic Sitcoms 1974-1984*, New York: Billboard Books, 2006, 79.

42. Mark Rothman and Eddie Mekka, Private communications with author, February 4 and 14, 2014.

43. "Lucie Wants Different Series," *San Antonio Express*, May 23, 1972.

44. Brant, *Happier Days*, 50.

45. Eddie Mekka, Private communication with author, February 14, 2014.

46. Melanie Mayron, Private communication with author, May 16, 2014.

47. Pegg, *Comical Co-Stars*, 236.

48. Rita Moreno, Private communication with author, November 25, 2013.

49. Morrie Gelman, "NBC Program Exex Attest to Testing Pilots on Cable," *Variety*, June 24, 1988.

50. Dwayne Hickman and Joan Roberts Hickman, *Forever Dobie: The Many Lives of Dwayne Hickman*, New York: Carol Publishing Group, 1994, 223.

51. Isobel Silden, "Barney Miller's Beat Stretches to Las Vegas," *The Pantagraph*, November 12, 1978.

52. Robert Sand, Private communication with author, December 6, 2013.

53. Jerry Mayer, Private communication with author, February 13, 2014.

54. Bob Ari, Private communication with author, October 4, 2013.

55. "Mac Davis Makes Series Effort in Spinoff from ABC's 'Webster,'" *The Paris News*, February 22, 1986.

56. Sam Weisman, Private communication with author, October 21, 2014.

57. Dave Kaufman, "On All Channels," *Variety*, October 12, 1987.

58. Barton Dean, Private communication with author, March 4, 2013.

59. Jeff Franklin, Private communication with author, April 13, 2014.

60. Al Franken and Tom Davis, *The Coneheads*: "The Cave," First Draft Script, June 7, 1983, 1-6.

61. Bradley Gregg, Private communication with author, January 27, 2015.

62. Ibid.

63. James Baio, Private communication with author, April 1, 2014.

64. Richard Hawkins, Private communication with author, May 20, 2013.

65. Ibid., 271.

66. Bob Denver, *Gilligan, Maynard & Me*, New York: Carol Publishing Group, 1993, 118-19.

67. Brandon Tartikoff and Charles Leerhsen, *The Last Great Ride*, New York: Turtle Bay Books, 1992, 32-33.

68. Michael E. Hill, "Jackee Becoming More Serious," *Altoona Mirror*, October 30, 1989.

69. John Mengatti, Private communication with author, February 14, 2014.

70. Deborah Pratt, Private communication with author, March 28, 2015.

71. David Ketchum, Tony DiMarco, and Jeffrey Ganz, "Presenting Kat Mandu," Revised shooting script, January 12, 1980, 18-19.

72. David Ketchum, Private communication with author, May 21, 2014.

73. Pratt, Private communication.

74. Harry Basil, Private communication with author, November 11, 2013.

75. Bill Persky, Private communication with author, January 13, 2014.

76. Craig Modderno, "Series in the Wings," *Los Angeles Times*, November 23, 1986.

77. Irma Kalish, Private communication with author, April 1, 2014.

78. Ted Bergman, Private communication with author, May 25, 2013.

79. Ibid.

80. Steve Granat, Private communication with author, March 10, 2014.

81. Ibid.

82. Richard Rossner, Private communication with author, October 23, 2013.

83. Mark Rothman, Private communication with author, February 4, 2014.

84. Stephen Cox, *The Munsters: A Trip Down Mockingbird Lane*, New York: Back Stage Books, 2006, 130.

85. Jo McDonnell Parker, Private communication with author, December 8, 2014.

86. Ibid.

87. "Strange Bedfellows," *News Record*, May 6, 1988.

88. "TV Followups," *Variety*, April 1, 1981.

89. Pegg, *Comical Co-Stars*, 152.

90. Natalija Nogulich, Private communication with author, April 1, 2014.

91. Harry Basil, Private communication.

92. Marcy Carsey, Private communication with author, December 22, 2014.

93. Tony Orlando with Patsi Bale Cox, *Halfway to Paradise*, New York: St. Martin's Press, 2002, 227.

94. "Another 'Three' for Taffner," *Broadcasting*, October 20, 1986, 46.

95. "Television in Review," *Variety*, July 25, 1984.

96. Ron Bloomberg, Private communication with author, May 28, 2013.

97. Mitchell Bank, Private communication with author, November 26, 2013.

98. Patrick Cassidy, Private communication with author, January 27, 2014.

99. Ibid.

100. Melissa Joan Hart, "Clarissa Now," www.tvsquad.com, March 15, 2011, retrieved July 19, 2013.

101. Jaimie Etkin, "'Clarissa Explains It All' Creator Talks New Book, Failed Pilot, That Ladder, Those Clothes and More," HuffingtonPost.com, August 21, 2013, retrieved November 29, 2013.

102. Melissa Joan Hart with Kristina Grish, *Melissa Explains It All: Tales from My Abnormally Normal Life*, New York: St. Martin's Press, 2013, 62.

103. Richard Gurman, Private communication with author, July 29, 2013.

104. Ibid.

105. Richard Katz, "'Seinfeld' Spinoff Spotted," *Variety*, July 19, 1999.

106. Gail Shister, "'Seinfeld' May Be Gone but Jackie Chiles Lives," *Chicago Tribune*, July 24, 1999.

107. Michael Weithorn, Private communication with author, March 3, 2014.

108. Gary Jacobs, Private communication with author, January 3, 2013.

109. Army Archerd, "Just for Variety," *Variety*, December 20, 1993.

110. Richard Gurman, Private communication with author, July 29, 2013.

111. William Lucas Walker, Private communication with author, September 19, 2013.

112. Ibid.

113. William Lucas Walker, "Treatment for a Gay Family Sitcom," September 21, 1995.

114. Steven Capsuto, *Alternate Channels: The Uncensored Story of Gay and Lesbian Images on Radio and Television*, New York: Ballantine Books, 2000, 362.

115. Writers First Draft, July 30, 2012.

116. Sean O'Neal, "NBC will still air that rejected *Office* spinoff, sort of," avclub.com, January 2, 2013, retrieved April 16, 2014.

117. Paul Tigue who played Mr. Waggit in the pilot provided the pilot summary to this author, November 23, 2014.

118. Timothy Sexton, "The Monsignor Martinez Live Action Spinoff from King of the Hill," Yahoo! Contributor Network, February 11, 2008.

120. Rene Rivera, Private communication with author, February 1, 2014.

121. Craig Bartlett, "Confirmed Notes about 'The Patakis,' Hey Arnold! – A Critical Analysis," tendraheyarnold.wordpress.com, retrieved December 1, 2013.

122. Stan Rogow, Private communication with author, June 25, 2014.

123. Bruce Ferber, Private communication with author, May 18, 2013.

124. Josef Adalian, "Why the Sitcom Spinoff Isn't Coming Back," Vulture.com, November 1, 2012, retrieved December 24, 2012.

Index

All in the Family 1, 4, 50, 51, 75, 88, 98, 99, 119, 130, 145, 150
Andy Griffith Show, The xiii, 15, 19, 21, 29, 35, 38, 40, 41, 45, 50, 53, 68, 69, 150, 203
Ann Sothern Show, The 24, 33, 81, 203
Arnold, Danny 52, 93, 95

Baio, Scott 83, 84, 85, 86, 99, 101, 154, 155, 161, 169
Brooks, James L. 50, 110, 153, 166, 173

Charles in Charge 117, 154, 155, 161, 163, 169, 170, 204
Cosby Show, The 97, 98, 124, 147, 148, 186, 204

Danny Thomas Show, The xiii, 2, 3, 19, 21, 22, 28, 34, 35, 39, 41, 49, 50, 53, 188, 204
Diff'rent Strokes 52, 96, 98, 101, 102, 114, 160, 204
Dobie Gillis 11, 32, 45, 54, 70, 91, 92, 106, 107, 109, 203, 205
Donna Reed Show, The 22, 28, 35, 44, 45, 95, 204

Facts of Life, The 52, 96, 98, 99, 100, 105, 106, 114, 125, 130, 132, 141, 153, 160, 204
Family Ties 96, 97, 98, 103, 104, 105, 144, 145, 204

Gilligan's Island 54, 60, 61, 62, 63, 74, 123, 139, 203

Gimme a Break! 98, 110, 111, 128, 129, 132, 133, 145, 204
Goldberg, Gary David 97, 105, 144, 145
Green Acres 3, 35, 58, 80, 163, 204
Gurman, Richard 160, 161, 172

Happy Days xi, 4, 7, 8, 52, 53, 54, 76, 81, 83, 84, 86, 87, 88, 99, 120, 122, 126, 154, 188, 204
Hart, Melissa Joan 157, 158, 181, 198

Jeffersons, The 4, 64, 98, 120, 124, 141, 142, 143, 146, 153, 160, 204

Komack, James 3, 54, 65, 70, 72, 89, 91

Lachman, Mort 98, 99, 111, 129
Laverne & Shirley 4, 52, 53, 75, 76, 84, 99, 111, 112, 118, 119, 122, 136, 204
Lear, Norman 48, 49, 50, 96, 98, 99, 101, 119, 120, 124, 125, 141, 142, 143, 151
Leonard, Sheldon 21, 22, 28, 49, 50, 52, 53

Married . . . with Children 124, 153, 160, 162, 172, 173, 205
Marshall, Garry 7-8, 48, 49, 52, 53, 75, 76, 83, 84, 85, 86, 87, 88, 99, 111, 118, 120, 122, 126, 127
Mary Tyler Moore Show, The 4, 49, 50, 59, 63, 64, 65, 97, 119, 153, 166, 182, 189, 190, 203, 205

M*A*S*H 4, 5, 50, 99, 100, 149, 150, 204
McKeever and the Colonel 32, 37, 205
Mister Ed 22, 25, 26, 27, 30, 31, 205

Rhoda 4, 50, 100, 109, 110, 182, 189, 205
Rifleman, The 6, 22, 42, 43, 205

Saturday Night Live 106, 114, 133, 134, 205
Schwartz, Sherwood 61, 62, 74, 75, 123
Silverman, Fred 4, 51, 53, 76, 88, 97, 133
Simpsons, The 110, 153, 154, 166, 191, 197, 205

Tartikoff, Brandon 97, 123, 128, 151
Thomas, Danny 21, 22, 28, 34, 40, 49, 50, 53, 54
Tinker, Grant 48, 49, 97, 99, 109, 128
227 98, 124, 130, 151, 152, 160, 205

Who's the Boss? 98, 112, 114, 136, 137, 205

www.ingramcontent.com/pod-product-compliance
Lightning Source LLC
Chambersburg PA
CBHW071228170426
43191CB00032B/1131